Walter Frere

Walter Frere

Scholar, Monk, Bishop

Edited by

Benjamin Gordon-Taylor and
Nicolas Stebbing CR

CANTERBURY PRESS

Norwich

© The Contributors 2011

First published in 2011 by Canterbury Press

Editorial office
13–17 Long Lane,
London EC1A 9PN, UK

Canterbury Press is an imprint of Hymns Ancient and Modern Ltd
(a registered charity)
13a Hellesdon Park Road, Norwich, Norfolk NR6 5DR

www.canterburypress.co.uk

British Library Cataloguing in Publication data

A catalogue record for this book is available
from the British Library

978 1 85311 868 5

Typeset by *Church Times*
Printed and bound by
CPI Antony Rowe, Chippenham, Wiltshire

A caricature of Walter Frere by an unknown artist, probably drawn in the 1930s, the original of which is at the House of the Resurrection, Mirfield.

Contents

Foreword[1]

Every night as I go to bed I say goodnight to the former Bishops of Truro whose portraits are on the walls by the stairs. There, at the corner of the stairs by the first landing, is a portrait of Bishop Frere, a copy of the one at Mirfield. In the Cathedral, processions normally form up in the South Transept and there, set in the floor, is a brass of Frere and I always try to stand near it or even on it, hoping, I suppose, that some of his holiness and learning may rub off on me. So Frere for me is not just a former Bishop of Truro, he is someone who reminds me always of how much I owe to the Community of the Resurrection and the tradition it represents.

I mentioned in the *Coracle*, our monthly diocesan publication, that I had been asked to write this Foreword and wondered if any readers had memories of Frere. I didn't expect many because it is 73 years since he was Bishop here. To my delight, I got several answers within days, even hours, of the *Coracle* reaching the parishes. One man, now aged 93, who as a boy sang in the Cathedral choir, remembered how Frere was wonderfully good at telling ghost stories which frightened him and other boys as they returned home in the dark. A lady, now well into her 90s, quoted word for word something that Frere had said in his address at her confirmation. One priest, now retired, remembered being told by his training incumbent that Frere sometimes wore shorts under his cassock. He knew this because Frere had talked about a letter of complaint from a person, who on a windy day, noticed that her incumbent was wearing only shorts under his cassock. Frere said: 'When the dear lady made a complaint to me, I thought it wise not to tell her that I was dressed in the same way.'

All very human, and it is well remembered that, just before he left, he said that he would leave half his heart behind in Cornwall. He isn't the

---

1 Written before Bishop Ind's retirement in 2008.

only Bishop of Truro who has done that, but there is no doubt that his liturgical and historical learning, as well as his holiness, has helped to shape the Diocese of Truro and every night as I climb the stairs I give thanks for that.

+William Truro

Introduction

NICOLAS STEBBING CR and
BENJAMIN GORDON-TAYLOR

Walter Howard Frere was one of the great scholars of the early twentieth century, but he was also something of an enigma. He was expert in many different areas of study, but more than 70 years after his death he is relatively little known: a few specialists in liturgy and Reformation history value his work, and his name appears briefly in certain ecumenical papers. Within the Community of the Resurrection, Mirfield (CR), which he helped to found and in which he lived for over 40 years, he is greatly revered. He had a huge impact on our formation, probably more than our acknowledged founder, Charles Gore. Yet to us, too, he is something of a mystery. No full biography of him has ever been written, only a collection of papers edited by C.S. Phillips, although this is valuable. Few stories exist about him. Even his formation of the Community appears to have been conducted by stealth; his name appears little in Chapter minutes and discussions. His influence is everywhere but he operated from behind the scenes. He was formidably intelligent, but also very well controlled. He came from the upper middle classes yet, like most early brethren of CR, was a convinced Christian socialist. He had family in the government, and friends throughout Europe, yet he was wholly a Community man. Members of the Community never felt he preferred his clever, famous or exciting friends to his brethren.

This book seeks to make Frere better known and to indicate the great range of his ability and interests. It begins with a masterly overview of his life by Alan Wilkinson in which the difference between his character and Charles Gore's makes for interesting reflection. John Davies then considers Frere's spirituality with its marked similarity to that of Lancelot Andrewes: the linguistic competence, the careful study of Scripture, the composition of beautiful prayers; it was a very ordered spirituality, but it produced a man whom many of his contemporaries described as a saint. Yet this scholarly, ascetic priest cared passionately about the disadvantaged. He insisted CR should live amongst the industrial poor and he helped start a College that made it possible for poor boys to become priests. Benjamin Gordon-Taylor looks at his teaching role and shows how this talented and fascinating teacher caught the imagination of his students, while at the same time propounding a vision of priesthood which was largely new to the Church of England.

Walter may have been a saint but John Livesley shows us how controversial he was as a bishop and how his very clear and historically rooted idea of how a bishop should operate did not always endear him to the people of Cornwall. Livesley tells us how some loved him and reckoned his influence to have been very great in shaping a new concept of episcopacy; his quirkiness and subtlety seem, however, to have alienated others so that he did not achieve all he could have done. Then in Alexander Faludy's essay on Frere as a scholar of the Reformation we see that meticulous attention to detail, to documents, to bringing together all the available resources and information that have made Frere's work fundamental to Reformation studies. Some of his conclusions were wrong and some of his prejudices were characteristic of his age, but in most aspects he was ahead of his time in his assessment of the Reformation period.

With Bernard Barlow's essay we enter a different area of Frere's work; that of ecumenist. Reading the account of his participation in Malines one is struck by how much could have come of those meetings, and perhaps did come of them forty years later. Yet there is a real sadness that more did not happen at the time. Frere and his colleagues were again well ahead of their contemporaries.

Much of Frere's reputation rests on his expertise as a liturgist, particularly in relation to the Revised Prayer Book of 1928. So it is fitting that two essays by John Livesley and Philip Corbett deal with different aspects of his work in this area. Both in their different ways show that, while Frere had a proper scholarly concern that the revisions should be accurate and should reflect the best results of liturgical research, at the same time his concern was fundamentally pastoral. He wanted the people of England to have a liturgy that was really adequate to their needs (which he felt 1662 was not) and he wanted it to serve the cause of unity between the different Anglican factions. Ironically, his main influence proved to be in the wider Anglican communion; though hundreds of churches in England did use the 1928 version it was a deep disappointment to him to have it rejected by Parliament and by Christians (such as Anglo-Catholics) whose Christian life he was trying to serve.

Something more of the enigmatic quality of Frere's work emerges in Peter Allan's essay on his study of the chant. Once again Frere shows astonishing technical competence, meticulous scholarship and some insights well ahead of his time, but he does not appear to have seen the immense contribution the chant can make to the formation and enrichment of the spiritual life of those who sing it. Perhaps the most important part of Allan's essay is his brief description of what could have been and still needs to be done in making us aware of the formative powers of plainsong.

In the final contribution George Guiver examines Walter's record as co-founder of CR. Here we see Walter acting almost by instinct to form the Community in monastic ways that he never expressed. Despite his great scholarship he shared with all other Anglican religious (and many Roman Catholics) a lack of monastic theology, a lack of interest in how it all worked. He got a lot right but his successors have had to fill gaps in creating an understanding of how men and women are formed to the service of God through the monastic life.

The book is not intended to be a comprehensive study or a full biography; rather it is offered as a first fruit of the work that deserves to be done on the many fascinating aspects of a remarkable person. For example, much more should be said of his ecumenical work, particularly with the Orthodox but also with the Student Christian Movement. Certainly, much more could and should be said about his liturgical scholarship and his work with the monastic chant. Our contributors have worked hard with archives and documents but there is much that remains untouched. There is plenty of material for a proper biographical study, and any of the essays could be usefully expanded to near book length. We don't apologise for the gaps that exist in what follows, and we hope very much that this book will inspire others to fill them and to place what we have done in a larger context.

We offer thanks, as is right and proper, to all who have helped us get this book going and ensure its completion: to the contributors themselves who have produced their work while coping with busy timetables and responsibilities; to the archive staff at the Borthwick Institute and other places of research who have been uniformly kind and helpful; to Christine Smith at Canterbury Press who has been patient with the many delays;

and above all to Ingrid Lawrie, our in-house editor, who has turned a rough text into what we hope is a respectable and pleasing publication.

N.S.
B.G.-T.
Mirfield, Lent 2011

1

A biographical sketch

ALAN WILKINSON

Early years

Walter Frere (1863–1938) came from a distinguished and ancient East Anglian family. *The Oxford Dictionary of National Biography* (2004) includes entries on nine of his relations, among whom, in the nineteenth century, was Sir Bartle Frere, a colonial governor and architect of empire. C.S. Phillips wrote of Walter Frere: 'In appearance and bearing, as also in his profound but gracious reserve, he was very much of an English aristocrat.'[1]

Five of the six founding members of the Community of the Resurrection were keen members of the Christian Social Union (CSU) established in 1889 by Henry Scott Holland (Charles Gore's closest friend) to promote Anglican social action and to form an Anglican social conscience.[2] Bishop Westcott of Durham, CSU's first President, believed that imperialism was an expression of Christian brotherhood and service, an image of the Kingdom of God, uniting many diverse organs into one body. Paul Bull, the most vocal imperialist in CR and an enthusiastic supporter of the Anglo-Boer War (of which Gore was a stern critic) entitled one of his CR pamphlets 'The Church and the Child Races'. Such moral imperialism provided the social and political context for CR's early missionary work in Africa, which began while Frere was Superior.

Walter Frere's grandfather, William Frere, became the second Master of Downing College, Cambridge, in 1812.[3] His niece married Christopher Wordsworth (nephew of the poet), who became Bishop of Lincoln in 1869. In 1837, Walter's father, Philip Howard Frere (1813–68), was elected

1 C.S. Phillips et al., *Walter Howard Frere, Bishop of Truro* (London: Faber & Faber, 1947), p. 13; see also Benedict Green CR, 'Walter Howard Frere', *Oxford Dictionary of National Biography* (Oxford: Oxford University Press, 2004).

2 See Alan Wilkinson, *Christian Socialism* (London: SCM Press, 1998), ch. 2 on CSU.

3 This account of Frere's early life relies on Phillips, *Frere*, ch. 1.

a Fellow of Downing and in 1839 Tutor and Bursar. Walter's mother was the daughter of a residentiary canon of Carlisle. Several members of the wider Frere family were clergy, including two cousins who were respectively the Bishop and Sub-Dean of Salisbury. Thus, when Walter was born on 23 November 1863 in Cambridge, his impressive and extensive clerical, political and university connections marked him out as a member of the ruling class.

But disaster struck Walter and his siblings. He was only four when his father died, and his mother died two years later. The arrangements that were made for the care of the orphans by the wider family were complicated. Not surprisingly, this unhappy period affected Walter permanently. He once remarked: 'I sometimes think that being an orphan is liable to make you a bit impersonal.' During these formative years he developed what Phillips called an 'etherealized naughtiness' which never left him, a strong sense of independence and an intense reticence which 'caused him to go out of his way to head others off from discovering his real grounds of opinion and action – a trait which puzzled not a few and, especially in his last years, diminished [his] influence'.[4]

At preparatory school he quickly distinguished himself by giving a speech on Speech Day with his typical lack of self-consciousness. He hoped to follow his grandfather and father to Eton but illness on the examination day wrecked his chances. Instead, he went to Charterhouse, where he enjoyed the community life, music and sport. In 1882 he went up to Trinity College, Cambridge, where many of his relations had been educated. He became secretary of the University Musical Society, sang, composed, learnt German, French and Russian. He took a First in Classics before proceeding to postgraduate theological studies. He was already demonstrating his capacity to keep several balls in the air at once.

His vocation to the priesthood ripened almost imperceptibly. If there were dramatic moments, these were concealed from others. He chose to go to Wells Theological College because it was soberly Anglican. Though he was a patrician, proud of his family and a bit of a dandy at Cambridge, before he left university he was drawn towards socialism. After a year at Wells, in 1887 he was made deacon in St Paul's Cathedral and priest two years later. He served in the parish of St Dunstan's, Stepney, under Edwyn

---

4 Phillips, *Frere*, pp. 16, 18, 20.

Hoskyns, later Bishop of Southwell, whose wife was a socialist in the William Morris tradition and a suffragist. Frere was in charge of the St Faith's district. Services were held in a schoolroom, but Frere also used a rubbish tip as a venue. At St Faith's he inaugurated what was probably the first 9.30 a.m. Parish Communion in the Church of England.[5] He was also elected as a Labour member of the local Board of Guardians, whose task it was to administer the Poor Law, and became secretary of the CSU for East London. In his spare time he studied the history of plainsong in the British Museum and researched and wrote up Stepney parish history. His devotions were also those of a scholarly mind: he wrote them in Greek, Hebrew and Latin and recited the daily psalms in Hebrew.

The Community of the Resurrection

In October 1887, the year Frere was made deacon, a number of clergy formed the Society of the Resurrection (SR) and elected Charles Gore, the Principal of Pusey House, as Superior. The Society was like a Third Order with its community focus at Pusey House. Gore hoped that out of the Society an Oratorian community would emerge. J.H. Newman, who founded his Oratory in 1848, conceived it as more like an Oxford college than a monastery, a brotherhood bound by the mutual affection of educated gentlemen rather than vows.[6] Gore seems to have conceived this new community on similar lines. Though he was not a monastic, he believed that there was an important role for communities of prayer and reflection. From a very early age, like Frere and others of his background, many of his most formative experiences had derived from living in a residential community – in boarding school, university and theological college. He also believed that religious communities should bear witness to, and strive for, social morality and justice and be paradigms for the right ordering of society. But Frere had a stronger belief in monastic life. During the summer of 1889, Gore began the further stages of the creation of a religious community at Pusey House. But he was psychologically incapable of giving himself totally to this one enterprise. He had a fear of being trapped with no exit. In 1889, apart from being creator of this nascent community, he was Principal of Pusey House; in June he took a

---

5 Donald Gray, *Earth and Altar* (Alcuin Club. Norwich: Canterbury Press, 1986), p. 159.
6 Placid Murray, *Newman the Oratorian* (Dublin: Gill and Macmillan, 1969).

leading role in the creation of the CSU; in November *Lux Mundi* was published. He was editor and he had contributed an essay that had caused national controversy; in December he sailed to India for three months to deal with the problems of the Oxford Mission to Calcutta.

In October 1891, two years after the community experiment had begun, Frere wrote to Gore as Superior of the SR, which he had recently joined. He had already considered joining a proposed community of friars in the East End, and had also visited the Society of St John the Evangelist in Cowley (founded by Fr R.M. Benson in 1865). He found them to be monks, almost hermits, whereas he felt called to be more like a friar, living in the world and ministering to those outside the Church. Though he realized it sounded presumptuous from a recently joined member, he proposed a mission house of SR in the East End but with a stricter rule. That would be better soil than Oxford 'where I know the seed is gradually maturing'. He would gladly hand over his private income of £300 a year. 'A common purse is to my mind an essential condition.' He declared himself impatient to begin.

This was a bold (some might think arrogant) letter for a young curate and a recently joined member to write to a religious Superior who was already an eminent theologian and ecclesiastic. He was suggesting that the new community was in the wrong place, that it needed a stricter rule and more urgency. There was an implicit contrast between his urgency and Gore's policy of gradual maturation. This is the first known of many instances where Frere with his clear objectives chivvied Gore to follow him. On 4 February 1892 Frere arrived at Pusey House to join the other potential members. 'I go to Oxford ... to see what they are up to with their brotherhood', he airily told a friend. The use of the phrase 'what they are up to' and of 'they' and 'their' showed his temperamental aversion to displays of emotion but also indicated that this was an enterprise which had not yet received his approval.

But why did he feel called to the religious life? He believed that the parochial system needed to be supplemented. He found the possession of money 'intolerable' (and eventually gave almost all his patrimony to CR). As a historian he knew the immense importance of religious orders to the church. He realized that his will required mortification and he needed the discipline of regular worship. He saw himself as supplying a Cambridge contribution to this embryonic community, as all the others were Oxford men. The others were dazzled by Gore, Frere was not. This independence from Gore was to become a crucial factor in the development of CR. Many years later he described to a potential biographer of Gore that he and Gore had never been at ease with one another and that Gore had been continually a 'disappointment'. Gore and Frere had very different temperaments: Gore was sombre, dramatic, prophetic, Frere was cool, detached and suspicious of anything histrionic. Gore knew how to amuse and fascinate, whereas (as a friend remarked) Frere was 'always battling with pride and intense reserve'. Gore was a theologian, uninterested in the detail of liturgical scholarship, which was Frere's academic passion.[7]

On 25 July (St James's Day) 1892, Gore and five other priests made their professions in the Pusey House chapel and so formed the Community of the Resurrection. They took no vows, but professed a lifelong intention, renewed annually. Frere's diary of 1892–5 and letters to other brethren reveal how loosely knit CR was in its early days and record his criticisms of Gore's lack of clear leadership. A week after the creation of CR they all dispersed for a month's holiday. Frere travelled with one of his sisters and another woman to Germany to enjoy the opera and to work in libraries. When everyone reassembled, George Longridge left for two years to help the Oxford Mission. 'I suppose it is right,' noted Frere in his diary, though clearly he did not. A few months at Pusey House deepened his conviction that Oxford was not the right setting for CR, but that lifelong vows were not essential as he had once thought.

On his first parish mission he felt stiff and academic. His work on the Sarum Gradual in various libraries was more congenial, but he continued with parish visits, missions, talks to groups and sermons. He preached to a 'swell audience' in Oxford, but was happier 'at the real work in the bosom of poverty' on missions in inner-city parishes. His attraction to socialism deepened under the influence of John Carter, a founding member of CR who played a leading role in the CSU. Frere regarded 'Evangelical Catholic' priests with particular warmth but disliked those who were 'papistical' or had no common life in their clergy houses. A few

---

7 See G.L. Prestige, *The Life of Charles Gore* (London: Heinemann, 1935); Alan Wilkinson 'Charles Gore' in *Oxford Dictionary of National Biography* (Oxford: Oxford University Press, 2004); Wilkinson, *Christian Socialism*, ch. 3; Wilkinson, *The Community of the Resurrection: A Centenary History* (London: SCM Press, 1992), p. 51; Phillips, *Frere*, p. 117.

years later he was a more relaxed missioner. At one Mirfield Mission he held 800 children spellbound day after day. Yet he had no tricks, no histrionics, just himself with his natural rapport with children.

In the summer of 1893 Frere was dismayed by the decision to move a few miles from Oxford to Radley, where Gore was to be vicar. 'All depended on CG's position at PH & suddenly he who had felt the difficulty of going to a town came out with a clear decision that he must leave & go into the country & get peace to read.' Many brethren had wanted to move to the industrial north. This now had to be postponed. CR had to give priority to Gore's needs. Yet paradoxically Gore said that it would be 'unendurable' to be called 'Superior'. Rather he wished to be known as 'Senior'. 'I cannot, as before God, who bids us not be called Rabbi, say to people *come & go*, as if I had authority to control their lives more or less absolutely.'[8] This was curiously self-deceiving, for the brethren almost always deferred to Gore's wishes.

Gore had never even been a full-time curate let alone a vicar. He seems to have envisaged Radley as a rural idyll where he could read and think. Instead he was constantly in a state of anguish about the compromised character of rural religion. He felt trapped. Even the accommodation was cramped. Inducted on 21 September 1893, he broke down before Christmas and went abroad. In March 1894 he returned for Holy Week and Easter but still was not well. In May he broke down again and was away for six months. He decided to resign as vicar. With Gore absent, the brethren were able to talk freely. Frere felt the tragedy keenly and quoted the opening chorus from *Agamemnon*: 'Cry woe, woe, but let the good prevail.' Gore did not return into residence until November, and he was now attracted by the offer of a canonry at Westminster Abbey. The brethren were startled, not least because it would mean splitting up the small community of six (one of whom continued at Pusey House) plus three probationers into two. Frere was horrified. In November 1894 he wrote in a letter that Gore would soon be in

another whirl ... what we want above all I think for this next year is to have the Senior at home quietly reading and pulling all our life together ... identifying himself much more with the Community than he has

---

8 Prestige, *Life*, p. 137.

been able to do so far ... It is of course an immense gain to the Community to have a commanding figure at its head but it may pay too dearly for the privilege.

The Community, he believed needed 'poverty and obscurity', but Westminster Abbey with its 'prelatical splendour' would stifle religion.

At Chapter on 29 November 1894, Frere courageously, but with pain, spoke out against Gore going to the Abbey. The acceptance of the canonry would be the triumph of 'the laxer view' of the Community. Rather it needed a parish for work among the poor and a stricter and poorer house than Radley. But everyone else agreed with the proposal – in any case it was only a week before the announcement. He commented bitterly in his diary: 'At present it seems the Senior's vocation v. the Community's.' He quoted again the chorus from *Agamemnon*: 'Cry woe, woe ...'. This startling declaration and dramatic quotation from such a laconic person as Frere convey the depth of his distress. As Gore became preoccupied and fulfilled at Westminster his health improved notably, but he also became marginal to CR. His house was a Community house for the next seven years with usually two or three in residence there. It was at Radley, however, that the brethren gathered for Chapter.

At Radley, some ordinands lived with the Community. Many years later one of them, J.M.C. Crum (then a Canon of Canterbury) recalled aspects of Frere's character. One was his ability to argue convincingly on both sides of an argument. Whereas other brethren had oddities that could be mocked, 'I think one looked at Frere as you look at some statue or picture which others tell you is beautiful.' He was an immensely scholarly historian, yet he could also sit down at the piano, sing ballads and German songs or equally play for village dances when the band was tired. The ordinands worried about Frere's health because he slept too little and drove himself too hard.

Frere continued to agonize about the Community. Both Radley and Westminster were too respectable to attract the type of person it needed. '*A really strong* [italics his] Community centre' was required, with no women servants, but household work, plain living, cassocks round the parish and the use of 'Father' (despite Gore's objections). By January 1897 Frere and his allies could wait no longer. A move to the north won almost unanimous approval. Various places were considered. The Bishop of Wakefield suggested a house in Mirfield. Gore did the preliminary negotiations. Frere and Cyril Bickersteth visited it and pronounced it very suitable. In September CR agreed to rent the house and grounds. Ironically for a community committed to simplicity of life with a pronounced social conscience, the house, extensive gardens and pasture were owned by the widow of the richest mill owner in the area, who had been President of the Conservative Club. Characteristically, Gore was far away in America for two months when this vital decision was made. In January 1898 the first two brethren moved in. At last in 1899 Gore agreed to the appointment of a brother in charge of probationers (as novices were called) and appointed Frere. So in effect Frere was now in charge of the future of CR.

Mirfield was totally different from Oxford, Radley or Westminster. A flourishing West Riding town since the fourteenth century, connected to the canal system in the eighteenth century, it was now a junction of two railways. The smoke from the many woollen mills mingled with the smoke from passing trains in the valley below the house. Local people reacted with some scepticism to the highly educated southern gentlemen who had come to do them good. In October 1901, Gore was offered the see of Worcester. He was thus rescued from the painful dilemma of having founded a community to which he was not able to give himself completely. CR left Gore to make up his own mind. As to be expected, Frere opposed this further elevation, believing that the call to the religious life transcended all others. But CR released Gore from his Community obligations.

Frere as Superior

In January 1902, Frere was elected Superior at the age of 38. This represented such a new development that some have regarded it as the 'Second Foundation'. CR was no longer composed of a distinguished Canon and his admirers (with one dissenter). Four years later Keble Talbot (who would be Frere's successor) arrived to test his vocation and reported that Frere was 'much the biggest man' at Mirfield. Frere came to the role with a clear understanding of what he wanted CR to be. This he explained in his *Commentary on the Rule* (1907), which is shrewd, humane and unpietistic. Talbot described Frere's style as Superior:

Light as were his hands upon the reins and sparing as was his use of the imperative, there was no mistaking Frere's governing touch upon the life of the Community, composed as it was in those earlier days of men of forcible character and strongly marked individuality ... He was more concerned to enlist their co-operation and to develop their initiative than to impose his orders ... The far sighted clarity of his mind, his detachment from the pressure of excited feelings and from all self-importance, the flexibility of his adjustment to unexpected situations enabled him to give the lead through all perplexities. Incalculable he often was; it was difficult to predict what line he would take. For one thing, he was generally two moves ahead of anyone else, and when you thought to come up with him he was away and beyond. And in matters which fall short of ultimate principles he was not greatly careful of consistency.[9]

Frere swiftly introduced changes and inaugurated profoundly important developments. He was at ease with the term 'Superior'. There were fewer servants. Brethren had to do more manual and domestic work. The term 'Father' became customary though not compulsory. Cassocks were more generally worn. Having been initially in favour of vows, Frere now accepted the idea of permanent intention instead. John Carter, a founding member of CR, lived in Oxford during term time where he promoted CSU. He had a pragmatic rather than a theological view of community life. He had a deep attachment to Gore, and, when Gore withdrew, so did he.

In 1902, CR decided to purchase the house and grounds at Mirfield. Of the £5,000 needed, Frere provided £2,000, a large part of his patrimony. CR now branched out in several new directions within a short space of time. At Radley, it had provided one aspect of ordination training by encouraging ordinands to share its life and worship. In 1897, it created a fund to provide bursaries for poorer ordinands. Brethren were deeply concerned that most Anglican clergy were drawn from the middle and upper classes and that it was difficult for potential ordinands with little money or education to be accepted. In 1901, CR investigated the work with this type of ordinand by the Society of the Sacred Mission (founded

9 Phillips, *Frere*, p. 54.

1893).[10] SSM offered an integrated course on its own premises. CR proposed a course which was also free of charge, but divided between a degree at the University of Leeds and a theological course at Mirfield.

In 1907, Frere gave some fascinating evidence to the Archbishop's Committee on the Supply and Training of Ordinands. He reported that there were 50 students at Mirfield and 12 at Leeds, selected from several hundred who had applied. Those who had been in full-time schooling were expected to pass Leeds Matriculation. Many had to be prepared for this over a year or more. The largest group had only elementary education. The men 'must be capable of polish ... We are anxious to have men from every class ... We find no difficulty about manners though they have to be learnt. We have to be careful in our selection about the difficulties of accent.' He considered that most students would be more at home with a middle-class high tea than a dinner party. They would not suit a rich congregation but would be more at home with a middle-class congregation than the average public school and university man. Students had to do their own housework and some cooking. The scheme only took men aged under 20, though the College would like to take men older than that. In his experience as an examining chaplain the most unsatisfactory type of ordinand was the man from Oxford or Cambridge with no training in the disciplined ministerial life. The best men were former elementary school teachers, 'the cream of the working class'. Later, in 1922, Frere was very critical of the Church's failure to continue to finance pre-ordination education training at Knutsford. In 1924 Frere and the Principal of the College of the Resurrection approached Billy Hand, a Norfolk priest who had been one of the first students at Mirfield, to set up a school in the grounds of his rectory at Tatterford to provide basic education for poor ordinands. It lasted until 1950.

Over a century after its foundation, the College at Mirfield flourishes at the centre of a diversity of other types of theological education, lay as well as ordained, on the site.

The third major development within a short time after Frere became Superior was the inauguration of work in South Africa, with the arrival

---

10 See David A. Dowland, *Nineteenth-Century Anglican Theological Training: The Redbrick Challenge* (Oxford: Oxford University Press, 1997); A. Mason, *History of the Society of the Sacred Mission* (Norwich: Canterbury Press, 1993).

of three brothers in Johannesburg in March 1903. While the British still governed South Africa, CR had ready access to leading members of the imperial establishment through CR's contacts within it. In 1900, Gore had urged upon CR the needs of South Africa, recovering from the war of which he had been such a stern critic. CR brethren were more sensitive to racial issues than many missionaries of that period, though they shared their attitude of benevolent paternalism. They engaged in pastoral work over vast areas and from the first pioneered the earliest systematic Anglican priestly training for blacks in South Africa. Between 1903 and 1977, CR trained nearly all the black priests in South Africa. Many of the white and black bishops (including Ambrose Reeves and Desmond Tutu) were also trained by CR, either in South Africa or at Mirfield.

In 1906, Frere visited Southern Rhodesia to investigate the possibility of taking over St Augustine's Mission at Penhalonga, after Bishop Gaul of Mashonaland had written explaining that he believed that community life was an essential basis for missionary work. It was not until 1915 that CR was able to take on the Mission in addition to the College, the Leeds Hostel, the work in South Africa and the new branch house in London. St Augustine's went on to make an outstanding contribution to lay and clerical education in Rhodesia. It also became the centre for trekking mission priests who covered huge areas on donkeys, caring, at one stage, for 42 churches and schools.

Another development with lasting consequences was the creation in 1903 of the Fraternity of the Resurrection, a type of Third Order. At first only men could join, but women were admitted a year later. The CR Quarterly also first appeared in 1903 and kept supporters in touch. Under Frere, numbers of the brethren continued to grow and extensions to the House were needed. The House chapel began to be inadequate. Some brethren thought that the building of a new church was not only a matter of having more accommodation but that it was an important proclamation that CR was in continuity with pre-Reformation monasteries. The foundation stone was laid by Gore (now Bishop of Oxford) in July 1911. The initial plans by Walter Tapper (which were never carried out) envisaged a church higher than Durham Cathedral, longer than Ripon and wider than Westminster Abbey. This reflected the optimism of CR about its future, though the Community acknowledged that the construction would be spread over a century. It is not known how enthusiastic Frere was about such opulence – he was distrustful of the flamboyant and expensive – but he had an acute sense of history. CR's decision to reject the Gothic style and adopt the Byzantine may have reflected Frere's attraction to Orthodoxy. Certainly the requirement that the building should be characterized by 'austerity and simple dignity' expressed Frere's spirituality. When in 1905 electric light was installed in the public rooms of the Mother House, Frere worried lest CR was slipping into luxury.

Controversies

Most CR brethren had a strong sense of *noblesse oblige*. With a mixture of self-sacrifice and naïveté they had moved north to try to bridge the gap between Church and working-class people while living in what a local Independent Labour Party (ILP) magazine called 'a capitalist's house'. The mill owner had specifically chosen the site to be above the level of the smoke from the mills below. The house looked not on the mills but on the open countryside the other side of the valley. In 1984, Joseph Hird, who in the early days of CR at Mirfield had been a young working man, a server and choir member at the local parish church, was still bitter in a personal memoir about 'T'Resurrection men': in his youth they had prayed for the workers who clattered past in their nailed boots but had no contact with them or the squalor in which they were living near-by.

In 1906 and 1907, however, CR, led by Frere, made a considerable effort to bring Church and Labour leaders together at two meetings in the Quarry in the CR grounds. Hitherto the main influence within the Liberal party and Labour movement had come from Nonconformity. CR was determined to demonstrate Anglican support for social reform. In 1905 Keir Hardie had asked for help from the clergy during the next General Election. During that election of 1906, Frere and Paul Bull (the leading CR missioner and the most ebullient of CR socialists) spoke for ILP candidates in Leeds and Dewsbury. They went on to organize a conference in May in the Quarry. The invitations were in the names of Frere and Bull, though CR had given the venture its blessing. Between 350 and 400 attended, mostly from the North. Frere, welcoming the delegates, recalled his days as a Labour Guardian and claimed that CR was 'communistic'. Both socialism and monasticism were essentially about community. Keir Hardie's arrival was greeted with a standing ovation. A collection was taken for locked-out miners. In July between 700 and 2,300 people attended the weekly Quarry sermons, this time on 'Christian Socialism'. In June the conference was followed by the formation of the radical Church Socialist League (CSL) in Morecambe by 60 priests and a few lay people. Those who signed the invitations to it included Frere, Bull and others who had attended the Quarry conference. Frere, Bull and five other CR brethren became members of CSL.

In April 1907, Frere and Bull organized another conference between Church and Labour. Frere proposed a resolution reaffirming the decision of the first conference to encourage cooperation between socialists and churchpeople to spread 'the principles of collectivism and develop a more aggressive propaganda'. The first conference had been attended almost entirely by men. This time a much larger number of women attended, including the suffragettes Emmeline Pankhurst and Annie Kenney. They and a number of other women delegates spoke in favour of a resolution proposed by Bull supporting votes for women. When the tradition of Anglo-Catholic misogyny is recalled, the presence of so many women and leading suffragettes is remarkable. Bull said: 'We must cease to look upon women as dolls and drudges, and ask them to be partners and companions in our life.'

No third conference was held at Mirfield, presumably because of the creation of the CSL, but also because these conferences and the open support of ILP candidates by Frere and Bull led to the accusation that CR was socialistic. Some supporters withdrew their contributions to the work of the Community, imperilling its future. Frere replied that the Community could not be held responsible for the views of its members. But critics said that since the public heard only socialist views from the Community it was legitimate to conclude that it was wholly socialist.

Samuel Healy, the most vociferous of the brethren, was a gift to critics. He both denounced Protestantism as 'founded by the devil' and was reported as suggesting that the assassination of capitalists would be an acceptable way to change the social system. In the Christmas 1907 edition of the *CR Quarterly*, Frere defended CR against charges of political bias, maintaining that while it was said that the Church should stand aside from politics, in the existing situation this meant that the Church should support Conservatism. In reality, he said, the Community was more representative of the Church as a whole because it included a wide range of political views.

In fact, the number of brethren who wished to identify themselves publicly as socialists gradually declined. Frere himself became more politically cautious. He ceased to be prominent in the CSL after 1912 partly because he thought a 'Remonstrance' to the bishops that year was too belligerent. Frere, nevertheless, was one of the eight brethren who joined 500 clergy in signing a Memorial to the Labour Party in 1923 on becoming the Official Opposition and offered their support. Frere believed that Labour must be offered a partnership in national life. In 1919, 1920 and 1922, during Frere's time as Superior, the local Labour Party held its garden parties in the Community's grounds.

Frere's first period as Superior was troubled by other controversies, some internal, some external. In 1903, the withdrawal of Hugh Benson, son of the former Archbishop of Canterbury, and his reception into the Roman Catholic Church fuelled accusations of popery. Caleb Ritson, the Warden (i.e., Principal) of the College had used his architectural skills to convert the stable block into the College. But he established a draconian regime. The students, as recipients of CR funds, were reluctant to protest, but eventually they did so. Ritson resigned and left CR in 1908. In 1910, Healy withdrew to work for the CSL. After he created another controversy by arguing that ancient church endowments were given to support a celibate priesthood, the brethren were naturally annoyed that, soon after leaving CR, he married.

Frederick Temple, Archbishop of Canterbury 1897–1902, was CR's first Visitor, but he never actually visited the Community. In January 1904, CR invited his successor, Randall Davidson to be Visitor despite the fact that he had little experience of and little sympathy for religious communities.[11] But CR's instinct was always to go to the top table. The invitation arrived when Davidson was under great pressure from Protestants to thwart the advances of Anglo-Catholicism. Davidson took five months to reply and objected to brethren being required to use sacramental confession. When CR modified this, he agreed to become Visitor. It was an inauspicious start to what was to prove a damaging relationship to CR. The Archbishop reluctantly agreed to preside at a meeting in London in May 1907 to raise money to build a Hostel in Leeds, to replace temporary accommodation for students attending the university. When he received

---

11 The correspondence about the Archbishop as Visitor is held at Mirfield and Lambeth Palace Library.

protests from Protestant groups, the modernist Bishop of Ripon and other bishops, he got cold feet. Surprisingly, Frere communicated to Davidson his own disquiet at the contents of some of the Community's popular booklets and invited him to appoint someone to examine them for doctrinal probity.

The Archbishop's appearance at Church House, Westminster, on 13 May 1907 was greeted with Protestant objectors handing out pamphlets denouncing 'Romanising Monks'. One tried to shout him down, another banged his umbrella on the table. The Archbishop, after commending CR's educational plans, denounced certain of the 'Mirfield Manuals' and asked for some to be withdrawn. In reply Frere was deferential. He said that he and the Community welcomed the Archbishop's help in bringing CR into line or keeping them in line with the Church's doctrine and discipline. In fact, Frere was playing a double game of seeming to the brethren to be standing up for them against the Archbishop while asking the Archbishop and the Bishop of Wakefield to strengthen his hand against those he regarded as troublemakers. Gore, however, speaking at a parallel fund-raising meeting in Leeds, denounced any censorship as 'tyranny'.

While Davidson was busy reading through 150 of the penny 'Manuals', Kensitites were organizing a protest meeting at Mirfield Town Hall for 6 June with an admission charge. Cunningly Frere arranged a meeting at the same time outside the Black Bull opposite, free of charge. He stood on a chair, was relaxed and amusing and persuaded the crowd that they were in no danger from 'The House of Correction' (as it was nicknamed) on the hill.

The correspondence between Frere and the Archbishop continued. After four years during which CR's name was dragged through the mud in local and national papers, Davidson resigned quietly at the end of 1908. During that time he had never set foot in a Community house. The issues raised during that period were important, not least how to achieve the right balance between individual and communal responsibility and what degree of liberty was desirable or possible for individual brothers. Frere mused upon these issues in his *Commentary* on the Rule, written in the midst of the controversies on board ship on his way to Africa in 1906 and published a year later.

Every brother must be free to develop his powers, his message and his work to the fullest extent, as God leads him. The Community could not tolerate for a moment that true liberty should be either violated by corporate action from without, or surrendered by the individual from within ... it will be prepared, if need be, to suffer through the mistakes of its members, regarding this as less of an evil than the coercion of any brother into uniformity where divergence is valuable or even tolerable ... The Community will demand of the individual that he should at all times bear in mind the relation that his sayings and doings have to the Community, and make a careful forecast of the effect that they are likely to have on the life and welfare of the body.[12]

Keble Talbot also caused problems for Frere. He had arrived at Mirfield in 1906, drawn by Frere's influence. Gore was one of his father's dearest friends. Talbot came from the heart of Liberal Catholicism. His father, as former Warden of Keble College, Oxford (later Bishop of Southwark, from 1911 of Winchester), had contributed to *Lux Mundi* (1889) its manifesto. His godfather was Henry Scott Holland. The fact that Talbot was not professed for three and a half years (when the probationary period lasted usually only a year or two) shows how divided in mind he was. This manifested itself on a number of painful occasions for Talbot, Frere and CR. During Talbot's probation, the Headmaster of Winchester College (Talbot was a Wykehamist) offered him the post of College Missioner. He was also offered work in India. The next year he was pressed to be Principal of Pusey House, not least by Scott Holland. In 1914, four years into profession, having refused these offers, he was urged by Gore and others to succeed his brother as Chaplain of Balliol. CR was divided. Frere was clear that the religious life was essentially corporate.[13] He moved in Chapter that a direct refusal should be made, the alternative being withdrawal from CR. Frere was no longer Superior but his judgement carried great weight. 'No doubt Frere's very penetrating and decisive views were the chief determining factor', Talbot reported to his brother. In 1920, the majority voted against him becoming Warden of Keble. Other offers later were more easily refused. Frere believed that his vocation was to help restore community life in the Church of England (as he told the Archbishop when he initially refused to become Bishop of Truro in 1923). In decisions about Keble Talbot we see Frere's view prevailing over the

12 *The Book of the Community of the Resurrection* (privately printed 1924), pp. 139–40.
13 For Frere's understanding of the religious life, see *Church Times*, 20 September 1901.

looser Oratorian understanding of community life held by Gore.

Over the years, Frere himself refused, or was relieved not to be nominated for, canonries at Southwark and Windsor, the deanery of St Paul's, and two professorships at Cambridge. But he accepted other part-time responsibilities outside the Community. He became spiritual advisor to the Order of the Holy Paraclete, Whitby, as it sought to work out its vocation before its foundation in 1917. He followed Neville Figgis CR as advisor to the Oratory of the Good Shepherd and received the first professions in 1919. He joined the board of Hymns Ancient and Modern in 1894, became a proprietor in 1903 and chairman from 1923 until his death. This helped CR's finances.

Frere as Superior had everything at his fingertips. When Talbot succeeded him in 1922 he said he felt like a 'cart-horse' succeeding a 'race-horse', a 'pen-knife' after a 'razor-blade'. But Talbot secured the votes of brethren precisely because (as Bull put it) Frere's 'very greatness and goodness has in a way paralysed the initiative of other Brethren. Walter does everything so much better than anyone else that the tendency has been to leave everything to him.' Frere had been Superior continually for 20 years apart from a break from 1913 to 1916. The cost of always appearing debonair and in control through crises and controversies was considerable. In 1904 his health broke down and he went abroad. In 1908, after an accident, he was away with neuritis for three months, mostly spent at St Paul's Deanery. In 1909 Longridge was recalled from South Africa to assist Frere and to prevent a total breakdown of his health. He was elected Superior from 1913 to 1916 to give Frere a break from ultimate responsibility. In 1916 Frere, now Superior again, appointed Longridge Prior at Mirfield in order to delegate domestic affairs to him. In 1930 as Bishop of Truro, Frere had a stroke, causing him to abort his presence at the Lambeth Conference. Four years later another stroke precipitated his resignation.

Culture

Frere made a cultural as well as a religious contribution to the Mirfield area. In 1910, for Commemoration Day, he produced the first play in the Quarry, *The Return of Ulysses*, by Robert Bridges. Music and songs by Frere were performed. In the following years, Elgar, Grieg, Stanford, Parry, Russian and sixteenth-century music were on the menu. Frere believed the church should elevate taste. He also shared in the culture of the wealthy houses of the area. He was the first President of the Mirfield Civic Society whose creation he and other brethren had promoted. When he lectured to the Society on 'Musical Form' he danced round the platform to illustrate it. He also lectured on medieval music to the Leeds Arts Club. Nothing daunted him. On board ship on the way to Canada, in the midst of a severe storm when magnates fortified themselves with champagne and elderly ladies were forcibly propelled across the deck, Frere walked to the piano with a light step, restoring a truant glass on the way, and played and sang for one and a half hours in most of the languages of Europe. Neville Figgis remarked that watching him walk made it easier to believe in the Ascension. Music was his passion, the one area in which he could let go. A visitor to Bishop Talbot's house once asked: 'Who is that man with a face like St Bruno, singing passionate Breton love songs?' Yet his preaching was unemotional, a drawback in Yorkshire accustomed to Nonconformist oratory. An elderly woman commented after one sermon 'I mak' nowt of Frere; he donna swee-at enough' ('I don't make anything of Frere, he doesn't sweat enough'). The Free Church *British Weekly* for 21 March 1907 provided a different picture of his preaching after a sermon at St Paul's: 'He is tall, slight, fair-haired, with features prematurely worn, and the forehead of a thinker ... both an intellectual and a tender preacher.' He spoke about suffering and asked:

> Have you ever, I wonder, had to do something to a pet dog which hurt it very much so as to get it well – to pull a thorn out of its foot or wash a wound, or something of that sort? ... It hurt tremendously, and yet there seemed to speak from his eyes trust of you ... as if he meant to say 'I do not in the least understand what you are doing, but go on.'

This homely illustration reminds us that there was a simple, direct side to Frere as well as the baffling and sophisticated aspects of his character.

Frere paid four visits to Russia between 1909 and 1914 at a time when travelling to Russia was almost impossible. Though he remained a Western Catholic, he warmed to Orthodoxy because of its 'timelessness' and 'its wonderful sense of fellowship with the departed'.[14] During the war, Serbian refugees, including monks and priests, were accommodated

---

14 *Church Times*, 19 June 1914; see also 26 June 1914.

at Mirfield and Frere helped to train Serbian ordinands in Oxford. In 1951, one of his former students, now a bishop, came to Mirfield to pray at his tomb. The Fellowship of St Alban and St Sergius, formed in 1928, elected Frere as its first Anglican President.

War

Spiritually and culturally, Frere was a European. So when war came in 1914, unlike so many he refused to preach Christian nationalism. War, he said in a Quarry sermon of 1915, was a 'clumsy way' to get things right again, but 'some better way must be found'. Like Davidson, George Bell and William Temple and other ecumenically minded Anglicans, Frere believed that, because European Christians could not worship together, it was easier for them to quarrel, and that the Christmas truce in the trenches, when enemies discovered each other as brothers, was a foreshadowing of what must be.[15] 'We cannot love our enemies if we believe we are wholly right and they wholly wrong. Some Germans were as distressed by the war as we are.'[16]

The National Mission of Repentance and Hope in 1916 was the Church of England's attempt to face the issues raised by the war.[17] Frere complained at one preparatory meeting: we have allowed ourselves to be paralysed by 'a prevailing spirit of Cathedral mattins which makes little demand on anybody but the choir'. He contended that: 'Prayer for the dead is one of our greatest levers & our neglect of it one of our worst faults.' He lamented Anglicans' disregard of the Eucharist and dumbness in the face of death, claiming that they preached too much and prayed too little.[18]

Frere and Gore

Gore resigned as Bishop of Oxford in 1919. In a letter to Frere, he ruminated about his future. Would the Community wish him to return?

---

15 *Community of the Resurrection Quarterly Review (CRQ)*, Michaelmas 1915.

16 *The Student Movement*, 1914–15.

17 For National Mission, see Alan Wilkinson, *The Church of England and the First World War* (2nd edn, London: SCM Press, 1996), pp. 70–90.

18 W.J. Sheils (ed.), *The Church and War* (Oxford: Blackwell, 1983), p. 343.

But he felt 'a certain carnal disinclination'. Frere replied at once, enthusiastically. His return was 'a long cherished hope'. If Gore had come back (as a Prelate Brother living under a modified rule), however, it would have been a huge mistake for Frere, Gore and CR. Many younger brethren were attracted to Anglo-Catholic papalism, which both Gore and Frere disliked. Gore and Frere were very different in temperament and academic interests. Gore was emotional, dramatic, prophetic, prone to pessimism but attracted disciples. Frere was a cool loner who shrank from courting the approval of others. Did Gore's refusal to return into residence awake Frere's painful memories of Gore's breakdowns at Radley and his exit to Westminster Abbey 20 years before? Was this the last straw for Frere? Certainly he later wrote about Gore with unwonted asperity to two potential biographers.[19]

Frere and Anglo-Catholicism

Unlike 'advanced' Anglo-Catholics, Frere and Gore were not apologetic about being Anglicans. Both refused to be deferential to the papacy. Frere in particular urged Anglo-Catholics to look to the East and not solely to Rome.[20] He was most attracted to Catholicism when it was leavened by Evangelicalism. He addressed the 1933 Anglo-Catholic Congress on 'The Debt Owed by the Church of England to the Evangelical Revival'. As Bishop of Truro he experienced the debt Cornish religion owed to Methodism: both its evangelistic zeal and the Tractarian stress upon the priestly were needed.[21]

At the 1923 Anglo-Catholic Congress, Frank Weston, the flamboyant and heroic Bishop of Zanzibar, sent telegrams to the King and Queen, the Archbishops and the Patriarch of Constantinople on behalf of the delegates. Then he proposed that one should be sent to 'the Holy Father'. (No telegrams were sent to Protestant leaders.) Two days later Frere told the Congress that it was a mistake (shouts of 'No' and some applause).

19 See letters quoted in Wilkinson, *Centenary History*, pp. 51–2.

20 See W.H. Frere, 'Christian Unity: The Eastern Orthodox Church', in *Report of the First Anglo-Catholic Congress, London 1920* (London: SPCK, 1920).

21 *Report of the Oxford Movement Centenary Congress, July 1933* (London: Catholic Literature Association, n.d.).

This incident widened the rift between himself and the papalists.[22] Dom Anselm Hughes of Nashdom Abbey implied, unpleasantly, that Truro was a reward for his opposition to the telegram.[23] Talbot reported that when the Archbishop pressed Frere to accept Truro because he would represent Anglo-Catholicism, he 'airily' said that in fact Anglo-Catholics regarded him as just another moderate with a kindly feeling towards them. However, a Nashdom monk grumbled, 'That rogue Bishop Frere defiled our high altar by using English at it.'[24]

Frere and the 'Women's Movement'

In 1981, Fr Philip Speight (then 94 and the oldest member of CR) told me that during the 1907 Quarry Conference between Church and Labour he had looked after Mrs Pankhurst and taken her a cup of tea. It is very difficult now to grasp how radical and daring was Frere's eagerness to preside over meetings that included Keir Hardie and suffragettes – almost comparable to today chairing meetings that included convicted terrorists. In opposition to the respectable and peaceable suffrage organizations, Emmeline Pankhurst founded the Women's Social and Political Union in 1903. To attract attention it turned to militant action including a campaign of arson, after which, in 1913, she was sentenced to three years' penal servitude. Yet Frere was not frightened off the issue by all this female militancy and the outrage it caused. In July 1914, in one of the Quarry sermons attended by 1,200 people, he posed the question: how can men and women be brought into fruitful cooperation? With civilization, he said, their relationship changed and woman's sphere of activity and responsibilities enlarged, so it was natural that she should now make a contribution to political life. He stressed that men and women were equal before God, that both were needed in religion and morality, and that it was quite inconceivable now that women should not work outside the home. The vote conferred status, but was also a weapon.[25]

---

22 H. Maynard Smith, *Frank, Bishop of Zanzibar* (London: SPCK, 1926) p. 304; W.S.F. Pickering, *Anglo-Catholicism: A Study in Religious Ambiguity* (London: Routledge, 1989), p. 52.

23 Anselm Hughes, *The Rivers of the Flood* (London: Faith Press, 1961), pp. 70–2, 74.

24 Colin Stephenson, *Merrily on High* (London: Darton, Longman and Todd, 1972), p. 55.

25 *Dewsbury Reporter*, 18 July 1914; *Dewsbury District News*, 18 July 1914.

Though Gore believed in male headship, he advocated a deaconess order and was an early and ardent advocate of votes for women in both Church and state elections.[26] Paul Bull continued to support a wider role for women. The Anglican feminist, Maude Royden, who once spoke on the same platform as Gore, felt a vocation to the priesthood. Her admirers (including Percy Dearmer) arranged for her to be able to conduct preaching services at a non-denominational centre in London in the 1920s. Among the list of her public sponsors, led by the Bishop of Kensington, were William Temple and Paul Bull.[27] Frere was a member of the Archbishop's Committee which reported in 1919 on the ministry of women. He complained that its members had spent a great deal of time on 'the curiosities of the Middle Ages' which were irrelevant. But they had never tackled the 'first and main question', the admission of women to the priesthood and episcopate. Though he was not in favour of the ordination of women, he lamented that no one in favour of such a change had been invited to give evidence and that there was only one woman on the Committee, which 'was out of touch with the greater part of the organised women's work as well as the aspirations of the younger women'.[28]

In view of Frere's support for the women's movement for over 20 years, it is surprising that he opposed the changes in the Marriage Service in 1927/28 which clearly reflected the influence of the movement: 'endow' became 'share' (worldly goods); the bride's 'obey' became optional. Frere wrote to protest that if the changes were made, the Church of England would no longer deserve to be called scriptural or Catholic and therefore schism or secession would appear a possibility to many. He claimed that the subordination of women in the family had Scripture and tradition behind it.[29] This is so unlike what Frere had been saying for 20 years that it sounds as if he was using these issues to strengthen his general repudiation of the results and procedures of Prayer Book revision, to which, ironically, he had made the largest single contribution. Archbishop

26 For historical background on gender and sexuality, see Alan Wilkinson, 'Three Sexual Issues', *Theology*, March 1988.

27 Nan Dearmer, *The Life of Percy Dearmer* (London: Book Club, 1941), p. 244 n.

28 Sheila Fletcher, *Maude Royden* (Oxford: Blackwell, 1989), p. 178–9.

29 R.C.D. Jasper (ed.), *Walter Howard Frere: His Correspondence on Liturgical Revision and Construction* (London: SPCK, 1954), pp. 110–14.

Lang thought that his change of mind owed more to psychology than theology. Yet Frere himself wrote to Dom Gregory Dix: 'I am conscious of no palinode.' He then with equal puckishness proceeded to authorize the use of the 1928 Book in the Truro diocese and used the eucharistic rite daily in his chapel.[30] In old age, however, his long-held support for the women's movement surfaced again. In 1938 he suggested that one altar in the new Community church should be dedicated to Holy Matrons and Virgins. But he was outvoted. Apart from one devoted to Our Lady and another to Mary Magdalene, the rest were dedicated to men.

Character

In 1941, Mervyn Haigh, Bishop of Coventry, a former Archbishop's Chaplain, recalled how when Frere stayed at Lambeth he would go to Sunday afternoon concerts at the Albert Hall, saying: 'I think we are always trying to give people more religion than they want.' He also described how Frere's complex manoeuvres in bishops' meetings often resulted in self-defeat. Especially towards the end of his episcopate, he 'staggered' the bishops by 'the increasingly paradoxical and seemingly "clever", subtle and even insincere kind of way in which he commended his views', often using arguments which everyone knew were not his own, but which he thought would convince those out of sympathy with him. 'This weakened his influence more and more until he almost ceased to have any.'[31]

In November 1934, Cuthbert Hallward CR (former Prior at Mirfield) visited Truro just after Frere had announced his resignation. It was (Hallward wrote) the end of 'a great episcopate', though, he added, he was skilled at concealing it, as with his other forms of self-mortification. He went on, that those who knew him only from Church Assembly were more familiar with 'that perversity in debate, which we know so well, and find him tiresome and puzzling' and do not realize his 'moral greatness'. Compared with Gore they find him 'flippant, unreliable, unstable, delighting over much in being unexpected, paradoxical'. Yet in fact, Frere was greater than Gore, 'more self-less'. Perhaps, thought Hallward, that

---

30 Phillips, *Frere*, p. 140; Jasper, *Frere*, pp. 173, 185.

31 Letter from Bishop Mervyn Haigh to Fr Keble Talbot CR, 29 September 1941 (Mirfield Archives).

'tiresomeness' was a camouflage to conceal his greatness? Keble Talbot wrote about Frere's 'technique of diplomacy and finesse worthy of a Renaissance Cardinal. But in the things of God he was utterly simple and direct.' In the conduct of business he preferred the knight's move in chess. Frere's own description of a pope could apply to himself: 'a strange mixture of saintliness and foxiness'.[32] He believed there was a 'menagerie of wild beasts' in everyone.[33] The liturgist Ronald Jasper, a student at Hostel and College who also knew him as bishop, said that he would make 'the oddest appointments' and that 'people were never sure where they stood with him'. Frere advocated 'holy guile'.[34]

Tacking evades capture and Frere seems to have had a deep fear of that. Another method of evasion is to become invisible. He was largely responsible for the *Historical Edition of Hymns Ancient and Modern*, but his name is not on the title-page. He once returned to Mirfield after a long absence. One of his bags had disappeared, in it the manuscript of a book upon which he had been working for 20 years. He showed no irritation, but was glad when it reappeared. When he was due to give an important speech, he sat on the platform correcting proofs until his turn came. In 1930, he was introduced to the House of Lords but did not bother to tell his family and seemed genuinely surprised when they were disappointed.

Retirement and death

Frere's time as Bishop of Truro is discussed in another chapter. CR never again repeated the experiment of making an episcopal residence into a house of the Community. Like Thomas Hannay (Bishop of Argyll and the Isles 1942–62) but unlike several other Prelate Brothers, Frere settled back happily in Mirfield. Gore retired to 'my beloved hovel' in Margaret Street, London. Frere had vaguely talked about retiring to South Africa for the warmth, or to some southern German town with an opera house. But he was through and through a Community man committed to simplicity of life. When he returned to the West Riding, he almost disappeared from view.

---

32 Phillips, *Frere*, pp. 52, 55.
33 Cambridge University Sermon in *Cambridge Review*, 1 May 1925.
34 Personal communication to author, 4 July 1988.

At first, he went away occasionally to conduct retreats or preach. A few months before his death he managed to go to Truro for the Cathedral's Jubilee. His address made such a lasting impression upon J.H. Hunkin, his modernist successor, that he reprinted a passage from it later in a book: 'The heart of religion, the entry of man into the fullness of this life, the joy of man in the life to come, is adoration.'[35] At Mirfield, he insisted on climbing up and down the steep steps to and from the crypt while the church was being completed. For the last two months, a daily mass was celebrated in his room. 'I live by that', he said.[36]

But Frere allowed himself a little relaxation. He grew a beard. He was permitted a wireless and a gramophone. When Edward VIII's abdication speech was broadcast, as CR had no radio, brethren crowded into his room to hear it through a huge horn, on which hung incongruously a photograph of Cardinal Mercier, a relic of Malines.

CR's mass – a rearrangement and amplification of 1662 – was an affront to Frere the liturgical reformer. He wrote to a priest in 1935: 'The liturgy of 1928 has full church authority; what is done commonly here has not and does not deserve to have. It is liturgically deplorable.' In his *Commentary* and elsewhere he insisted upon the corporate nature of the Eucharist; private masses were medieval deformations. But now the novice master exerted powerful pressure on novices to say private masses daily. Frere had his own method of staging individual protests against liturgy he disliked. Hugh Bishop (later Superior) in his unpublished autobiography remembered: 'He was an old man in his seventies when I was a novice, but that did not prevent him from attempting to sing the elaborate melodies in a cracked and tuneless voice which effectively wrecked the efforts of the cantors and the rest of the choir.' Ronald Jasper confirmed this: 'He often disapproved of the way things were sung to Plainsong, so he happily sang *his* way out of time with everyone else ... Thomas Hannay [the Precentor] got furious; as students we loved it and Walter happily sang on!'[37]

Frere preached at the College Festival in 1935, asking what was the main topic of conversation in clergy houses – was it the externals of

---

35 The Bishop of Truro, *The Gospel for Tomorrow* (Harmondsworth: Penguin Books, 1941), p. 81.

36 Phillips, *Frere*, p. 202.

37 Personal communication, 4 July 1988.

religion, rather than the saving of souls? A reliance on ecclesiastical machinery sometimes replaced faithful visiting and pastoral work; 'priestly individualism had often run riot, and reduced the Church to confusion.'[38] College students after his death remembered his lectures with slides meticulously tabulated; his voice which conveyed a culture and spirituality which made listening to it an 'aesthetic joy'; the intense simplicity of his sermons. For them, he was not merely a learned scholar, a cultured gentleman or a shrewd and humorous judge of character but a saint.[39] He lectured at the College until five days before he died.

He made his final liturgical protest in printed form a few weeks before his death. In the preface to *The Anaphora* (1938) he charged that the Liturgical Movement was being met 'in a small but influential part of the Anglican world, by a determined obscurantist and retrograde movement which poses noisily as catholic, but is really anarchic in method though medieval in outlook'. Dom Gregory Dix was dismayed by what he regarded as Frere's defective scholarship and bitter language. Frere, unrepentant, replied with a light-hearted Elizabethan verse:

Spend thy bolts; I care not
fal la la la la la la.[40]

His friend Evelyn Underhill thought CR (which she admired) had no idea how to look after Frere in old age. But he was not the person to agree to 'the small comforts and ameliorations' she wished for him. He once remarked 'I regard sitting on the least comfortable chair as very important.'[41] When, a day or two before he died, he was asked to choose ways in which his comfort could be increased, Frere replied crisply, 'I think I would prefer to do what I'm told.'[42]

Walter Frere died on 2 April 1938. He was 74. A few days earlier, he had completed the form of consecration for the new Community church. A Solemn Requiem was celebrated by the Superior on 6 April in the presence of four bishops, including his successor at Truro. The ashes were

---

38 *Mirfield Gazette*, Trinity 1935.
39 *Mirfield Gazette*, Trinity 1938.
40 Phillips, *Frere*, pp. 142–3.
41 Phillips, *Frere*, p. 181.
42 Phillips, *Frere*, p. 201.

placed in a stone tomb in front of St Basil's altar. On the north side in front of St Benedict's altar a similar tomb contains the ashes of Charles Gore. So the two founders of CR and the two founders of Western and Eastern monasticism were given equal recognition. Above St Basil's altar, a Russian Orthodox nun painted a triptych of icons given by the Fellowship of St Alban and St Sergius. On either side are St Basil and St Seraphim, in the centre is Christ in majesty. Frere had grown to love the Orthodox tradition: 'The *lex orandi* is more wholly treated as the equivalent of the *lex credendi* here than elsewhere: partly because it is essentially a worshipping Church, and partly because it has never been forced ... to make confessions of faith.'[43]

Now he is gone [wrote Keble Talbot in his obituary] light-footed he trod this world, even while with all diligence he plied the tasks which God ordained for him in it. He walked in its dream as one who wakes to sights and sounds beyond it. May the brightness of God's Presence shine upon him. (*CRQ* John Baptist 1938)

---

43 *Church Times*, 19 June 1914.

2

The spirituality of Walter Frere[1]

JOHN DAVIES

The word 'spirituality' may be used in both a narrower sense, indicating one's devotional life, 'inner life', characteristic way of praying, and a broader sense, referring to one's whole characteristic style of belief, life and practice, of which one's devotional life is an especially significant part. The broader sense has long been discussed and categorized[2] (*via negativa*, affirmation of images, the mystical way, etc); what is recent is calling it 'spirituality', and applying it to communities (Cistercian, Quaker, Russian, Celtic) and to individuals.[3] This chapter begins with the broader and works toward the narrower, as is particularly appropriate with Frere. In him the two were notably integrated and congruous. Though he wrote about prayer, he said very little about his own devotional life. We can infer much, however, and especially from a remarkable and invaluable body of evidence: the eight private books[4] he used over many years, through which we may watch him at his studies and overhear him at his prayers. Three aspects of Frere's spirituality will be examined: its basis, its evidences and its characteristics.

---

1 I am greatly indebted to Mrs Joan Brunnschweiler, who word-processed my manuscript into usable form, with kindness and unfailing patience with many revisions. I am likewise indebted to Fr Thomas Seville CR, the librarian at Mirfield, for his invaluable help and guidance since 2005, and to the archivist, Fr Steven Haws CR.

2 As by Charles Williams; see the characters of Durrant ('the sacramentalist') and Richardson ('the mystic') in *The Place of the Lion* (London: Victor Gollancz, 1931).

3 Recent in general currency, of longer use by specialists; see G.P. Fedotov (ed.), *A Treasury of Russian Spirituality* (New York: Sheed and Ward, 1948) and the discussion of the word in the Preface.

4 These are actually published books, but are heavily annotated by Frere (see below), and show the wear and tear of constant use. They are kept in the CR archives at Mirfield.

Basis

By this is meant what Frere received from his family, upbringing, education and training – the things from which he fashioned his spirituality (not that he was merely passive to them, or ever left their influence behind). The secular and religious bases are distinguished, although they were intermingled in his experience.[5]

Frere's family was eminent, able, familiar with public affairs, and included members with outstanding gifts and achievements. It was natural for him to use his gifts, to serve others, to take on large responsibilities, to move confidently in the public domain (and to know the place of diplomatic manipulation in complex human affairs). His background also contributed to his lack of self-consciousness and self-importance, and to his reticence and reserve. His natural gifts were great: health, energy and stamina; a swift, subtle and complex intellect; versatility and wide interests; extraordinary diligence; particular abilities in historical study, languages and music. His education developed all these, equipping him with exact and rigorous scholarship; capacity for long-term and large-scale planning; grasp of detail; fitness to lead and readiness to collaborate; and the ability to handle a variety of tasks in parallel. His character included a sense of humour and great capacity for enjoyment; a will 'inclined to be imperious';[6] and a strong and warm family sense[7] which resurfaced in the communities of school and college, where he was happy in company and made lasting friendships. Beneath the reserve was love for others: the family motto *Frere ayme Frere* extended beyond the natural family.

Frere was brought up in Anglican homes and schools and seems to have absorbed from them serious religion and an Anglicanism of an undemonstrative Catholic kind. Perhaps he was, like Keble, a 'once-born' high churchman, with no need to look elsewhere for Catholicity. This continued at Cambridge and Wells.[8] He cannot at Cambridge have been unaware or unappreciative of the flourishing evangelical tradition,

---

5 C.S. Phillips et al., *Walter Howard Frere, Bishop of Truro* (London: Faber & Faber, 1947), chs. 1, 6, 9, and *passim*.

6 Keble Talbot in Phillips, *Frere*, p. 44.

7 Phillips, *Frere*, pp. 20–1 and ch. 6.

8 'His own views were old fashioned High Church, learned from his guardian Mr Gordon ... when I asked him why he was choosing Wells as his theological college ... he said, "I don't want them to make a ritualist of me"' (Phillips, *Frere*, p. 27).

whether or not he took any active part in it;[9] he later praised 'a real Evangelical Catholic', and was one himself.[10]

Evidences

Scripture

The Bible was fundamental and pervading in Frere's spirituality – easily overlooked because he published little about it.[11] In the course of the Prayer Book daily office, he read the entire Bible, with a few minor omissions, every year,[12] reinforced by the eucharistic lectionary, and brought to mind by the daily reading of Psalm 119 in the little Hours.[13] He practised and taught systematic scriptural meditation,[14] which was part of the CR horarium; the prayers he composed for his own use and others' had a high scriptural content, and he had a penchant for devotional scriptural catenae (see below). His sermons and addresses are expository – text, exposition, implications for the hearers. Reference to Scripture occurs in numerous contexts.

He studied the Bible assiduously, and here we can examine four of his eight private books. The first is a Bible with Apocrypha, Authorised Version, with the Prayer Book bound in at the front and 164 blank pages at the back. It is inscribed 'Radley Vicarage' and 'March 1895'. Its

---

9 Phillips quotes from a Cambridge University Sermon of 1935 the sentence 'Men and women have found here their Saviour in their undergraduate days' – the very language of evangelicalism.

10 Alan Wilkinson, *The Community of the Resurrection: A Centenary History* (London: SCM Press, 1992), p. 42.

11 There is one publication on the nature of Scripture in the light of modern critical method: Mirfield Manual 44 *The Bible* (c.1905). Divine revelation reaches perfection in Christ; it is recorded and interpreted by 'necessarily imperfect' human writers; and critical method is a welcome enrichment. The essay can be read with profit today. Its substance would have adorned *Lux Mundi*, and was embodied in a retreat address of 1911, 'The Study of the Bible', printed in the *Christian World Pulpit*, of great power (see note 13 below).

12 This was the case with the 1662 and 1871 Lectionaries; Frere and CR probably used the latter.

13 Ps. 119 is traditionally used by Christians as referring to the Christian Bible. The 1911 address starts from Ps. 119: 105, 'Thy word is a lantern unto my feet.'

14 W.H. Frere and G. Longridge, *Meditation* (Little Books on Religion, 42. London: SPCK, 1926). In Frere 'meditation' means meditation on Scripture.

condition (falling apart and many pages worn thin with use) suggests that it was used as an office book for mattins and evensong. Its heavy annotations, in blue/black and red ink and in Frere's minute yet clear handwriting, show that it was equally an instrument of detailed and learned study. The text has many re-translations, mostly for correction and clarification. The margins contain cross-references, especially between Old Testament – Apocrypha and New Testament. Noteworthy is 'word-linking' (my term): the underlining, and linking by thin lines, of the occurrences of significant words and word groups. The pages thus exhibit a network of significant word studies, thickest of all from Romans to the Apocalypse. The blank pages at the end are used for two systematic schemes: first, lists of references under words and subjects (glory, soteriology, etc); second, synopses of the Gospels, written out in full in Greek – the four gospels for the Passion and Resurrection, the synoptics for the Ministry. All this thorough, detailed, highly laborious work centres on the text and meaning of Scripture, culminating in the history of Jesus and the theology of the New Testament. Thus it was from his own methods that he advised an early Mirfield student to take 'a Bible and a Concordance, choose particular words, and trace them through Holy Writ'.[15]

The second private book is a Hebrew Bible. No purchase date is inscribed, but everything points to the same period. This is annotated similarly but more sparsely and selectively. Frere knew and used Hebrew,[16] but he is perhaps chiefly using this book as background study for teaching.

Third is a Hebrew Psalter, a German edition of 1880 with a blank page bound in between every page of text. The text is word-linked throughout in red ink. Every blank page is filled with about 50 textual and linguistic notes relating to its facing page of text. The purpose is to elucidate the meaning, for this is both a study book and a prayer book, and it shows the close relationship in Frere of scholarship, study and prayer.

The fourth book is a Greek New Testament, the Westcott and Hort edition of 1885, inscribed 'St James' Day 1893' and 'Radley.' Here the

---

15 Remembered by a pre-1914 student in an obituary letter, in the *Mirfield Gazette*, 1938.

16 A Syriac Grammar and New Testament, bought in the nineties but hardly marked, suggest that he began but abandoned this line of study.

annotation is complete, very full and directed to one end: a word-based compendium of New Testament thought. Every page has its network of word-linking. In the top and bottom margins each key word has its list of occurrences in other NT books. At the beginning of each book, each word has a list of its occurrences in that book. The effect is of a concordance of keywords. On the front and rear blank pages are lists of references to key subjects (parables, Christology, grace, etc.) – a skeleton NT word-book. Frere has equipped himself for meditation, preaching, study and teaching, embarking on the task on settling at Radley. Doubtless it rests upon his three years of reading classics and his fourth year of theological study when 'he attended professors' lectures, particularly Dr Hort's.'[17] That was in Hort's, and Westcott's, Cambridge heyday. Frere shows affinities with them and kept the anniversaries of their deaths (see below).

Liturgy

This, Frere's supreme field of scholarship, was his supreme means of worship, and that in its turn arguably his supreme interest. 'It was impossible to live with Walter Frere without being impressed by the fact that what he really lived for was worship.'[18] The Eucharist and the daily office made the framework of his spirituality.

The Eucharist was central: he introduced the Parish Communion[19] at Stepney, and its equivalent Sung Eucharist was the chief Sunday service at Truro. It was communal; non-communicating masses and individual priests' masses he rejected. Reservation for the sick he promoted; extra-liturgical devotions before the sacrament he opposed. He used and commended the Prayer Book rite, while working to improve it; and his long and devoted work towards the 1928 rite was 'in the interests of truer and fuller worship'.[20]

---

17 Phillips, *Frere*, p. 27.

18 Bernard Horner CR, 'Foreword' in R.C.D Jasper (ed.), *Walter Howard Frere: His Correspondence on Liturgical Revision and Construction* (Alcuin Club. London: SPCK, 1954).

19 The pioneer, according to Donald Gray, *Earth and Altar* (Alcuin Club. Norwich: Canterbury Press, 1986).

20 Gregory Dix in Phillips, *Frere*, p. 141.

The office was likewise 'essentially corporate',[21] though usable individually, as the Rule (II.3) expects when brethren are away from the Community. To the secular priest's duty of Prayer Book mattins and evensong, CR added the little Hours, using *Prime and Hours* from 1898,[22] and Frere's own copy remains. Here we can quote one of his rare statements about himself, for when Mowbrays published a new edition of *Prime and Hours* in 1929 there appeared the following opposite the title page:

> Over 30 years have passed now since the previous edition of *Prime and Hours* appeared with the commendation by the Archbishop of Capetown in 1897. He hoped that the little book would prove fruitful, and it is certainly fruitful still. To many people who value the saying of Offices as private devotions this particular form of them has made itself very dear.
>
> For myself I may say that it has been my constant companion throughout the whole of these thirty years and more of its existence. Now that the new edition comes out with some enlargement and improvement, it falls to me to give what the Archbishop of Capetown gave before, namely, a warm commendation of the book, and to continue the hope that *Prime and Hours* in its new form may serve a new generation and provide a worthy model for their prayers.
>
> WALTERUS TRURON: Lis Escop, Truro, August 1, 1929.

Note the personal warmth, 'my constant companion', and the commendation of liturgical forms as both medium and model for private prayer.

The practicalities of liturgy – conduct and ceremonial – were important to Frere; he was in charge of them at Stepney, influential at Mirfield, and in charge again at Truro where at that time the Bishop was

---

21 Commentary on the CR Rule in *The Book of the Community of the Resurrection* (1924 edn), p. 102.

22 *Prime and Hours: According to the Use of the Church of England, with Other Devotions* (Oxford: Mowbray 1897), adopted in January 1898 (Chapter Minutes). It was an extract from *The Priest's Book of Private Devotion*, and Frere had used it for the *Wells Office Book* which he compiled in 1896. CR, after some years of deliberation in the 1930s, replaced it with a Community office book.

also Dean.[23] One of his last tasks was to compile the elaborate dedication service (text and rubrics) for the completed church at Mirfield in 1938. His general book, *The Principles of Religious Ceremonial*, appeared in 1906,[24] and there were numerous particular works.[25] He was a leading light (and president for many years) of the Alcuin Club, wrote on practical points in the *Truro Diocesan Gazette*, and was a one-man encyclopaedia of ceremonial to individuals (often Anglican bishops) who wrote from near and far.[26]

The religious life

CR, as well as enabling Frere to fulfil his desire for the religious life, elicited his chief printed exposition of spirituality, the *Commentary on the Rule* written in 1907 and subsequently printed with the Rule and Constitution.[27] In his first paragraph he defines the religious life as 'a life which aims at union with God in Christ by means of certain bonds and detachments, which are not those of ordinary Christian life ... not indeed different from them in kind ... but in an emphasized form.' It is for those 'called to seek after the glory of God and the perfection of their life in other surroundings than those which form the usual medium of Christian perfection'. It is thus not the way, but one way, of perfection; so that what he goes on to say about it illuminates 'ordinary Christian life' also. Some examples of this are: (a) The distinction between rule and ideal; obedience to the rule is instrumental for loyalty to the ideal.[28] (b) The balance between the individual and the community, requiring effort and self-abnegation from both sides.[29] (c) Renunciation is for positive ends; thus poverty is an aspect of community of goods, which includes it and is 'more far-reaching'.[30] (d) The religious community is analogous to

---

23 He compiled a directory for the Truro Sung Eucharist in 1937.

24 Revised edition 1928.

25 E.g., *The Use of Sarum* (Cambridge: Cambridge University Press, 1898–1901) and the new edition of Daniel Rock, *Church of our Fathers* (London: John Hodges, 1903–4).

26 See letters in Jasper, *Frere*.

27 *The Book of the Community of the Resurrection*, 1924 edn (page references are to this edition).

28 *Commentary*, pp. 70, 71.

29 *Commentary*, §4.

30 *Commentary*, §7.

(and can learn from) the natural family, as is shown by CR's preferred term 'brother' and use of one another's Christian name.[31] (*Frere ayme Frere*, as Frere doubtless observed with pleasure.)

Preaching

Preaching, especially for missions and retreats, was a major work of CR, and Frere took full part in it all his life. The *Commentary* aligns CR with the active orders, like the Franciscans and Dominicans, as 'missionary, evangelistic and, above all things, active'.[32] A large body of Frere's sermon texts remains. Some of his more public sermons were printed in full – Cambridge University Sermons in the *Cambridge Review*, others in newspapers and the *Christian World Pulpit* – and one survives in his handwriting. These are on large topics treated generally (though never vaguely). Most of what remains is in the form of notes, for mission and retreat addresses, to particular churches and mostly to committed hearers. There are approximately 600 of these,[33] many preached on several occasions. They show that he usually preached from notes, and on a system evidently perfected over the years. There are numbered headings, single words and phrases, key sentences, tabulations, brackets, 'plus', 'minus', 'therefore' signs, all in his small very clear handwriting. Their subject is Christian belief, life, devotion – spirituality in fact – and they cover an immense range. They often explore, and always presuppose, the pattern of sin – conversion – sanctification, and particularly the long process of sanctification through prayer, sacrament, discipleship and practical goodness. It is the two-fold pattern (particularly its second part) proclaimed in a sort of manifesto in the *Mirfield Mission Hymn Book*: 'The Evangelical assertion of the power of the Cross, and the cleansing of the Precious Blood, lead on to the gifts of Grace which flow from the Risen Life of our Saviour in the Fellowship of the Catholic Church.'[34]

---

31 *Commentary*, §9, especially p. 118.

32 *Commentary*, §3, especially pp. 86, 87. Compare the Della Robbia plaque of Dominic and Francis set over the front door at Mirfield.

33 In the Borthwick Institute. For the present purpose I have had to be content with a representative sample of about 150.

34 1948 edn, Preface, p. iii.

Lancelot Andrewes

Frere admired Andrewes, resembled him and in important respects followed him. Our earliest evidence is that in 1887, when at Wells, he bought and started to annotate Andrewes's *Preces Privatae*.[35] In 1892 he bought a new edition of it and took the process further; in 1898[36] he lectured on Andrewes as 'a representative of Anglican principles'; in his 1904 book on the Reformation[37] he gave Andrewes prominence as the major exponent of the Catholicity of the Church of England; and he adopted Andrewes's methods of devotion. Both men were scholars, historians, linguists, apologists and preachers. Some words by F.E. Brightman about Andrewes are remarkably applicable to Frere:

> His extraordinarily minute knowledge of the Holy Scriptures is plain to everybody: and his command of it and of the rest of his learning, is such that it perhaps serves to conceal his originality ... To one to whom knowledge is so large an element in life and is itself so living a thing; whose learning is so assimilated as to be identified with his spontaneous self, and has become as available as language itself, originality and reminiscence become in a measure identical; the new can be expressed as a combination of older elements ... He took up what he found and fused it into a new whole.[38]

Here we examine two more of the eight private books: the two editions of Andrewes. The first is an 1828 edition, Greek and Latin, by P. Hall. It is inscribed '1887' and 'Wells', and has 20 blank pages bound in at each end. In 1937 Frere gave it to Osmund Victor CR, who added his own notes. Frere annotates the text sparsely and for his own clarification, as one learning his way round it. In the blank pages he supplements it; at the front with prayers from eucharistic liturgies, and with a hand-drawn blank kalendar into which he enters anniversaries (mostly of deaths) of

---

35 Also known by other titles; this is the least confusing.

36 Church Historical Society lecture.

37 Frere, *The English Church in the Reigns of Elizabeth and James I* (London: Macmillan, 1904). Frere's interest in seventeenth-century Anglicanism persisted; one of his last works was the first published edition of *A Devotionarie Book of John Evelyn of Wotton* (London: Murray, 1936).

38 In his English edition of the *Preces Privatae*, trans. F.E. Brightman (London: Methuen 1903), p. xxix.

family, friends and other individuals important to him, for example, 'Bishop Wilberforce 1873', 'J.H. Newman 1890', 'Dr Hort 1892'. In the pages at the back are extracts from Tauler and Thomas à Kempis, and a variety of prayers. He is absorbing, using and supplementing Andrewes.

The second copy is an edition of 1892 by P.G. Medd.[39] The printed text contains numerous blank spaces, representing the lacunae in the Laud manuscript, and an additional 20 blank pages have been bound in, so Frere has plenty of room for the annotations that have become his settled habit. But he uses this book rather differently from the earlier one. Here his own entries build upon Andrewes in character, content and even in form; as when he catalogues, for praise and thanksgiving, his temporal blessings of circumstance and of human benefactors.[40] There are other whole pages reflecting Andrewes indirectly; as in the long Latin prayer addressed to Jesus as he appears in St John's Gospel, and in the page headed XAPA (Joy): a Greek catena of New Testament texts about joy, followed by a 'wheel of perpetual rejoicing' where the key phrases of Romans 5. 1–10 are displayed as the 16 spokes of the wheel – a pleasant, unexpected metaphysical conceit. To these and other prayers we shall return.

Prime and Hours

The seventh of the private books is Frere's personal copy of *Prime and Hours*. It is inscribed 1898, the year CR adopted it. It shows many signs of being his 'constant companion' both in choir and in private; it has had bound into it *Prayers from Sursum Corda 1908* (a 36-page week's scheme of private prayer) and 24 blank pages. The annotations are voluminous, including Truro items, and the latest entered date is 1936.

The book has a kalendar with blank boxes for each day; here Frere continues the practice of filling them with individual anniversaries. It is much fuller than in *Preces Privatae* 1887 – Hort is joined by Lightfoot and Benson, and T.H. Huxley and R. Wagner both get a place. The chief part

---

39 This is based on the Laud manuscript, an Andrewes manuscript given to Archbishop Laud, and shorter than the text underlying the 1828 edition; the textual history of *Preces Privatae* is complex.

40 Closely following part of Andrewes, 'Another Particular Thanksgiving' (Brightman edition, pp. 229, 230).

of the book is the text of the Hours, and these pages are annotated for use in choir; all four margins of each page are filled with plainchant staves in red with the antiphons noted in black. The pages of the week's scheme devoted to intercession are filled with lists of all the Truro parishes, two rural deaneries each day. The blank pages contain personal prayers, Greek, Latin or English, evidently composed by Frere; and a number of short prayers, some for the Hours, are on loose sheets between pages. Their range, from the intensely personal to the corporate-liturgical, suggests that for Frere private and liturgical prayer are parts of a continuum.

Sursum Corda

Sursum Corda: A Handbook of Intercession and Thanksgiving. Arranged by W.H. Frere and A.L. Illingworth[41] was published by Mowbray in 1898. An obituary of 1938 called it 'probably the most popular and most widely used of all his books'[42] and it was frequently re-issued in the inter-war years.[43] It looked a typical devotional book of the period, but was anything but typical in its emphases. It has double importance for us, as Frere's one devotional book written for Christians in general,[44] and – since he used it himself for the rest of his life – the eighth of his private books.

It is clearly inspired by Andrewes's *Preces Privatae* in plan and tone. Its backbone is a seven-day scheme of intercession and thanksgiving. The many prayers, mostly brief, some litanies, are on one topic a day; the user is to be selective, and to write personal notes for which plenty of blank

---

41 Agnes Louisa Illingworth (1860–1936), wife of J.R. Illingworth, a contributor to *Lux Mundi* and rector of Longworth, near Oxford, where the 'Holy Party' met in the 1890s. CR, then at Pusey House and Radley, had contacts with Longworth, and Frere was evidently included. She tells how, when the parish needed £27 for a heating system, 'it seemed a case for prayer. I asked H.S.H., W.F., and one or two more to join us at the time, and at the Cottage meeting we prayed for funds. By return of post came £27…'; E. Raikes (ed.), *Agnes Louisa Illingworth* (London: SPCK, 1938), pp. 20, 21. She and Frere evidently appreciated one another, and *Sursum Corda* followed.

42 'which he arranged with Mrs A.L. Illingworth in 1893'; *Church Times*, 8 April 1938.

43 In 1905 was published the 'Small Edition', smaller in format, without blank pages, but with an expanded Thanksgiving section. It is printed in red and black, with a frontispiece showing the Elevation, and seems intended as a presentation edition. In 1908 appeared *Prayers from Sursum Corda*, extracted from the Small Edition and consisting only of the seven-day cycle of Intercession and Thanksgiving, simpler and much shorter.

44 Though presupposing some degree of education, like most devotional books of the period.

space is provided. The seven topics for intercession are the ministry, the laity, the world, mission, people connected with the user, sinners, the suffering. For thanksgiving they are Christ, the saints, revelation, redemption, creation, the hope of glory, the plan of salvation. An introduction to the two kinds of prayer precedes the scheme, and prayers for special purposes follow it. There is (as in *Prime and Hours*) a kalendar with blanks for the user's own entries.

Frere's own copy is inscribed 'To "my true friend in Christ" W.H.F., St Faith's Day 1898', in what must be Mrs Illingworth's writing. It is as worn as his *Prime and Hours* and even more fully annotated. What becomes clear is that it was Frere's habitual intercession book (and thus complementary to *Prime and Hours*). The annotations fall into four categories:

The Kalendar. This is much fuller than the previous ones already noted, whose contents have been transferred to it. The years noted for each entry show that Frere kept it up until his last years. Wagner has gone, and Brahms and Stanford arrived; there are Mrs Illingworth's birthday and the Illingworths' wedding anniversary; Lightfoot, Westcott and Hort are all present. Most of the days of the year are filled.

Lists. These fill the blank pages and spaces of the intercession section. Some are lists: family, religious communities (some including every individual), foreign missions, one that is perhaps the parishioners of Stepney. Many are by initials only, and a cross has been added for the departed. ('ALI[†] 1936' shows him updating into his last years). The number of individuals is immense. And the use of mere initials shows frequency of use.

Maps of Truro. Frere has extended the deanery lists in *Prime and Hours* in an extraordinary way. On some of the blank pages in the intercession section he has drawn maps of each Truro deanery, in red and black. The map shows the parishes with their names and a number; at the foot is a list of the clergy, each with his corresponding parish number. Thus each day Bishop Frere's intercession has its vivid, detailed visual aid.

Written prayers. Collects and other forms are written on the pages, and a few on loose slips between pages. Many are intercessory (e.g., 'for those I have absolved', and an untitled prayer which is perhaps of the time of the General Strike), some not (e.g., a catena dated 1931 from

I Timothy on Timothy's calling, probably for Frere's meditation on his own calling as bishop). Here we note also that the thanksgiving cycle has been enriched by pasting in seven fine prayers (perhaps by Frere) which had been added to the 1905 edition of *Sursum Corda*.

Prayers written by Frere

For one who used so readily prayers written by others, it was natural to write prayers for his own and others' use. We have seen that there are many written into his private books, and none of these has been published. He wrote two sets of prayers for publication: a sequence of six prayers of personal devotion, *Suspiria Animae Vix Amantis Deum* (Sighs of a Soul Scarcely Loving God),[45] and some of the collects in *Black Letter Saints' Days*.[46]

We shall quote examples later, but here some general points may be made. First, we may take these prayers as indicators of Frere's spirituality whether written for himself, for the private use of others or for liturgical use; there are no inconsistencies arising from the difference of users. Second, the links with Scripture, liturgy, the prayers of others (e.g. Andrewes) are plain and frequent. Third, we note the combination of considered composition (in form, sequence and expression) and the qualities of directness, depth of thought and fervency of spirit. We note also the variety of forms and styles: collects and terse prayers of a Latin directness; longer prayers of a Gallican or Orthodox expansiveness and richness; reminiscences of Andrewes and other seventeenth-century writers; and the scriptural catenae, probably as media for meditation, which he seems to have found especially congenial.

Two further points are the pleasure taken in visual arrangement on the page – symmetry, parallel columns, occasionally such a conceit as the 'wheel of rejoicing' – and, in the unpublished prayers, the free use of English, Latin, Greek and (less often) Hebrew.

Last, there follows the one prayer existing as part of a private diary. He was not a diarist habitually, it appears, but in the early years of CR he kept

---

45 Or '… a Soul Loving God with Difficulty' (St Mary's Wantage 1899, reprinted 1920). See Phillips *Frere*, p. 175, where it is not clear whether 'for others' implies 'at the request of others'. No records remain of the genesis of the *Suspiria*.

46 *Black Letter Saints' Days* (London: SPCK, 1938).

a journal which surfaced only in 1984.[47] It begins with a 'Retrospect in Gratitude to God' and at one point breaks into this prayer, and then resumes the diary mode:

O my God indeed I thank Thee for all this. Things looked dark enough when I was torn away from Stepney distracted in my outlook and only trying to follow blindly: but now Thou hast set my feet in a large Room: this is all beyond my best hopes: O God keep us faithful and lead us to our next step in dependence on Thee alone.

Other sources

Frere contributed much to the *CR Quarterly* from its beginnings in 1903 to his departure for Truro, and to the monthly *Truro Diocesan Gazette* during his episcopate. The latter contains Pastoral Letters, 'Bishop's Notes' (mostly administrative) and articles of which some are reprinted in Arnold and Wyatt.[48] Indirect evidence is found in the CR Chapter Minutes and the CR Chronicles and archives.

Frere wrote many letters, official, advisory, of spiritual direction and personal. Of the last two categories, few remain; he put together a bundle of letters which might later be useful historically,[49] and we may infer that he destroyed others – no doubt any of an especially private and personal kind. Fortunately a few of the personal ones are quoted in the books about their recipients. There is no evidence that Frere ever kept a personal journal after that of the 1890s (his reticence and his self-effacement make this unsurprising).

Lastly, there are the memories, accounts and assessments of those who have written or spoken of him since his death: obituary notices and letters in the press;[50] the books by Phillips and Wilkinson, both of which report conversations as well as letters from people who knew Frere personally (as did all the contributors to Phillips); and histories and biographies in

---

47 Martin Jarrett-Kerr, 'A Lost Journal of +Walter Frere CR', *CR Quarterly* No. 325, St John Baptist 1984, pp. 12–19. Cf. Wilkinson, *Centenary History*, p. 42.

48 J.H. Arnold and E.G.P. Wyatt (eds), *Walter Howard Frere: A Collection of his Papers on Liturgical and Historical Subjects* (Alcuin Club. London: Oxford University Press, 1940).

49 CR archives. Reprinted in Jasper, *Frere* (see Introduction, p. xi).

50 A very full collection of cuttings is kept in the CR Chronicles.

which he figures, however briefly. While these are secondary material, they are full of value, particularly the testimonies of those who knew him in life, and who sometimes report his spoken words.[51] Everything Frere wrote is potentially relevant, whatever its subject; his spirituality may surface at any point.

Characteristics

Anglicanism

Anglicanism is not just a background to Frere's spirituality; it was its continuing framework and practical basis. And its various elements, so often contrasted or antagonistic, were in him present and integrated to an unusual degree.

He held that the Church of England was the Catholic Church of the nation, and had been from its beginnings, though separated from the Papacy at the Reformation on justifiable grounds,[52] as Parker had seen and Andrewes witnessed.[53] It was established (though not Erastian) and its responsibility to the nation extended into the British Empire. Its liturgical tradition was authentic, and, though capable of improvement, needed no interpolations from other rites. In all this Frere was of the same mind as Gore, and had the same unperturbed confidence in the Catholicity of Anglicanism.[54] In doctrine he was a 'liberal Catholic' like Gore and *Lux Mundi* – incarnational, 'grace perfecting nature', the Church

---

51 Three pieces not to be missed are Talbot (Phillips, *Frere*, ch. 3), A.S. Duncan-Jones ('Introduction' in Arnold and Wyatt, *Walter Howard Frere*) and Horner ('Foreword' in Jasper, *Frere*).

52 'The Place of the Papacy in the Organisation of Christian Unity' (1895), in Arnold and Wyatt, p. 1, and 'What Is the Position of the Roman Catholic Body in England?', Church Historical Society Lecture 5, 1896.

53 *The English Church*, chs IV, X, XX.

54 Arrived at by a different route: Mr Gordon's parish of Barley (near Cambridge), Charterhouse, Cambridge, Wells. His enthusiasm for Parker and Andrewes ('the founder of the Cambridge movement', *The English Church*, p. 344) suggests a conscious notion of a Cambridge tradition of high-church Anglicanism. Frere's family life was Cantabrigian, and he retained his academic connection with Cambridge (see Dix in Phillips, *Frere*, pp. 144, 145).

continuing the work of Christ – but he did not neglect sin or the Cross,[55] as his addresses and devotional aids to Holy Week show.[56] It was he who proposed the CR cassock-belt badge,[57] a Western-style, three-dimensional crucifix with the Agnus Dei of the resurrection on the flat reverse side; and it was in his years as Superior that the prominent crucifix was erected at the Community cemetery.

This recalls the evangelical element, already noted in his approval of 'a real Evangelical Catholic', and in the *Mission Hymn Book*'s manifesto. Phillips records Frere's sister saying 'Wally, what a Protestant you are really!'[58] and Underhill wrote 'had he not been a Catholic, Bishop Frere would have been a fervent Evangelical of the best type',[59] In his historical works he gave honourable place to puritan and evangelical in the Church of England.[60] His evangelical affinities may be seen in his emphases on the Cross, conversion, personal discipleship and growth in grace; in the pervasiveness of the Bible in his thought, preaching and prayers; and in the tone of his personal devotions.

A further note of Anglicanism has been its appeal to reason and learning. The place of these in Frere is demonstrated throughout this book, and his spirituality is no exception. It employs his intellectual force, depth of reflection and clarity of thought and expression; it readily draws upon his knowledge of Bible, liturgy and devotional writing; it expresses itself in the deliberate composition of written prayers; and it employs the devices of scholarship: annotation, tabulation, arrangement, system. All this is used in the service of prayer, preaching and worship. It does not displace the inward thought, the spirit, the will, the aspiration; but is wholeheartedly used as their instrument and medium – sacramentally, in fact. Perhaps there was here a particular debt to 'Dr Hort' who pre-eminently exhibited the partnership of critical method and positive theology, of intellect and faith, of scholarship and devotion.

---

55 As the *Lux Mundi* school has been accused of doing (see Wilkinson, *Centenary History*, pp. 8, 9).

56 E.g., Frere, *The Stations of the Passion of Our Lord and Saviour Jesus Christ* (Oxford and London: Mowbray, 1896).

57 Chapter Minutes 11 July 1914, 'Walter's proposal that we shall have a Community Cross'.

58 Phillips, *Frere*, p. 30 (see note 63).

59 Phillips, *Frere*, p. 181.

60 A. Hamilton Thompson in Phillips, *Frere*, pp. 150–1.

Affirmation

Frere shared the fundamental world-affirmation of Gore and *Lux Mundi*. He repudiates

> that element so prominent in much monastic asceticism, which … tends to look upon God's world as evil. As 'Sons of the Resurrection' we shall see in the Incarnation that which sanctifies afresh the world of God's making, and leaves only the world that refuses God, 'lying in the Evil One'.[61]

There remains the problem of 'using the world and not abusing it'.[62] In the 1913 address *Our Relation to the World* he begins from the affinity and the disharmony between the physical-spiritual world and physical-spiritual man.

> God means us to be brought into harmony that we may rightly use the world. He has made all these things for us that we may have them to enjoy. Harmony is there between us and our surroundings; it remains for us by the grace of God to perfect it by self-discipline, by intelligence, by spiritual meditation, by the countless forces that will bring us more completely into touch with God's world, and will clear away the discords and reinforce the harmonies.[63]

But then comes the crucial proviso: 'Man can only be in right relation to the world by being simultaneously in right relationship with his Maker', and that (though this address does not expound it) requires our redemption and sanctification. Here, and elsewhere before the Great War,[64] Frere

---

61 *Commentary*, p. 135.

62 The phrase is from I Corinthians 7.31 (AV) where it refers to the Corinthian Christians. In Greek it stands at the head of §III of the Rule, and Frere expounds it in the *Commentary*, for the religious life; and for Christians in general, in two sermons at St Paul's Cathedral, 1908 and 1913. C.S. Phillips clearly saw Frere as an example of the phrase, since the Greek version, duly in the singular, appears on the title page of *Frere*.

63 St Paul's Cathedral, 10 March 1913: printed in *The Christian World Pulpit*, 2 April 1913 (Borthwick). Its 'text' is Ken's 'That with the world, myself, and Thee, I ere I sleep, at peace may be.'

64 Cambridge University Sermon, 26 October 1913, and perhaps the address just quoted.

sometimes seems to view the future of the world, and of the Church's world mission, with some of the optimism commonly ascribed to the Edwardians and the incarnationalists. Even in 1917 he could see the Russian Revolution as a dawning of liberty and democracy.[65] After the Great War there is a change, as he surveys the world, the hostile powers at work in it, and 'the serious menace that the un-christianised world is'.[66] The discords are now as prominent as the harmonies.

Frere's background, gifts and training doubtless predisposed him to world-affirmation. It underlies much of his activity throughout his life: the scholarly and educational work, the adoption of the active religious life, the promotion of CR's works at home and abroad, the embracing of Cornwall during his episcopate there. It shows also in his love of communities natural and supernatural, his care for individuals and their proper fulfilment, and his unquenched love of music.

Renunciation

Nevertheless, renunciation is an essential element in the practice of the Christian life, lay and secular as well as clerical and religious. The trouble with the world is that 'it is obtrusive, like some individual who ... always manages to push himself into the front row ... to talk rather the loudest.'[67] One way of keeping it in its place is renunciation. In a sermon 'How to Use the World',[68] addressed to lay Christians living normal world-affirming lives, Frere suggested a practical method of renunciation, consisting of the regular conscious recollection that the worldly blessings we rightly enjoy, like family life or satisfying work, could be given up willingly if circumstances removed them from us. Whatever we may think of this as a practical suggestion, the sermon does illuminate the place of renunciation in 'using the world'. The matter is clearer when in the *Commentary* Frere deals with the specific renunciations required by the religious life. They are in no way minimized; but they are put into an

---

65 Frere, *Some Links in the Chain of Russian Church History* (London: Faith Press, 1918), 'Introduction', quoting a letter of similar hopefulness from a Russian priest.

66 Addresses on post-war malaise (Borthwick): *Truro Diocesan Gazette* 1926, 'A Lenten Pastoral' (February) and 'A Pastoral' (October) concerning 'the serious menace'.

67 The 1913 address.

68 St Paul's Cathedral, Trinity XX 1908 (typescript in Borthwick). This is closely related to the 1913 address.

affirmative context, explained as so many means to larger and positive ends. Thus poverty is dealt with in the section on 'Community of Goods'; the community and its members pursue 'poverty and simplicity of life' and 'far greater still … the mortification of the lust of private ownership' which 'develops that detachment from material ties which must go with closer attachment to God'.[69] Celibacy

> is good in itself as an act of renunciation in response to God's call and for his glory; it is good in its result when it leads to detachment, to concentration, to efficiency in work, to the forcible taking possession of the kingdom of heaven.[70]

Obedience 'is not so much one of the ideals of the Community as a necessary postulate for them all', each brother 'merging himself in the Community and seeking by all means to share its common mind'.[71] Perhaps most striking of all, on the subject of recreation:

> A right use of the world is as important as a right detachment from it, and perhaps as difficult … The objects of beauty, the means of delight, the untainted pleasures, the healthy recreations – all these embodiments of God's goodness in the world we must learn to use by learning first to be detached from them. The things which at the call of Christ he renounced, the religious receives back, and in a new, true and safe sense possesses (as he realizes his own vocation more and more), according to the promise of our Saviour which he annexed to his call … and the title of our community is a continual reminder that the true end of mortification is resurrection to newness and fulness of life.[72]

Frere obviously embraced the grand renunciations of the CR Rule. Certain of his personal renunciations were noted:[73] the repudiation of personal wealth, the spare diet, the preference for cheap accommodation when travelling, choosing the least comfortable chair, making do with an

---

69 *Commentary*, pp. 108–10.
70 *Commentary*, p. 113.
71 *Commentary*, pp. 124, 129.
72 *Commentary*, pp. 135, 136.
73 E.g., Phillips, *Frere*, pp. 49–50, 106 (note), 181.

inferior radiogram at Truro. He welcomed menial work in CR life, and mistrusted installing electric light at Mirfield as tending to luxury. He pursued detachment and accepted disappointments.[74] He practised self-abnegation; in the first ten years of CR he accepted a number of decisions contrary to his own views. In his years as Superior he was not an autocrat, though obviously outstanding among the brethren in many ways; in his *Commentary* he emphasizes the high value set in the Rule on the contribution and fulfilment of every brother. He was no doubt aided in all this by his natural inclinations to efficiency and high standards of work, and to self-effacing service of others. One also senses a natural pleasure in having high aims and in stripping for action in pursuing them; a natural athleticism of mind and spirit, like that of his body. It brings to mind R.H. Benson's enthusiastic description of him in 1902: 'a lean man, a theologian, liturgiologist, hymnologist, scholar, musician, preacher, athlete, and a saint! ... and withal a very pleasant human person'.[75]

Community

It is not surprising that a priest, bishop, high churchman, liturgist and historian should have a strong sense of community. But in Frere this sense is exceptionally strong and pervasive. He was a devoted pastor of the flock at Stepney and Truro;[76] and he chose the intensified common life of a religious community, whose unity, for all its affinity with family life, 'must be greater and closer ... Because the community ideal demands a more complete merging of the individual in the whole.'[77] And that community was set aside by neither his bishopric nor his retirement.

This rested on a strong natural inclination. He and his siblings remained close, perhaps the more for their early loss of their parents. He took happily to the life of boarding school and Cambridge, and enjoyed the essentially common pleasures of sport and music.[78] In the secular

---

74 Phillips, *Frere*, pp. 48–9. (He must also have been seriously disappointed at the failure of *Hymns Ancient and Modern*, 1904. See note 86.)

75 C.C. Martindale, *The Life of Monsignor Robert Hugh Benson* (London: Longmans, 1916), vol. I, p. 171.

76 Phillips, *Frere*, chs 2, 5, 6, and his contributions to the *Truro Diocesan Gazette*.

77 *Commentary*, p. 119; 'more complete' does not imply 'total', as the *Commentary* makes plain elsewhere.

78 Phillips, *Frere*, chs 1, 6, 9.

realm he was an educationalist, and a communitarian politically and eco-
nomically, as in general was CR. His scholarly interests were the Christian
Church's common history, common prayer and common music. Scholarly collaboration marks much of his output: joint works,[79] completions
of unfinished works,[80] revisions and new editions of other men's works.[81]
He supervised Freestone's *The Sacrament Reserved*,[82] advised and assisted
authors,[83] contributed to collaborative and reference books,[84] drew up
syllabuses.[85] His name did not always appear; he was content with being
merged in the scholarly community too.[86] *Frere aimait confrère.*

We shall revert to this community-sense, but we note here three
particular ways in which it figures in his prayers and his provision for the
prayers of others. There was his enthusiasm for praying via the liturgies
and devotions bequeathed by his fellow Christians. There was the practice
and promotion of intercession – the most community-minded of all the
'parts' of prayer. And there was the cult of the Saints. Thus in *Some
Principles of Liturgical Reform*, 1911, he proposed 78 Black Letter Days
for a future Kalendar; most of them appeared in the 1928 Prayer Book.
But there they only had common collects; so Frere, arguing that each

---

79 E.g., Frere and Langton E.G. Brown (eds), *The Hereford Breviary* (3 vols., London:
Henry Bradshaw Society, 1904–15).

80 E.g., Frere (ed.), *The Use of Sarum* (2 vols, Cambridge: Cambridge University Press,
1898–1901).

81 Briggs and Frere, Procter and Frere; Rock, *Church of our Fathers.*

82 W.H. Freestone, *The Sacrament Reserved* (Alcuin Club. London: Mowbray, 1917).
William Freestone CR was killed in 1916 shortly after completing the book, which was
seen through the press by Frere and L.S. Thornton.

83 E.g., J. Willis Clark (ed.), *The Observances in Use at the Augustinian Priory of S. Giles
and S. Andrew at Barnwell, Cambridgeshire* (Cambridge: Macmillan and Bowes, 1897), p.
vi: 'Frere "went through the proof-sheets with me more than once, and ... explained to
me much that I should otherwise have failed to understand" [a considerable labour]'.

84 E.g., chapter on Plainsong in P.C. Buck (ed.), *The Oxford History of Music* (Oxford:
Oxford University Press, 1929), articles in H.C. Colles (ed.), *Grove's Dictionary of Music
and Musicians* (3rd edn, London: Macmillan, 1928).

85 E.g., for the Mirfield course at Leeds, and the Knutsford Test School, R.V.H. Burne,
Knutsford (London: SPCK, 1960), p. 7.

86 As in the *Wells Office Book* (1896), and *Hymns Ancient and Modern* (London:
William Clowes, 1904), in which he took a prominent part (in that book none of the
contributors was named). In his massive and erudite *Historical Edition of Hymns Ancient
and Modern* (London: William Clowes, 1909) he is named as author only of the long
historical Introduction.

collect should bring out its saint's individuality, authorized for Truro a set of proper collects in 1935[87] (subsequently published in 1938).[88] In the diocese of Truro he promoted the cult of the Cornish Saints, and in 1933 authorized for that purpose a Cornish Church Calendar.[89] Note that his sense of the community includes this strong awareness of the individuality of its members, whether living or departed.

Private prayer: the trio of modes

We are fortunate to have Frere's general theory of individual prayer, in a sermon marked 'Oxford Jan 31. 1915'.[90] It is evidently addressed to a general congregation; Frere, at 52, is offering a considered rationale of private prayer, based on his own experience, as a possible pattern for his hearers. He may also be consciously offering an alternative approach to the mystical which had been so much expounded in the previous decade or so. For he begins from Scripture, Romans 8.26, and with a scriptural perspective:

> What an absorbing mystery is this intercourse between man and God! an attempt to bring together two incommensurables – a condescension, infinitely gracious, on the part of the Most High God, and a straining beyond his own tiny power on the part of the ambitious soul of man. Behind these two advances or between them is the agency of the Holy Spirit, helping the infirmity of us who know not how to pray as we ought, interceding and interpreting for us ... But none the less, it is the simplest thing in the world. One word, and it is done; when having received the Spirit of adoption we cry 'Abba, Father'.

---

87 *Truro Diocesan Gazette*, January 1935. He writes that the collects owe a good deal to *Prime and Hours, English Liturgy*, and A. Campbell Fraser, *An Aid to a Devout Use of the Minor Holy Days of the Book of Common Prayer: Containing Collects for Each of the Black Letter Days and an Appendix* (London: Elliot Stock, 1917). He typically says nothing of his own part, though Phillips says 'A large number of the Collects were composed by the Bishop himself' (*Frere*, p. 91).

88 *Black Letter Saints' Days*.

89 Phillips, *Frere*, pp. 90, 91; *Truro Diocesan Gazette*, September 1933.

90 In the Borthwick. It is the only sermon handwritten in full. Everything suggests a considered statement, perhaps even a manifesto.

God is the Most High; prayer is directed upwards; as from adopted children to their Father.

He then distinguishes and expounds three distinct but interrelated modes of prayer. First comes 'formal prayer', taught in home, school and church, by words, forms, actions; simple rituals at first, liturgy and written prayers later. This 'remains as the strong core of our worship both in public and in private'. We soon acquire the second mode, 'informal prayer', where we speak freely to God in our own words. Both modes are necessary, and mutually supportive: the formal gives proportion and stability, and corrects subjective limitations and preoccupation with the needs of the moment; the informal gives immediacy and relevance to the current situation, and corrects formalism and unreality. Both modes are verbal, but sooner or later 'we are bound to reach the point at which words fail us', and then we move to the third mode, 'mental prayer'. This supervenes typically at times of depression and of exaltation, but in any case it takes a larger place in our prayers as we progress and as we increasingly realize the inadequacy of our words and thoughts and desires. Then 'man is upheld not by his grasp of attention, nor by his own soaring of soul, but by the power of the Holy Spirit'; as 'even the dust is held up aloft on the breath of the wind that supports it'.

All three modes have their proper value and purpose, and Frere explores them all thoroughly, the verbal modes in eight pages and the mental mode in six. The last is clearly the crown, and at its climax he draws upon 'St Theresa that consummate psychologist and teacher of the art of prayer'. But the verbal modes are in no way discarded; they 'remain' with their permanent intrinsic value, and Frere expounds all three modes with enthusiasm. Talbot's words tally with the sermon: 'One may only uncertainly surmise the heights to which the spires of his prayer soared. What is certain is that they sprang out of a fabric of great architectural elaboration and strength.'[91]

Evelyn Underhill wrote that Frere's 'devotion seemed to demand embodiment, and he sought it by preference in liturgic and historical forms'.[92] This tallies with the first and very positive section of the sermon,

---

91 Phillips, *Frere*, p. 51.
92 Phillips, *Frere*, p. 180

but not with the equally positive last; and 'by preference' implies that he had 'less ... sympathy with formless prayer'.[93] But this the sermon (which she cannot have known) surely disproves; all it shows is that he preferred to approach 'formless prayer' via verbal prayer, rather than take the direct approach of the mystics. As to the latter's various methods, he speaks briefly:

> it is true that Mystical Schemes of terminology have been created from time to time by the masters of spiritual experience: some small features of them have become parts of the common heritage: those drawn from scriptural writers have had the best chance, and the best success in gaining currency.

But most of them 'have become familiar only to the few'. The implication is that his threefold system is Scheme enough – as it clearly is for him – and a good Scheme for most of us, certainly for some of us.

This may explain Underhill's words 'in the technical sense he could not be called a mystic'[94] and 'he was a realist'.[95] 'Realist', and her later term 'realistic Christocentricism',[96] appear to mean 'sacramentalist', which he was, even in his theory of private prayer. Thus his use of mode one affected his mode two – 'a distinguished Presbyterian said ... that it was a revelation of what strength and depth could be given to extempore prayer by a mind nourished and schooled by habituation in the classical forms of liturgical worship'[97] – and we have seen that his modes one and two carried his mode three. It was a congruous scheme for a man of his

---

93 Phillips, *Frere*, p. 181 Underhill illustrates her point with an anecdote that Frere 'used to tell – a bit against himself – of a student discussion on prayer which was opened by a Cuddesdon student with an account of his own methodical devotions: carefully prepared daily meditations, special intercessions and thanksgivings for each day of the week.' "I was just thinking", said the Bishop, "how nice all this is! How *very* nice!" when a Russian girl exclaimed in a voice of horror: "But I thought we were going to discuss Prayer."' Underhill clearly thought that the girl had the right idea. Frere would perhaps have thought that she could learn from the Cuddesdon man as well as he could from her.

94 Phillips, *Frere*, p. 182 – the 'technical sense' as then understood; a wider sense of 'mystical' has been proposed in recent discussion, e.g., Melvyn Matthews, *Both Alike to Thee* (London: SPCK, 2000).

95 Phillips, *Frere*, p. 180.

96 Phillips, *Frere*, p. 182.

97 Phillips, *Frere*, p. 52.

cultural scholarly intellect, communal sacramental religion, and deep personal devotion. But he was a realist in another sense, well aware of the down-to-earth conditions of prayer, as when he advised the end-of-the-day-weary to 'kneel down and say "O God I am tired" and then jump into bed'.[98]

Intercession

Intercession is a prominent element in Andrewes, who may have been the initial stimulus to Frere's own emphasis on it. This was certainly reinforced by his friendship with Mrs Illingworth, as the end of the Preface to *Sursum Corda* shows: 'It only remains for the compilers to add that this book has arisen out of their keen sense of their own failures in grappling with the work of Intercession.'[99] In the Introduction, Frere offers his theory of intercession: it is a duty, an 'exacting task' though 'full of its own joys and encouragements'. It has to be learnt. It grows as our knowledge grows of the world and its needs, till it comes 'to embrace all men and all things' and even becomes 'some poor copy of the boundless love of Almighty GOD'. It benefits the intercessor because it arouses hope and 'takes the sting out of anxiety' as we learn to 'turn worry into intercession'.[100]

Frere practised intercession in detail, volume and system. Only a scrutiny of his lists will reveal their extent, and his care in updating them, especially in noting people's deaths. In this last, intercession passes into commemoration of the departed, since the latter doubtless included commending them to God; so the living and the departed are both objects of intercession. Some of his own written prayers are for different classes of those he ministered to, like the prayer 'for those I have absolved'. Even in prayers for himself, it is often for himself-as-pastor, and thus has others – those he ministers to – in mind: as though the thought of others is never far away, the intercessory impulse always strong. Thus the Latin prayer to the Johannine Jesus addresses him in his various beneficent relations to others and asks that Frere may imitate him, for example (translated):

---

98 Recalled by a College student in 'W.F. The Last Years', *Mirfield Gazette*, 1938.
99 *Sursum Corda*, p. vii.
100 *Sursum Corda*, p. 1 and ff.

Saviour of the sick man at Bethesda, may I
be a helper of the sick:

Rememberer of others even in death, give me
the love that forgets itself;

Consoler of the Magdalen, make me a solace
to the sorrowing.[101]

Frere continued to urge intercession upon others, in *Sursum Corda*, in many addresses, and in the *Truro Diocesan Gazette*, where he taught its importance and called for it on specific occasions, for diocesan needs, for mission, for the world. In 1931 he called for *Intercession for a Troubled World*. He composed the following prayer, clearly for public use and surely for the General Strike of 1926:[102]

O Lord make haste to help our land
in this hour of contention, mistrust
and perplexity; that, seeking only
what is just/fair among men and what
is right before Thee, we may find
the way out of present discord towards
the goal of generous goodwill and
mutual service, in the love of Jesus
Christ our Lord.

Thanksgiving

This, the second strand of *Sursum Corda*, is also prominent in Andrewes and a joint concern with Mrs Illingworth, as is even more strongly put in the Preface, following the passage quoted above: 'and out of their difficulty in even realising at all that there is such a work as Thanksgiving'.

---

101 The elegant pithiness of the Latin is worth a note. The original petitions are:
    Salvator aegri in Bethesda   aegrotantibus subvenire
    Memor alium etiam in morte   da caritatem sui obliviscentem
    Magdalenae consolator   lugentibus fac solatium.
102 A loose sheet in his *Sursum Corda*.

In the Introduction he gives it more space than Intercession, perhaps out of a conviction that its neglect was general (in the 1905 edition the thanksgiving sections are expanded). Such neglect, he writes, has two bad effects: 'depression about the world at large or the salvation of our own souls', and the delusion 'that there is more in the world to cause us depression than there is to evoke our thankfulness'. In particular, thanksgiving puts our sin in perspective; penitence there must be, but 'when our sins are forgiven, penitence has done its work and thanksgiving takes its place'. Similarly 'thanksgiving must overpower the sense of shame, because GOD's mercies are after all so much greater even than our sins'. Compare Mrs Illingworth, recalling an occasion when she

> heard her husband and his friends discussing what was the instinctive attitude of the Christian's mind towards God. All agreed that it was one of sorrow for sin. 'I smiled to myself' said Mrs I., 'but I said nothing, for my first thought is always one of gratitude.'[103]

Frere returned to the point in 1905 when in the Rule of the Fraternity of the Resurrection he writes 'their sorrow [for sin] shall find its best expression not in brooding over past sin or present sinfulness, but in the outpouring of loving thankfulness to God for his mercy, and in fervent intercession for the careless and the godless'.[104]

But thanksgiving is not just a remedy for gloom. 'Rather it must be the constant companion of every day and hour, by its continual presence brightening what is dark, and lightening up that which is already bright with unearthly radiance.' Like intercession, 'it has to be recommended, has to be doggedly practised, has to be laboriously learnt', for 'the natural heart of man is hard and insensible to GOD's mercies, is cold and ungrateful even when it is conscious of them'. But when thanksgiving is learnt, it brings happiness, and becomes the way to adoration; it 'runs up into the more impersonal act of worship, wherein ... we lose ourselves in the presence of GOD in glorifying GOD for being what he is' (an example of Frere's second mode of prayer rising to the third).[105]

A good example of Frere's own practice is his Andrewes-inspired

---

103 Raikes, *Agnes Louisa Illingworth*, p. 22.
104 *CR Quarterly*, Michaelmas, 1905.
105 Quotations in this paragraph from the Introduction to *Sursum Corda*.

'Commemoratio Temporalium',[106] a catalogue of his blessings: his existence, his earthly blessings, his Christian experience, his family, friends and benefactors (the last listed by their initials). It is thanksgiving, and again we encounter his sense of community; and we may surmise that thanking God for people involved interceding for them.

We can see thanksgiving implicit in other types of prayer by Frere, as in the following example.[107] It is a petition that we may know God in knowing his created works, but it implies thanksgiving for them (and for the natural sciences that illuminate them):

Grant we beseech Thee Almighty God that as we grow in knowledge of the wondrous works which Thy mighty hand hath ordered and created and still doth daily and hourly sustain: so we may grow in knowledge of Thyself, of Thy Son through whom Thou madest them, and of the Holy Spirit who filleth them all; with whom Thou livest and reignest Three persons in the One God for ever and evermore. Amen.

Sanctification

Frere's community-sense in no way undervalued the individual; indeed the freedom and fulfilment of each member is one of the Community's positive aims. Thus the *Commentary* emphasizes it, while also requiring the due balance of the Community's and each brother's needs. (As bishop, Frere respected the diversities and even eccentricities of his clergy.)[108]Most important was his sense of the individual Christian's relation to God, the life-long discipleship, the growth in personal virtue and prayer, the pursuit of perfection – sanctification in fact, though Frere seldom uses the term.

For sanctification was Frere's primary spiritual concern. His teaching was mostly addressed to the already committed, in *Sursum Corda*, the *Commentary*, and in the hundreds of sermons and addresses. Talbot judged his preaching best fitted for 'the spiritually awake' and too cool for arousing the unconverted. (That was Paul Bull's *forte*, and when he and Frere conducted a mission 'they achieved a combination of heat and

---

106 See note 40.
107 Another loose sheet.
108 Phillips, *Frere*, pp. 92–5.

light that had a high evangelistic efficacy'.)[109] Frere's constant aim is that his readers and hearers may grow, in prayer, understanding, virtue, practical goodness, the love of God and man. Aspiration, growth, learning, work, progress, are constant themes, even ambition and a 'spiritual enthusiasm for progress'.[110]

If, as the scanty evidence indicates, Frere was a 'once-born' Christian, his own experience was of a life of growth. Not that he forgets conversion; as an Evangelical Catholic he shared over many years in missions seeking to convert. His last Cambridge sermon[111] was on the subject, based illuminatingly on Revelation 1.12–17, summarized as 'I turned and saw: and I fell at His feet.' Conversion is fundamental: it can be experienced in different ways, and renewed 'while life lasts' – 'there is call, turn, and vision for all of us right up to the end'.

Sanctification is an active pursuit, fuelled by 'true spiritual ambition', 'seeking that which is more excellent'.[112] Intercession and thanksgiving are 'difficult and exacting tasks' learnt over a lifetime of 'detailed and systematic habit'. It is an exacting pursuit – one retreat address is entitled 'The Cost of Discipleship'. We work out our salvation, and Frere, with his active temperament and (arguably excessive) work programme certainly did. But he did not, in life or teaching, forget that it is God who works in us; he returns often to divine grace, providence, the light of Christ, the power of the Spirit, 'the gifts of Grace which flow from the Risen Life of our Saviour'. A whole retreat on 'Grace in the Soul' devotes ten addresses to providence, conversion, justification, the new life, temptation, personal gifts, action and endurance, sacraments and prayer, the Church. And at the end of his life he said of the daily Eucharist: 'I live by that.'[113]

To individuals he taught the way of sanctification by advice, confession and spiritual direction. For this there can be little direct evidence, but there are a few letters, and the reports of some who received his help. An obituary recalled him at Stepney as 'one of the most gentle confessors of Holy Church'.[114] In advice and direction he 'never failed to give from the

---

109 Phillips, *Frere*, p. 59.
110 *Commentary*, p. 77 (even 'spiritual rivalry').
111 Phillips, *Frere*, pp. 177–8.
112 *Commentary*, pp. 99.
113 Phillips, *Frere*, p. 202.
114 *Church Times*, 8 April 1938 (CR Chronicles).

stores of his own knowledge and profound spirituality';[115] he was sympathetic without softness, methodical without rigidity, penetrating and decisive in a crisis.[116] But 'it was not always easy to get definite advice or opinions from him, for his humility always made him diffident and tentative in his approach to other souls.'[117] Perhaps it was not only humility, but a distrust of 'strong' direction: 'he had nothing of the urge to penetrate the secrets of others and to assume responsibility for their lives which has marked many great religious leaders. He had an unfailing respect for personality.'[118]

Here his relation to Evelyn Underhill is illuminating. He was her spiritual director from about 1928 to 1932, and her warmly appreciative account of him in Phillips doubtless rests upon that experience. In one letter to her he suggests that she should stop thinking about 'the symptoms' of what is troubling her ('a sort of moral cancer' perhaps) and ask God to remove the underlying cause.[119] In another, about her fitness to advise others, he tries to divert her from worrying about her sins: 'that isn't penitence. Penitence is a swift prostration, and then on again. Don't let your mind then hang about your faults ... St Paul boldly forgets in order to reach forward. He was so sane and bold over it.'[120] One senses that he distrusts too much spiritual introspection, and avoids it himself (a counterpart to his general reserve about himself and others); and since Underhill changed to a 'stronger' director (Somerset Ward) she perhaps needed what Frere would or could not provide.[121]

Frere's own pursuit of holiness exemplified his teaching. He chose the religious life with its devotions, renunciations and constraints; within it he used his gifts, worked diligently, accepted responsibility and surely found fulfilment even though he wore himself out in the process.[122] Most

---

115 Phillips, *Frere*, p. 178.
116 Phillips, *Frere*, p. 182.
117 Phillips, *Frere*, p. 182.
118 Phillips, *Frere*, p. 178.
119 C.J.R. Armstrong, *Evelyn Underhill* (London: Mowbray, 1975), p. 247.
120 M. Cropper, *Life of Evelyn Underhill* (London: Longmans, 1958), p. 154.
121 See Armstrong, *Underhill*, pp. 245–9. They remained friends (Phillips, *Frere*, chs. 6 and 10, Cropper, *Underhill*, pp. 154–5). He had helped ('my dear and kind friend Bishop Frere') with Underhill's *Worship* (London: Nisbet, 1936); her *Eucharistic Prayers from the Ancient Liturgies* (London: Longmans, 1939) is dedicated 'In Memoriam Walter Howard Frere'.
122 Phillips, *Frere*, p. 200–2.

of his work was for others, in the service of God. He seems in general to have looked not inwards at himself but outwards to others and upwards to God. He attended to himself chiefly in thanksgiving for his blessings and prayer for his fellows, with penitence as a necessary sideline. But personal devotion was at the centre, as a few of his mainly personal prayers will illustrate (none are in print).

First, the prayer-sequence *Suspiria* (see note 45), written by Frere in his thirties, before CR moved to Mirfield:

LOVE

My God, I desire to love Thee perfectly:
With all my heart which Thou madest for Thyself,
With all my mind which only Thou canst satisfy,
With all my soul which fain would soar to Thee,
With all my strength, my feeble strength,
which shrinks before so great a task,
and yet can choose nought else but spend itself in loving Thee.
Claim Thou my heart, Fill Thou my mind,
Uplift my soul, and Reinforce my strength,
That where I fail Thou mayest succeed in me,
and make me love Thee perfectly.

FEAR

I fear Thee, O my God.
O righteous Father,
With a filial awe,
O Judge inexorable, with guilty dread,
O Holy Ghost, with terror born of sacrilege.
I fear Thee, O my God:
And fearing Thee I fear naught else;
Not life, nor death, nor hell,
Not man, nor fiend,
But only Thee,
My God

TRUST

O Father, I will trust Thee:
For all the known and all the unknown good that I have ever had
has come from Thee.
Sweet Saviour I will trust Thee:
Thy grace is all-sufficient for my soul,
As mighty as Thy power and as matchless as Thy love.
Blest Spirit, I will trust Thee:
How can I ever dare to trust myself,
To think, or speak, or act apart from Thee?
O God, my God, my Hope and Stay,
Who knowest and orderest all that is best,
I know not what to will or do aright;
Then make me ever love to choose and do Thy will.

SERVICE

My God my heart is set on serving Thee;
To serve the world is hard, unsatisfying,
To serve myself is the most cramped of slaveries,
But to serve Thee is perfect joy and liberty.
My God, my heart is set on serving Thee.
Here would I consecrate to Thee and to Thy cause
each faculty and power
Of intellect or learning, Of heart or sympathy,
Of spiritual fervour, Of influence or guidance,
All come from Thee, All shall revert to Thee,
I only have the usufruct and that I give to Thee.[123]
Take all and use it for Thy holy purposes,
Use me to glorify Thee.

DESIRE

Lord, I desire, I desire,
I cannot say how much:

---

123 'Usufruct' – the right to use and enjoy the property of another – neatly summarizes
the Christian attitude to life, as belonging to God but used and enjoyed by man.

I only know I stand in need of all things.
And would that my desire were as great as is my need!
Lord, who alone canst satisfy the human heart's desire,
And fill with all Thy fulness the abyss of human need,
Hear now how I desire all good things,
And Thee, Thyself, my God, above all else,
Who givest all.

PATIENCE

My God I can wait   If Thou uphold me:
I can endure If Thou sustain me:
I can give up If Thou reward me:
I gladly will do all   If Thou command me:
O righteous Judge, Thou art both strong and patient,
I will be patient if Thou make me strong.

Second, three separate prayers written into his private copy of *Sursum Corda*. The first, undated, has similarities with the *Suspiria*; the other two are from his time in Truro, written in his sixties.

O Lord Thou hast the knowledge and the power and the will
to carry out the welfare of my soul
I poor creature have neither the knowledge nor the power
nor even the will to desire it as I should
Therefore O Lord of generous mercy
Do Thou so order for me and so arrange for me as Thou
knowest to be for Thy good pleasure and for my most certain welfare.

O Father let me know Thee well enough
to be very patient
O Saviour let me know Thee well enough
to understand others
O Blessed Spirit let me know Thee well enough
to avoid mistakes
O Sacred Trinity let me know Thee better
day by day and hour by hour.
Amen   (Easter 1926)

Is it today that Thou wilt call me?
Then Lord make me ready for Thy call.
If not today, but on some morrow,
Then while it is called 'today'
Let me make haste to amend.

(June 1930)

Sanctity

Some judged that Frere had gone far enough on the way of perfection to be called a saint. In 1935, when he retired from Truro, a poem to that effect appeared, subscribed 'Truro. March, 1935. D.L.' The first four verses run:

A saint once lived amongst us and moved on –
And we, so foolish were we, never realised his worth
Till he had gone away.

What was he like, our saint? Thin, keen and tall,
Though not by height alone o'ertopping all the rest
But by his character.

Stern to himself, and, if occasion need,
To others too, but ready to respect each prejudice,
And to efface himself.

Loyal to all who called him overlord
E'en to his own undoing and his hurt and pain,
Such was the man our saint.[124]

In 1947 Bernard Horner CR, who had known him since the 1900s, wrote in a review of Phillips:

---

124 Communicated by Fr Dominic Whitnall CR (who was confirmed by Frere at Truro). I am indebted to him for both information and much encouragement.

we shall never get a right appreciation of Frere if we forget that we are dealing with a saint. A saint is a man who loves God supremely and his love compels him to the consecration of all his powers and faculties to promote the glory of God; and also compels him to an active charity towards man. The saint does not consider that he is giving glory to God either by ignoring or by despising what He has created.[125]

Talbot[126] found his 'spiritual quality' reminiscent of the description of the divine Wisdom as 'quick of understanding, holy, subtle, freely moving, clear in utterance';[127] and though he does not call him 'saint', his portrait of Frere is certainly that of a notably holy man. Talbot also gives attention to Frere's faults and foibles, as do other contributors to Phillips.[128] They have received further attention in more recent study (see Chapter 1 of this book). He was a complex person, and had to deal (at some cost to himself) with some situations and persons not amenable to straightforward solutions. His shortcomings must not be given undue weight (nor must the views of his detractors). But in any case faultlessness is not a prerequisite of sanctity. A 'saint' is one in whom his fellow Christians agree that they have seen signally manifested the presence and the working of God; and Frere may well be recognized as such a one. He would certainly qualify for inclusion in that motley procession, the *Common Worship* Calendar.

His spiritual writing is little known today. Even in the voluminous anthology of specifically Anglican spirituality, *Love's Redeeming Work*,[129] none of it appears. It has not been easily accessible.[130] Frere would not complain. He avoided the limelight and has succeeded in staying out of it. Perhaps he will become more widely known and honoured.

---

125 *CR Quarterly*, Christmas 1947, p. 35. The words quoted here reappear, slightly altered, in Horner's 'Foreword' in Jasper, *Frere* (n. 18).

126 Phillips, *Frere*, p. 52; cf. the whole of pp. 47–52.

127 Cf. *Wisdom of Solomon* 7: 22 (RV).

128 Talbot, in Phillips, *Frere*, pp. 48, 50–4, 60, 201–2; H.F. Stewart, p. 28, Dix, pp. 140–4, also in Phillips.

129 G. Rowell, K. Stevenson, R. Williams (eds), *Love's Redeeming Work* (Oxford: Oxford University Press, 2001). Frere is not mentioned in Gordon Mursell, *English Spirituality* (London: SPCK, 2001), or in C. Jones, G. Wainwright, E. Yarnold (eds), *The Study of Spirituality* (London: SPCK, 1986).

130 The private books being at Mirfield, and the relevant printed works long out of print and forgotten.

3

'Brilliance and suggestiveness': the Educator

BENJAMIN GORDON-TAYLOR

Walter Frere was one of the pioneers of theological education, especially in the formation of ordination candidates in the context of a religious community. This was already happening under Fr Kelly at the Society of the Sacred Mission at Kelham, but Frere was no mere version of Kelly any more than CR was a mere version of SSM. While he encouraged the Community of the Resurrection to take note of the Kelham approach, what emerged was unique and reflective of Frere's personality and determination: the College of the Resurrection at Mirfield and its associated institution, the Hostel of the Resurrection in the University of Leeds. As well as a founder and shaper of theological institutions and curricula, however, Frere was also a teacher of liturgy and church history, as much – in the case of liturgy – to his diocese of Truro and the Church of England as a whole as to classes of ordinands at Mirfield.

Theological education for ordinands: the College and Hostel of the Resurrection

Frere's significant contribution to the adequate training and formation of candidates for the priesthood may be divided into two parts: his general views on the subject, and their concrete application in the founding of the College at Mirfield and the Hostel at the University of Leeds. Indeed, the foundation of College and Hostel undoubtedly gave further shape to the ideas.

Although as Superior Frere was undoubtedly supportive of the possibility of CR training ordinands at Mirfield, it appears to have been Fr Paul Bull CR who did much of the necessary gathering of information, not least the assessment of Kelham under its founder Fr Kelly as a model of a monastic context for formation. Bull visited Kelham in May 1901 and reported his experience to the brethren of CR in July 1901; the outcome was a proposal to associate training at Mirfield with the taking of a degree at what was about to become the University of Leeds. A key element in the thinking behind the scheme was to enable young men from impoverished backgrounds to be ordained, not hitherto possible since both social status and suitable financial means were effectively qualifications for orders in the Church of England: 'a new form of simony', as Charles Gore called it. Nevertheless, it was the impeccable social and intellectual credentials of the young Community of the Resurrection that gave the Mirfield scheme a necessary boost; as Alan Wilkinson has noted, while 'CR lacked anyone of the craggy originality of Kelly ... because the CR scheme included an element of university education and had the backing of Gore, Frere and [Keble] Talbot it was eminently respectable.'[1] As Wilkinson further notes, the notion received the highest approbation from the Archbishop of Canterbury himself, Dr Temple: 'I rejoice to see that you contemplate preparing all your men for a degree in Arts before they become theologians.'[2] As an implicit indication of Frere's thinking, this is revealing in that it confirms his instincts to range widely in thought and enquiry, reflected in his own teaching and research but inevitably rubbing off to good effect on students at the College and Hostel. That it is implicit characterizes the surprising difficulty of pinning down precisely Frere's influence on the College in its early years, although it is undoubtedly and very significantly there. Clues are everywhere, yet Wilkinson gives the impression that Frere, though Superior, encouraged from behind rather than led from the front. To put it another way, it is true to say that Frere's guiding hand is evident, but never overwhelming or immediately to the fore. Initially, indeed, it may have been less present than it ought to have been. It seems extraordinary that Frere did not earlier notice, correctly interpret or take action in respect of the problematic period in office of the first Warden of the College, Caleb Ritson CR. However, this episode may explain the clearer evidence of his firmer influence which is to be found in successive reports on the College, signed by Frere, to the Chapter of the Community,

---

1 Alan Wilkinson, *The Community of the Resurrection: A Centenary History* (London: SCM Press, 1992), p. 279.

2 Letter to Hugh Benson, 1902, quoted in Wilkinson, *Centenary History*, p. 279.

which are extant from 1907. These were almost certainly written (in typescript) by the new Warden, Bernard Horner, but did not receive the Superior's *imprimatur* without the latter's manuscript corrections where necessary. Frere was no romantic when it came to governance, and if he had taken his eye off the ball in Ritson's time his attention was thereafter fully focused, and included the fortunes of individual students, on whose progress or otherwise he could be very sharp. In the 1913–14 report the typescript reads that a student 'has left the College', but has been amended in Frere's hand to 'has been dismissed as intellectually insufficient'.[3] This is typical of Frere's attention to detail in the matter of the College in the years following the Ritson era, which extended to precision and a certain modesty on the sufficiency of the training offered. The Report for the year 1912–13 includes an assessment of the two-year period spent by students at Leeds before the Mirfield-based element of their training commenced. The original typescript reads:

In the majority of cases [the two years at Leeds] make a distinct and valuable contribution to the development of a man's character and give him a much wider outlook. Indeed the [College] Council consider that such an interval is essential to a complete course of training for each student.[4]

Frere has amended the last sentence so that it refers to 'a *satisfactory* course of training' – Frere was never one for complacency, and recognized the limits of what was being attempted, although it was deemed a success. There may also be a deliberate theological implication here: in the final analysis it was God who made priests, not CR.

In less tangible, but for students of his time equally important, ways, Frere influenced the ethos of the College, and therefore the formation of the students for priesthood, by his personality and example. There was, as Wilkinson has said, 'a lot of fun and stimulus ... and regular cricket matches between brethren and students',[5] and Frere was at the heart of this. There exists in the College archives a tiny photograph on the back of which is written 'College vs. Community, Summer 1914'. College students

3 MS College Annual Report to Council (hereafter MS CollRpt) 1913–14, p. 5.
4 MS CollRpt 1912–13, p. 7.
5 *Centenary History*, p. 281.

stand behind brethren seated on the grass at the edge of the cricket field, in a spot still clearly identifiable today. It is a very relaxed photograph. All wear various incomplete versions of cricket whites, in the case of some of the brethren semi-clerical. Frere sits on the grass in dark trousers and collarless white shirt, his legs tucked beneath him, cigarette in hand, smiling at the camera, his warmth obvious. It is a poignant photograph, given its date on the brink of the First World War, but Frere's appearance in it seems to confirm what students typically said of him with overwhelming affection.

These were the men from all backgrounds whom the brethren gathered at the College. But even Frere could not wholly throw off the class distinctions of the day. In the 1907 report to an Archiepiscopal Committee on 'The Supply and Training of Candidates for Holy Orders', Frere remarks that

the men must be capable of polish ... We find no difficulty about manners though they have to be learnt ... I do not suppose our average

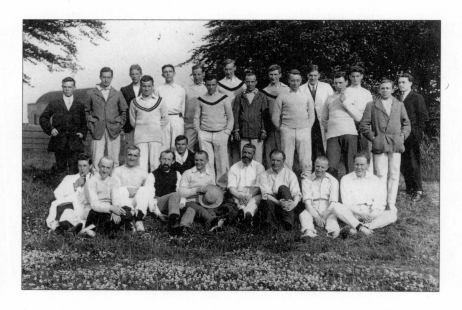

Community v. College cricket, summer 1914 (see above). Frere is sitting
second left in the front row, smiling at the camera. The first part of the
Community Church to be completed is visible in the background.

man would know what to do at a dinner party ... As regards the accent we find the cockney dialect to be the most prohibitive.[6]

It is perhaps unfair to single Frere out when such views and their implications of social attitude would have been common even in what must have seemed to many a radical social experiment like CR. Frere was a man of his time, then, but the impression of his genuine warmth and concern for the students is still evident.

Two of Frere's published papers stand out as of particular importance in understanding his thinking on theological education, the first appearing in the *Church Quarterly Review* in 1910, the second in his collection of lectures to a Russian audience, *English Church Ways*, of 1914. There is inevitably some overlap, but both need to be considered as examples of the manner in which Frere disseminated his ideas and the practice they had inspired at Mirfield.

Frere's manifesto: A word to the Church of England

In 1910, in a *Church Quarterly Review* article entitled 'The Training and Examination of Candidates for Orders', Frere had the opportunity to set out in detail for a wider domestic audience his views on theological education in the Church of England. As in the corrected annual reports, Frere's lack of complacency, directness of view and a certain caution and evenness of judgement are present from the very outset:

> Ten years ago it might properly have been supposed that the supply of candidates for the ministry was falling off. The number of clergy ordained was certainly diminishing, and the position was alarming. At the present time, though the position remains serious, it cannot be said that the cause of the seriousness is a decline in the number of men who wish to give themselves to the priesthood.[7]

Although he does not mention Mirfield by name, the particular contribution the Mirfield scheme had made in its first eight years of

---

6 Quoted in Wilkinson, *Centenary History*, p. 283.

7 'The Training and Examination of Candidates for Orders', *Church Quarterly Review* 1910, p. 333.

existence is implicit: the addressing of the problem of lack of access to theological training on the part of candidates from poorer backgrounds. In this something of Frere the Christian Socialist is apparent:

> The changes which had taken place in the universities and public schools had had the effect of depriving many a poor home of its opportunity of sending up a son to school and college to be trained for the ministry. The ancient endowments that were given for this purpose, among others, were diverted from the poor to the rich, and from the men of average ability, who could qualify, to men of exceptional ability who could win scholarships, or to men whose parents could secure for them an elaborate and expensive preparation for school or college. This change, together with the general fall in clerical incomes, was paralysing, especially to the clergy.[8]

Frere continues with a thinly veiled criticism of the continuing failure of the Church as an institution to address the fact that 'we have lost so many men for the ministry':

> We have learned, in short, a few of the lessons of our failure, and are beginning to make up a little for what has been lost; but there are many lessons which still remain to be learned, and a great deficiency still to be overcome.[9]

This amounted to a robust challenge; the Mirfield scheme, it is again implied, had shown that it could be overcome with imagination. Frere continues with a discussion of finance, arguing with withering emphasis for a real sea change in attitudes at all levels towards funding for theological education, such that

> the training of the clergy must be made one of the primary charges upon church finance ... we may insist that the support of candidates for the ministry should be one of the first claims upon any system of church finance, whether reformed or unreformed.[10]

---

8 'Training and Examination of Candidates', pp. 333–4.
9 'Training and Examination of Candidates', p. 334.
10 'Training and Examination of Candidates', pp. 334, 335.

Having dealt robustly with finance, Frere turns to educational matters, his true forte, and 'the most difficult part of the present problem'.[11] What follows may be said to encapsulate his developed thinking. He argues for variety in methods of training – Mirfield not being the only way – but this variety must be 'not only on theological grounds, but on others widely separated from theology'. Three considerations are in view. First, 'the preliminary testing of the candidate before any definite responsibility is incurred on his behalf'; secondly, 'there is the general education needed as an introduction to [thirdly] the study of theology and the technical training for the work of the ministry'.[12] In other words, Frere is calling for a more conscious and deliberate integration of identifying and nurturing vocation with the necessary encouragement and nurturing of mind and competence in pastoral effectiveness. He is critical of the one-year course at theological college followed by many ordination candidates, while recognizing that 'It is an immense gain that it has now been secured in most instances.'[13] This is classic Frere argument: praise for a step in the right direction with very clear insistence that there is nonetheless more to be done. The single year will not do, and the evidence is to be seen in the junior clergy, who are typically

enthusiastic workers, zealous and wholehearted in their practical labours, but not theologians, not convincing preachers, not interested in the theological aspects of life in which the laity are interested, not as well trained for their purpose nor as interested in general matters as the average doctor or lawyer.

What in consequence is needed is 'a fuller and more adequate professional training'.[14] This is again a withering assessment, and may not have been wholly fair, but it does contain two interesting assumptions on the part of Frere. The first is that clergy ought to be interested in, take note and reflect on what concerns the laity, the 'general matters' of the world's turning – obvious today, perhaps, but pioneering at the time in its suggestion of a thoroughly incarnational and, in modern terms, 'street-

---

11 'Training and Examination of Candidates', p. 336.
12 'Training and Examination of Candidates', p. 336–7.
13 'Training and Examination of Candidates', p. 337.
14 'Training and Examination of Candidates', p. 338.

wise' priesthood which very shortly came to typify Mirfield-trained priests in the tough urban parishes of East London and elsewhere, and as chaplains in the trenches of the Great War. Given this concern, it is no surprise that the contemporary College pamphlet, *More Men*, is anxious to point out that 'People who do not know anything about it suppose that the Mirfield course is necessarily a "narrow seminarist training", such as can only turn out delicate hot-house plants of a particular type. Nothing could be further from the fact.'[15] The second, and perhaps more surprising, assumption in the 1910 article is that priests should be regarded as professionals like doctors and lawyers, and should therefore be given a professional training. This is an issue of competence. Frere sees a need for priests who can be good at what they *do* because of what they *are*; as a realist and not the romantic his medieval enthusiasms might seem to suggest, Frere recognizes that priests have to be given the means to get on with it, equipped with at least a minimum standard of competence, if they are to be free to minister to their people effectively. For this reason 'technical training', as he calls it, is vital, and implicit is the assertion that superior social class or independent financial means are no guarantees in themselves, if they ever had been, of effective mission and pastoral care. Indeed, one feels Frere is suggesting they could be a hindrance.

An arresting contrast with today follows in Frere's discussion of the needs of various ages of potential ordinands, and the recognition of the possibility of a vocation commonly at a very young age:

there should be schemes of prolonging the education of the boy who receives his call at 14 or 15 and has so far had little schooling or unsuitable schooling, or perhaps has even left school already ... during the intervals of business hours, there should be more organized supervision and more definite encouragement from the authorities to whom he attaches himself.[16]

No one could accuse Frere of discouraging younger vocations. Indeed, he regards those who receive the call 'rather later' as those of 16 or 17 years

---

15 *More Men: The Crying Need of the Church. Some Account of the Attempt at Mirfield to Supply Them* (2nd edn., Mirfield 1910), pp. 9–10.

16 'Training and Examination of Candidates', p. 339.

of age. His concern is with readiness for collegiate life and study, with the possibility that such a candidate 'be put back into school in view of the new prospect which is opening out in front of him'.[17] Many years later, in 1925, CR was to supply an answer to such preparatory needs at Tatterford in Norfolk, under the direction of the Rector, Billy Hand, who had been one of the first students greeted by Frere at Wakefield railway station over 20 years before, and one of the first to be ordained in 1908.[18] But the vision had been Frere's for many a year, as evidenced by the 1910 article. The Knutsford Test School founded after the First World War was to answer the specific needs of demobilized soldiers who were ordinands, but here too Frere's hand was on the educational tiller from the outset.[19] It may be concluded that Frere was not merely a critic expecting others to do what he thought necessary – it was simply that the War intervened. His vision was never dimmed, and was realized in the end. In fact immediately before the War he had an opportunity to explain his philosophy of education for the priesthood simply and directly to a Russian audience, in his *English Church Ways* of 1914, based on lectures given in St Petersburg in March 1914. In the talk called 'Clerical Life' he emphasizes that 'the clergy are but a small part of the Church, but an immense deal depends upon their training'.[20] The Knutsford and Tatterford schemes, and overwhelmingly that at Mirfield, are testimony to his tenacity and determination in pursuit of this conviction. In spite of all this, he did not believe a man of over 30 should be accepted for training, again a stark contrast with today, feeling that, if the way were completely cleared of obstacles for those of younger age, it would not in any case be necessary. This is a very different view of vocation from that of today – Frere insists on the reality of vocations across the social classes, but suspects or perhaps even refutes those of older men, although he does admit that there may be 'unusual circumstances'.[21] For a person of such vivid imagination and fervent vision perhaps this is surprising, but hardly untypical of his time.

---

17 'Training and Examination of Candidates', p. 340.

18 See Wilkinson, *Centenary History*, pp. 285–6.

19 See R.V.H. Burne, *Knutsford: The Story of the Ordination Test School, 1914–40* (London: SPCK, 1960), *passim* and p. 7: 'we had our own syllabus, drawn up by Fr Frere CR'.

20 W.H. Frere, *English Church Ways* (London: John Murray, 1914), p. 52.

21 'Training and Examination of Candidates', p. 342.

After some discussion of missionary studentships, very much in accord with other work of CR, Frere's next target in the 1910 article is the final stage of training, and follows the usual Frere style of argument, in that 'The present system of bishops' examinations is cumbrous, uneven, and unsatisfactory. Some approximations to something better have been made, but more needs to be done.' Here Frere repeats his concern for 'technical' as well as intellectual training to produce a consistently competent junior clergy. Examinations should therefore include 'technical and spiritual' matters.[22] The paper begins to sum up with emphatic calls for change and

> fresh experiment. We must not be afraid of trying novelties ... there must be more use of the newer universities and less clinging to conservative methods in sending men at great cost to the older universities who would be both more suitably and more economically trained at the newer universities.[23]

And then another typical Frere touch: 'we must not be surprised or dejected if some of the novelties prove unsuccessful', and in conclusion an unflinching and rousing challenge which could be said to lie behind everything that CR under Frere hoped to achieve by its own scheme:

> Above all, it is imperative that the Church as a whole should be awakened to a sense of its responsibility for the discovering, encouraging, training, and financing of the vast number of its fine sons who are eager in heart to respond to a call which they have heard, but hardly dare recognize or mention because of the atmosphere of discouragement within which the Church, through its insensibility, its class prejudice, and its parsimony, has enveloped them hitherto.[24]

Some of the phrases in this passage echo the College prayer, which speaks of 'an eager response' to God's call. Frere must have had this in mind as he wrote this last paragraph, and it may indicate that he was the author

---

22 'Training and Examination of Candidates', pp. 343–4.
23 'Training and Examination of Candidates', p. 344.
24 'Training and Examination of Candidates', p. 344.

of the prayer in its original form. That prayer and effective action should be so closely aligned is no surprise in Frere or his community.

Frere's manifesto: A word to the Russians

Frere's lecture 'Clerical Life', for a Russian audience and reproduced in the volume *English Church Ways* (1914) is a much more concise, clearer distillation of his thinking, and it reveals an even clearer preference, after a few more years of experience, for his Mirfield scheme. This may be thought understandable, even obvious, yet, given his audience, he presents what appear to be general remarks on the principles of theological education almost as if they were the universal conviction of all involved in such work in the Church of England, when in fact he has Mirfield in mind throughout. More is also revealed of his political leanings, how these influenced his thinking on the nature of priesthood, and how this was put into practice at Mirfield – again, not all would have shared his views on the social and economic state of the nation and its people, and it is to be supposed that his pre-revolutionary Russian ecclesiastical audience would not have been that enthusiastic to apply the same principles to their own society either. Nevertheless it is a lucid summing up of Frere's thought and work as a theological educator up to the brink of the First World War.

He begins with the need to avoid a priesthood that is too detached from the society which it purports to serve:

> There are, indeed, some elements in the priest's calling which necessarily separate him off from others; but our theory is that, apart from these elements, he should be as much like others in upbringing as possible, so that thus the disadvantage may be avoided of the clergy forming, through isolation, in their most impressionable years, a class apart from the rest of their fellows.[25]

The manner in which they were to be trained was crucial to the encouragement and achievement of this. Frere thought that 'small groups' were best for 'final preparation', although he includes in this colleges with

---

25 *English Church Ways*, pp. 52–3.

'sixty to eighty students'.[26] His social views and the implicit wisdom of the Mirfield scheme further emerge in his assessment of the 'new universities', of which Leeds was one, in contrast to those in which he had received his own education:

> the new universities are not expensive and aristocratic institutions, like Oxford and Cambridge. These new facilities make it possible that, before long, there will be required normally of all candidates for the priesthood a university education and a degree, together with a special theological training as well.[27]

This is exactly what has been fully realized only in recent years in the theological colleges of the Church of England, in that almost all candidates for ordination now read for a degree or diploma through the college's association with a university, including Oxford or Cambridge. Frere was nothing if not visionary. Here, though, he continues on his social theme, declaring that 'we have suffered a good deal in the English Church from being too aristocratic ... the clergy have so largely (in fact, almost exclusively of late) been drawn from the wealthier classes'.[28] This is more than a sideswipe of a committed Christian Socialist: rather it is introducing the social justification for Frere's egalitarian philosophy of clerical education, as a result of the practice of which 'the change is coming about which will enable the Church to fulfil its duty more fully to all classes'.[29] Further to this was the need to deal with the problem of accessibility to theological education, at the very heart of the motivation to establish the College at Mirfield to address 'a great disadvantage that the priesthood was so largely closed, as it was, to the sons of those who had only moderate or small means', and he could report that 'funds are being provided, and colleges have been set up where men who have their vocation from God can get a proper training for the priesthood at the Church's expense'.[30] Or, in the case of CR, at the Community's expense; he is, however, too modest to say this, although Mirfield is very close to

---

26 *English Church Ways*, p. 53.
27 *English Church Ways*, p. 54.
28 *English Church Ways*, p. 54.
29 *English Church Ways*, p. 55.
30 *English Church Ways*, p. 55.

the surface of this apparently general sketch. Frere's emphasis on 'vocation from God' is significant: this indicates his passionate belief in the priority of the divine initiative, in the way of which no unjust or unequal social system should be allowed to stand. Again, one wonders what his Russian audience made of this.

There was a further concern that Frere believed needed to be addressed in the training of clergy for the Church of England: that such training kept up with and incorporated the wider intellectual life of society and the scientific advances of the day. Here is more evidence of Frere's desire to ensure that clergy were not 'separate' in the practice of their ministry, and also that they should be enabled to engage with all sections of society. He was convinced that ordinands should be

> in touch with all sides of intellectual life. It is of crucial importance that they should be able to set the teaching of the faith in a proper light before the well-educated classes as well as before those of less intellectual attainments. Theology must continually be absorbing into itself all the new acquisitions which God continually gives in the growth of human knowledge; so that all the treasures revealed as knowledge increases, may be utilized in expounding more perfectly the 'faith once delivered to the saints'.[31]

This is a plea for the integration of faith and life on an intellectual level so that it may be placed at the service of the whole of society, not just a part. Again, it is expressive of Frere's visionary capacity: he wrote this as the fabric of society and its seemingly unchanging unchangeable strata were about to be uprooted irreversibly by a war the nature and social consequences of which no one in 1914 could have predicted. This was to be as true for his Russian audience as it was for the England (and its Church) of which he spoke. Yet here too is an enduring and valuable principle for all involved in theological education: that ordinands must be aware of the world's turning and the currents of knowledge and experience that shape society past, present and future, in order that as priests they may confidently interpret these for others as well as themselves. The task was and is a challenge, as Frere recognized: the

---

31 *English Church Ways*, pp. 55–6.

teachers of the faith 'must also be prepared to meet the objections, scruples and difficulties of the day. Such things are always presenting themselves as hindrances to the believer, but in varying forms in each succeeding generation'.[32] In the early twenty-first century, here is a particularly vivid example of 'he, being dead, yet speaketh'. Indeed, remarkably contemporary seem Frere's reflections on the importance of science in relation to faith alongside the traditional emphasis on the humanities as the basis for theological method, partly in necessary response to attack:

> Now, our traditions of general education are still very much bound up with mediaeval precedents. Philosophy, mathematics and rhetoric (or arts), with a sound knowledge of the classical languages of Latin and Greek – these still form the traditional studies preparatory to theology. But in these days, historical science and natural science are to a considerable extent taking their places in the scheme of university studies: and this change is having an effect upon the training preparatory to theology. It is from these sides that a special, and somewhat novel, form of attack upon the faith is being made. It is important therefore that there should be among the clergy men trained in the science of historical criticism and in the various branches of physical science, as well as those trained upon the old lines in philosophy and letters.[33]

There is thinly veiled criticism of the bishops of the Church of England in this respect:

> far too few of our candidates are educated in the physical sciences. It is difficult to combine such studies with the philosophy that is needed for theological competence and the knowledge of Greek and Latin, which our bishops still regard as a *sine qua non* in theological candidates.[34]

Unusually for him, Frere does not attempt to suggest how this difficulty

---

32 *English Church Ways*, p. 56.
33 *English Church Ways*, p. 56.
34 *English Church Ways*, pp. 56–7.

might be overcome, and is merely content to note that the universities are producing 'some men' with the appropriate knowledge. But it is nevertheless interesting to compare his ideal in 1914 with the fact that today graduates in all disciplines offer themselves as candidates for ordination, and there is in the contemporary Church a healthy intellectual culture in the field of science and theology which takes its place in the curricula of theological colleges as well as having a prominence in public life; in other words, the ideal has been realized to a considerable degree.

It is in the next section of his lecture that Frere focuses on the principal elements of the curriculum in his own time, and here again we should note that he is talking about his *own* curriculum, largely designed by him, in its context at Mirfield, with an unspoken but implicit desire that it be followed by all institutions; and again, therefore, for his Russian audience the picture is not quite as universal as his confident presentation might make it seem. He identifies 'three principal departments of theological education with a view to ordination: theological, spiritual and technical', all in the context of 'a strong corporate life, which shows itself not only in the common intellectual training, but also in common services and devotions, in social life, and – as you would expect of Englishmen – in athletics as well'.[35] Here is Frere's scheme in a nutshell, an integrated dynamic in which each element has its own vital importance in relation to and interacting with all the others. Those who have been students at Mirfield ever since will, allowing for the passage of time and inevitable adjustments, recognize this immediately as true of their own experience of the College, although for some (many?) with the exception of the alleged automatic disposition to physical exercise attributed to 'Englishmen'. The fact that this is so shows yet more clearly how powerful Frere's influence was in the early direction of the College, and how enduring his legacy in this respect.

The outline curriculum repays study. The theological element comprises five strands: Dogmatic Theology, Bible, Church History, Patristics and Liturgy, or 'Liturgical Science' as Frere calls it. Compared to today there are some notable absences, partly reflecting the subsequent development of theological study and methodology which would later change the emphasis. Frere's particular interests are perhaps reflected in

---

35 *English Church Ways*, p. 59.

the prominence of liturgical studies, another aspect of his influence on the College which remains today. But it is also important to note that he has a view of the whole curriculum, and we know that he was largely responsible for its design at Mirfield and at associated 'feeder' institutions at Knutsford and Tatterford. His social concerns were also vitally in view, another giveaway that we are hearing 'Mirfield' in what is being described. Thus 'some elementary knowledge of economics' is necessary in preparation for priests' encounter with 'the industrial questions, and the social problems of all sorts', in relation to which, he claims, 'a great society of churchmen, many of them clergy' seek 'to claim for the Christian law the ultimate authority to rule social practice'. He mentions by name the Christian Social Union and the particular concern with 'the practical application of Christian ethics to the questions of the day'.[36] Again, here is Frere the Christian Socialist advancing the opinions of his confrères and their application at Mirfield, and not the universally held view of all involved in theological education.

The spiritual dimension of the curriculum (although Frere would never have believed that prayer could be taught intellectually) 'is concerned with the inner life of the priest', and here we see through Frere's eyes the heart of what today is called ministerial, and specifically priestly, formation. Frere is direct and unequivocal in stating of a candidate for ordination that:

> Particularly during his time of close preparation, he must be testing the reality of his own vocation to the priesthood ... looking up to Jesus Christ like the converted St Paul, asking, 'Lord, what wilt thou have me to do?'; and by learning the answer in his own soul, he must be giving the response and making that surrender of his whole self in sacrifice to God, which the priesthood requires.[37]

Later in the lecture he returns to this theme in a moving passage which admits the challenge faced by every ordinand, and again with which ordinands in our own time and experience can identify. It is a passage which stands out in tribute to Frere's wholehearted and unswerving

---

36 *English Church Ways*, p. 60.
37 *English Church Ways*, p. 61.

commitment to the outworking of his own vocation in the hands of God:

> Many a time, it may be, the student will feel overwhelmed by the greatness of the task which lies before him, and by his own unworthiness. But if the call of God is real, and his own response is honest, he will learn more and more to offer up his life in sacrifice to God and to the cause of the Church; and already the reassurance of the Holy Spirit will begin to steady his purpose, to clear his outlook, and to deepen his surrender.[38]

It is in pursuit of this that the corporate life of a theological college ought in Frere's vision to be ordered. The passion with which this is written – and we may imagine the passion with which the spoken version was delivered – is typical of Frere the priest, who has known this in himself and who generously gave of himself that it might be realized in others, especially those for whose training the Community had responsibility. In an early College magazine at Mirfield, there was a regular column entitled 'Heard in the Clough', the latter being an unmade road, still in existence and still partially unmade, which descends steeply from beside the College gates to the main Huddersfield road in the valley below, and often used by students on walks. In one such column, we read that a student was heard saying to another: 'Walter just about saved my soul last night.' In that casually overheard remark is a great deal of what Walter Frere's own sacrificial priesthood meant to him and to those among whom he exercised it. What was heard in the unmade road pointed to the unmaking and remaking which is the work of God in calling and forming, with which work of grace Walter Frere freely and selflessly cooperated; or, as he put it in a dramatic phrase, by God's grace 'the rough metal is being tested and forged into a weapon apt for the Master's use'.[39] This is not mere hagiography: every account of his personality and most of his writings to some degree, however unconsciously, communicate that Frere was a willing bellows-boy to the blacksmith of souls.

Alongside this vision of spiritual purpose it would have been understandable if Frere had placed relatively little emphasis on what he

---

38 *English Church Ways*, p. 63.
39 *English Church Ways*, p. 62.

terms the 'technical' aspect of theological education, but his integrated conception of that task meant that this was far from the case, if only in that Frere was anxious to emphasize what was not capable of total assimilation by 'instruction' alone. He notes – and here again is the hint of disapproval – that 'There is much variation in the amount of technical training given at different colleges', although all teach a minimum of basic matters such as preaching, 'the technical details of the administration of the sacraments' (what we would now call liturgical presidency), pastoral competence and spiritual guidance. The real point, however, is that these can only be 'taught' to a degree, since 'there are many things in which instruction given to a student is too empirical to be of much value. Each man must learn by experience.'[40] Then comes the first and indeed only direct reference to Mirfield, although he has effectively been describing it all along: finally he gives in when he says in connection with the ongoing task of practical experience that:

> In our college at Mirfield it is the custom for our old students to reassemble, a year after they left college, and others with them, for a week of pastoral and practical instruction. It is much easier then, than earlier, to give detailed instruction as to the special duties of the priesthood that are soon to come upon them, especially the hearing of confessions and the celebrating of the Holy Mysteries.[41]

Deacons' Week, as it is known, continues today, although in addition to the content to which Frere refers, contemporary methods of theological reflection are also offered, but with the same purpose of helping those about to be ordained to the priesthood to prepare for what is 'soon to come upon them'. It is another living legacy.

It is extraordinary that the most direct and concise statement of Frere's views on the nature and content of theological education with a view to ordination should be in the form of a lecture to Russian church people, yet it is of an importance that places it alongside the 1910 *Church Quarterly Review* article as a refined and still more convinced exposition of his position, and of remarkable prescience.

---

40 *English Church Ways*, p. 62.
41 *English Church Ways*, p. 62.

Frere at Mirfield: the College, war and peace

At Mirfield, the Great War undoubtedly had as significant an effect on the College and Hostel as on any institution. Many students enlisted, although the national emergency did not prevent another expulsion for the typically Frereian reason, in the 1914–15 annual report, of 'intellectual insufficiency'.[42] It soon became clear to Frere and the rest of the Council that the College could not continue as normal:

> In the present state of National anxiety the Council is convinced that all must be free to put themselves at the service of their Country. They do not therefore propose to admit to the College in September any new men who might *reasonably* be serving the Country in the active prosecution of the War. This decision, coupled with the fact that some 32 of the resident students have enlisted, has compelled the Council to shut the College and transfer the Mirfield students to Leeds *with the newcomers for* next term.

> The Council has decided to offer the College Buildings to the War Office on the understanding that the War Office must be responsible for the management and finance of the Buildings so long as they occupy them.[43]

The final part of this indicates that Frere had not lost his sense of care and prudence even in such a calamitous time. There is also no suggestion of any principled opposition to the War.

The record after 1915 is understandably sparse, with no full annual report until 1917–18, although there does survive a half-yearly report dated January 1916 and handwritten by Frere on four pages torn from an exercise book. There was, after all, not much to say: 'The College buildings are closed.' There is, however, considerable comment on the matter of enlistment by students, and the conclusion: 'The Council is purposed to support an application of theologians for exemption from Military Service, but not Arts Students. W.H. Frere, Chairman.'[44] The

---

42 MS CollRpt 1914–15, p. 3.
43 MS CollRpt 1914–15, p.11, Frere MS additions in italics.
44 MS CollRpt Jan 1916, pp. 1, 4.

annual typewritten format is restored for 1917–18, and normal service is resumed. Nevertheless, Frere's last major documented occasion of involvement in the governance of the College before his elevation to Truro does concern the effects of the wartime closure on returning students:

> The difficulties inevitably connected with the reopening of the College have been less than might have been expected. There was some unrest during the Michaelmas Term, which was probably accentuated by the dirtiness of the kitchen staff and the unsatisfactoriness [a very Frere word] alround [sic] of the food. The Warden [Horner] had several interviews with the Theologians [final year students] at which care was taken that he should hear everything that had been considered ground for complaint. After the grievances and wishes of the students had been classified, the Warden dealt with those that were temporary or fell within his regulation: the Chairman of the Council [Frere] had further interviews to discuss the more permanent and fundamental.[45]

We do not know what the grievances were, aside from the catering issues, but it is clear that they were serious enough for the Superior to be personally involved. We may be seeing here an uncomfortable echo of the early years under Ritson where food was concerned, and Frere's consequent resolve to be sure to avoid a repeat of that crisis.

Thereafter, Frere's influence diminished, in fact seems to have been wholly absent once he was in Truro, but he had done more than enough in the first 20 years to stabilize the College and Hostel, indeed the whole Mirfield scheme, for many years to come. He was to return in 1935, retired, once again to be revered by the students and, as will be seen below, for one final fling in the classroom before his death in April 1938.

Frere at Mirfield: curriculum and classroom

Frere's scholarly interests ranged beyond liturgy, so it is not surprising that he taught not only that but also at various times Theology and Church History at the College of the Resurrection, and had concern for the whole curriculum at Mirfield and institutions directly associated with

---

45 MS CollRpt 1919–20.

its main purpose of formation for the priesthood. Frere's profound and leading influence over the curriculum in the early years and beyond is exemplified and unequivocally stated by a booklet produced several years before the Great War entitled *More Men: The Crying Need of the Church. Some Account of the Attempt at Mirfield to Supply Them.*[46] Its author is anonymous but may well have been Frere, although he is referred to in the third person: 'The Theological Course [at the College] is directed by the Superior of the Community, the Rev. W.H. FRERE, D.D. and other brethren of the Community are also upon the theological staff.'[47]

It is likely that Frere taught much more than Liturgy and History at the College before the Great War. In 1909 it was reported that 'the Superior [Frere] and Keble [Talbot] have been engaged in Theological instruction, and Paul [Bull] has given a course in Preaching.'[48] In 1914, while Frere was giving the lectures in St Petersburg that formed the basis of *English Church Ways*, it is stated that 'Chad [Wager] lectured on Liturgics during Walter's absence in Russia';[49] this confirms that Frere normally taught it. After the War, during which the College was closed, he almost certainly resumed the teaching of Liturgy before his appointment to the See of Truro.

Frere's absence from Mirfield while Bishop of Truro in 1922–35 appears at first to have had a negative effect on the place in the College curriculum of 'Liturgics' (as the annual reports often call Liturgical Studies, suggesting that the term is not after all exclusively North American, as is usually thought). In 1934–35 it is revealed that Fr Lawrence Wrathall CR had recovered the situation somewhat, although he was then about to relinquish the Liturgy teaching:

We are losing Lawrence who has done excellent work in Liturgics, and has made the students really interested in a subject which had come to be regarded as somewhat of a parergon [*sic*: a by-work]. The proof of this is to be seen in the number of 'benes' gained in the Liturgics paper

---

46 *More Men*.
47 *More Men*, p. 17.
48 MS CollRpt 1909, p. 3.
49 MS CollRpt 1913–4, p. 8.

last year and this. Victor [Shearburn CR, later Bishop of Rangoon] is taking over his work.[50]

This suggests that the academic life of the College without Frere was significantly different, and not for the better. Back at Mirfield in retirement, it was Frere's return to teaching as a stop gap just prior to his death in early 1938 that gives the present chapter its title. As the annual reports show, there was something of a crisis also in the provision of teaching in Church History in 1936–37 which continued into 1937–38:

> Our weak point again has been History, which has been subjected to make-shift arrangements unworthy of the dignity and importance of the subject ... Mr John Dickenson of Leeds University lectured through the Michaelmas Term, and was most welcome as a lecturer and a guest. Walter [Frere] then carried on until a few days before he died with all his old brilliance and suggestiveness, but he left a good deal untouched. Hugh Bishop is to begin lecturing this next year, and I hope he will prove capable of taking even more of it.[51]

Thus Frere came to the rescue at the end of his days, and thus are neatly linked the swansong of Frere and the beginning of Hugh Bishop's involvement in the College which would see him appointed Principal in 1956 before his election as Superior in 1966.

The teacher of 'Liturgics' and Church History

The areas in which Frere made particular mark as an educator were Liturgy (including music) and Church History. His scholarly work on the liturgy is itself deserving of a much more detailed study than can be attempted in the present collection, although key aspects of it are studied in the essays by John Livesley and Philip Corbett. It was, indeed, the crucial underpinning of his communication of the history and nature of the Church's liturgy to a variety of audiences. Four main aspects can be discerned: the production of accurate, scholarly editions and monographs

---

50 MS CollRpt 1934–35, pp. 7–8.
51 MS CollRpt 1937–38, p. 5.

to place at the disposal of students and fellow scholars; the specific revision and rewriting of Francis Procter's *History of the Book of Common Prayer*, thus supplying a standard text on the Prayer Book from the beginning of the twentieth century down to at least the 1960s, and still very valuable today; the education of the Diocese of Truro, its clergy and its cathedral church in aspects of liturgical history and practice; the responses to requests for advice and help from fellow bishops and others; and the teaching of students at the College of the Resurrection and other groups, with the aid of lantern slides, some of which survive and give some idea of his teaching methods.

Frere is perhaps best known for his contribution to liturgical research and teaching, but his expertise was much wider. Elsewhere in this collection Alexander Faludy comments in detail on Frere's contribution to the study of the Reformation, and Peter Allan on his musical scholarship, but alongside these not inconsiderable achievements it was his admittedly often overlapping liturgical concerns that occupied the majority of his time. Frere's contributions to the published series of the Alcuin Club and the Henry Bradshaw Society represent painstaking, meticulous research which took him to libraries across Britain and Europe. Many of his manuscript notes survive, most of them in the care of the Borthwick Institute at the University of York but some still to be found today tucked inside the back cover of books in the Community's library at Mirfield, where in the margins of many mainly liturgical volumes are annotations often of significant interest and assistance to the present-day reader. To discover these and to learn from them is to see evidence of a consummate scholar's dedication and attention to detail, on further aspects of which John Livesley comments in his essay in this collection, 'A scholar's scholar'. It is also to realize that Frere the teacher is teaching still, but nevertheless inviting us to pick up the baton, to follow the 'suggestiveness' and see where it leads.

Frere the lecturer: the lantern slides

What were Frere's lectures like? There exist some tantalizing references by students to his voice and vocal mannerisms as well as allusions by brethren to the excellence of the product. There are no extant lecture notes, which could simply indicate the very real possibility that he needed none, but there survive at Mirfield at least some of the glass lantern slides he must have used in the teaching of Church History and Liturgy, and thus it seems likely that he often spoke to accompany the slides. It is clear that the collection is incomplete, but what remains is highly instructive and gives a real flavour of his scholarly interests and his translation of these into effective pedagogical method for students of Liturgy at Mirfield and conceivably elsewhere. By digitizing the slides it has become possible to use some via modern means of digital slide projection to bring his work to the attention of current students. Many are pictorial or photographs of pages in books, but the most interesting are those written (on the glass slides) in Frere's instantly recognizable (and often multi-coloured) hand, for this purpose a little larger than the minuscule version typical of his annotations and private papers. The scope of the slides is classic Frere: the Book of Common Prayer and the development of the Eucharist feature prominently.

The textbook: Procter and Frere

In 1855 the first edition of Francis Procter's *History of the Book of Common Prayer* was published. In 1901, Frere's revised and enlarged version appeared, and became known to generations of theological students of all theological traditions in the Church of England and in the

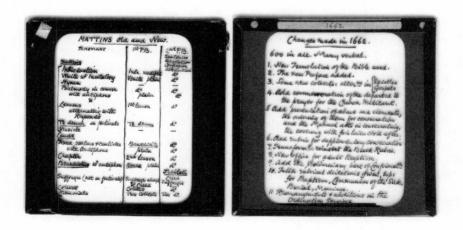

Two typical lantern slides made and used by Frere in his teaching of liturgy (see above).

Anglican Communion as 'Procter and Frere', still in print in at least 1961, an extraordinary record even for what was by many used essentially as a textbook, but which bears all the marks of Frere's scholarly thoroughness and the value of his detailed research, and which made his teaching more widely accessible beyond the gates of Mirfield.

It is an instructive though complex exercise to compare Procter's original with Frere's revision. In the preface to 'Procter and Frere', dated December 1900, Frere looks back over the half century since the first edition of Procter's book, published in 1855:

> Nearly half a century has passed since the first edition ... a period full of enthusiasm for liturgical studies which is almost, if not quite, without parallel. While these facts speak eloquently of the solidity and value of Mr Procter's work, they also explain amply the reasons why it was necessary that it should undergo considerable change. In fact, while the general outline and plan has been retained, the greater part has been rewritten.[52]

Everywhere there is evidence of Frere's correction and addition. It was hoped to give here an example in parallel text of changes he made, but it cannot be done in any meaningful way, such is the skilled integration of original and revision. There is indeed a case to be made for questioning the continuing attribution to Procter aside from the outline structure, but to have eliminated him would have been at odds with Frere's keen sense of scholarly integrity and tradition in the sense of continuity – rather like, it might be argued, his own view of the Book of Common Prayer itself. The work of scholarship was a shared endeavour, as his gracious acknowledgement of assistance in the Prefaces to the first, second (1902) and third (1905) impressions show: 'Many thanks are due to kind friends and strangers who have pointed out mistakes both great and small.'[53] These thanks did not mean he was in agreement with everything suggested to him, and he was certainly prepared to test alternative theories in order politely to dispatch them. In the 1902 Preface he alerts the reader to the fact that, in that edition,

---

52 F. Procter and W.H. Frere, *A New History of the Book of Common Prayer* (3rd impr., London: Macmillan, 1961), p. v.

53 Procter and Frere, *A New History*, [1905] p. xi.

a far clearer statement of the genesis of the Elizabethan Book is given. Dr Gee [in his *The Elizabethan Prayer Book*] has lately put forth a new theory on this point, but acknowledging how much he has done to clear up the subject, I cannot but feel that a searching scrutiny of the records leads to a different conclusion, which when stated, moreover, carries more conviction with it.[54]

Thus the opening remarks in the first Preface of 1900 give credit where it is due to his principal forerunner while gently alerting the reader to the existence of more recent evidence that must supplement and sometimes supplant the conclusions of 50 years before. It is testament to Frere's work that his own version remained in print for well over half a century more, and is still of value today, even though, as in the century and more since the first edition of Procter and Frere, study of the Prayer Book has moved on still further, as Frere would himself have assumed that it would. Indeed in his contribution to the Prayer Book revision debate he became an important part of that which would be studied by others: the student has become the studied.

Walter Frere's commitment to the accurate provision of information to the student was total, and his approach was a version in his time of what the higher education of the present day knows as research-led teaching. Without the hours spent in libraries, the meticulous tabling and annotating, not to say what must have been a prodigious memory, Frere would not have been the excellent teacher he clearly was. 'Procter and Frere' is a monument to this in that it brings the solitary endeavour into the public square to a degree other published scholarly works of Frere do not, at least not with the same immediacy. This is perhaps borne out by the ease with which, even now, his surviving lantern slides on the Book of Common Prayer can be matched up with the corresponding sections in the book. Here, indeed, we may come as close as we may to the spirit of Frere's lectures.

The liturgical educator of the Church of England

Frere was brought in at the suggestion of Gore to the heart of the fraught

---

54 Procter and Frere, *A New History*, pp. ix–x.

debate about the revision of the Book of Common Prayer precisely because of his proven expertise. Effectively he became, along with other contemporary liturgical scholars like his friends Brightman and Dearmer, the liturgical educator of the Church of England, a position consolidated by his elevation to the See of Truro. While much of this work became political, and unavoidably so given the tendency of liturgy to focus theological dissonance, at its heart there remained the concerns of the scholar to advise and teach on a well-informed basis with a view to improvement and good practice. Again, today it would be said that Frere had a commitment to liturgical formation. Pieces he wrote for the general reader in the *Truro Diocesan Gazette* suggest how aware he was of the possibilities of his wider authority as a bishop in diocesan terms and nationally.

Frere even taught practical liturgy to Charles Gore when the latter became Bishop of Worcester in 1902, supplying him with handwritten instructions as to episcopal ceremonial on various occasions.[55] Much later, in 1930, having been a bishop himself for eight years, he did the same for J.A. Hollis, the Bishop-designate of Taunton, in which correspondence Frere clearly sees himself as the authority on the matter, and with an intention to publish:

> I know no decent book on the subject; I tried to stop the publication of a very bad one on the subject the other day but didn't succeed. Bit by bit I have been trying to build up a scheme, but very little of it has got onto paper yet; but Bishop [James] Nash [CR] and I are hoping to work something together now he has come home and has leisure at Mirfield.[56]

It was not to be (and any written material has not come to light), but Frere's reply to Hollis survives as a mature and quite detailed view, although in its author's modest opinion simply 'one or two obvious things that probably you will recognize at once'.[57] As an example of Frere's modesty this is very representative, yet the letter also shows that he could

---

55 G.L. Prestige, *The Life of Charles Gore* (London: Heinemann, 1935), p. 239.

56 R.C.D. Jasper (ed.), *Walter Howard Frere: His Correspondence on Liturgical Revision and Construction* (Alcuin Club. London: SPCK, 1954), pp. 277–8.

57 Jasper, *Correspondence*, p. 278.

be very forthright in his opinions and aware of his own fund of knowledge, which he undoubtedly possessed.

Frere the Educator: 'Brilliance and suggestiveness'

The aim of this chapter has been to give an impression of Frere the educator, not a detailed analysis of the several fields in which his talents in this respect were employed, nor an assessment of his academic research. What we hope to have suggested is that Frere is the single most important figure in the founding and shaping of the College of the Resurrection, a significant thinker on the nature of theological education in relation to the needs of his time, a masterly designer of suitable curricula for different categories of student, and a skilled teacher especially of Liturgy and Church History in the classroom itself and in more personal and diffuse ways as priest and bishop.

4

Bishop of Truro 1923–1935

JOHN LIVESLEY

The task set before me ever since I was up at Cambridge has been to take a hand in recovering Community life for our Church. It was set before me there graphically – I have never forgotten the road, the gate, the beyond which framed the task.[1]

A new model of episcopate: by design or default?

The one previous published assessment of Walter Frere's time as Bishop of Truro has characterized his episcopate as 'the unfolding of an idea and the realization of an ideal of a chief pastor's office in the Church'.[2] Frere apparently set 'a type and standard of episcopacy' (perhaps, it is implied, a superior type or standard) 'which had disappeared from the English Church, though known in the Anglican Communion elsewhere.'[3] Whilst, as this chapter will seek to demonstrate, this argument is a forceful one, and Frere's episcopate certainly displayed a remarkably different ethos and style from that of his Anglican predecessors, it is also important to remember that both Frere himself and his Community as a whole had

---

1 W.H. Frere, letter to Randall Davidson, Archbishop of Canterbury, 27.8.1923 Davidson Papers, vol. 11, folio 67, Lambeth Palace Library.

2 G.W. Hockley and W.R. Johnson, 'Truro' (ch. 5), in C.S. Phillips (ed.), *Walter Howard Frere* (London: Faber & Faber, 1947), p. 76. This essay was produced by two figures who, as Archdeacon of Cornwall and Prebendary and Rector of St Ervan respectively, were intimately associated with Frere's administration of the Diocese as Bishop (see further note below). Their portrait of Bishop Frere, therefore, is attractive as affectionate and admiring, but verges on the hagiographical and refuses to engage with the more controversial aspects.

3 Hockley and Johnson, 'Truro', p. 80.

previously considered their own vocation to be basically incompatible with that of a bishop in the Church of England. As yet, no member of the Community of the Resurrection who had been made a bishop had continued as a full member: Charles Gore had essentially left the Community on being made Bishop of Worcester in 1902, and when James Nash was made Bishop of Cape Town (1917) the semi-detached status within the Rule of Prelate Brother had been invented to accommodate his new role. For Frere, the primary architect of the Community's Rule,[4] the call of the Community life must always take priority over any potential preferment, as his letter to Archbishop Davidson, quoted above, demonstrates. As Alan Wilkinson points out, Frere had opposed both Charles Gore's Westminster canonry in 1894 and his acceptance of a bishopric in 1901. He had recently led the opposition to Keble Talbot's desire for detached service.[5] He had also refused for himself the King's offer of a canonry at St George's Chapel, Windsor, as recently as 1921.[6] Whereas, with hindsight in 1941, Frere's episcopate may well have appeared to his many admirers as the 'realization of an ideal', in 1923 Frere himself seemed to be aware of no such vocation, either for himself or for any other member of his Community.

Frere first learned of his nomination to the See of Truro by letter from Stanley Baldwin, the Prime Minister, in late August 1923. True to his principles, Frere immediately refused the offer without consulting anyone else, 'begging' Baldwin, as he put it to Davidson, not to submit his name to the King.[7] C.S. Phillips's account of the negotiations that preceded Frere's acceptance gives the impression that, whilst his refusal was completely genuine, Davidson's persistence and 'further correspondence' opened a relatively easy way to his acceptance, once it became clear that he could remain a full member of the Community.[8] The reality was much more complex. As Frere wrote apologetically to Davidson, when he finally

---

4 See Alan Wilkinson, *The Community of the Resurrection: A Centenary History* (London: SCM Press, 1992). Frere's own handwritten copies of the Rule are still held in the Community's archive at Mirfield.

5 Wilkinson, *Community*, pp. 161–3.

6 C.S. Phillips, 'Elevation to the Episcopate' (ch. 4), in Phillips, *Frere*, p. 62.

7 Frere to Davidson, 27–23; Frere's correspondence with Baldwin is not with the Davidson Papers at Lambeth, but the order of events is clear from the Frere-Davidson correspondence.

8 See Phillips, 'Elevation', p. 67.

accepted the nomination a month after Davidson's first letter: 'it must have seemed to you a slow and even perverse way that I have gone. But it has been, both for me and the Community, a complete reversal of plans and hopes.'[9] It is worth considering the process in detail because many of the key issues which were faced along this 'slow and ... perverse way' were to remain key issues throughout Frere's episcopate.

Presumably because of his attitude to the Windsor canonry in 1921, Davidson had expected that Frere might well refuse the formal offer from the Prime Minister, and so wrote to Frere on 13 August to try to pre-empt Baldwin by explaining his reasons, although in the event Baldwin's letter arrived first and Davidson's plan was spoiled: 'It has long been my wish to have you with us in the Episcopal College, and Truro seems to afford the very opportunity.'[10] It is important to notice, as Wilkinson does,[11] that, to Davidson at least, Truro's needs were secondary to the perceived needs of the national Church, although, as his letter states, Davidson had consulted the departing Bishop, Guy Warman, as to the appointment. With this apparently urgent priority before him, and perhaps irritated by the disturbance to his Scottish holiday caused by what he later described to Baldwin as Frere's 'somewhat impetuous refusal',[12] Davidson went on to exert considerable pressure on Frere to accept, persuading the Prime Minister to ignore Frere's refusal until Davidson had had sufficient time to work on him further.[13] In the ensuing correspondence between them, Davidson always writes with sympathy and encouragement and sometimes with affection, but he makes it quite clear that 'the highest public considerations' and the opinions of 'those whose judgement ought to weigh with you'[14] must outweigh Frere's 'inward' refusal and his 'so dominant a sense of divine purpose' towards his life in the Community, a sense which Davidson could surely never fully understand.[15]

---

9 Frere to Davidson, 13.9.23, Davidson Papers, vol. 11, f. 78.

10 Davidson to Frere, 13.8.23, Davidson Papers, vol. 11, f. 68.

11 Wilkinson, *Centenary History*, p. 163.

12 Davidson to Baldwin, 18.9.23, Davidson Papers, vol. 11, f. 79; Davidson also complained to his journal some weeks afterwards that Frere's nomination had given him 'abundant toil, telegraphically and epistolary during these weeks' (Archbishop Davidson's Journal, dictated 28.10.23, Davidson Papers, vol. 14, ff. 228–230).

13 See Davidson to Frere, 28.8.23 (1st letter), Davidson Papers, vol. 11, f. 70.

14 Davidson to Frere, 28.8.23 (1st letter).

15 Frere to Davidson, 27.8.23.

So what were these 'highest public considerations' urging Davidson to nominate Frere? As he wrote to Frere himself on 28 August, in a letter often quoted elsewhere, he felt the bishops must have among their number a representative 'of what is called, however inadequately, Anglo-Catholicism', but one who would 'yet be able to regard these questions largely, sanely, and with the equipment of scholarly knowledge'.[16] Perhaps also because of his age, Frere was to Davidson the ideal, responsible representative of Anglo-Catholicism, a movement that he recognized must be regarded seriously though not uncritically. Writing about Frere's nomination in his journal in October 1923, and shortly before his consecration on 1 November, Davidson acknowledged that 'his advent to our body portends, I think, a good deal more discussion of controversial matters than has hitherto been our wont', but he nevertheless insisted that 'the younger spirit ... must have its full say in the coming years and ought not to be snubbed though it may have to be resisted.'[17] Many Anglo-Catholics, however, questioned Davidson's motives, and how truly representative Frere was of Anglo-Catholicism as a whole, given his scrupulous opposition to the famous telegram of greeting to the Pope from the first Anglo-Catholic Congress of July 1923.[18] But the latter, much less quoted, part of Davidson's letter of 28 August makes it clear that such

---

16 Davidson to Frere, 28.8.23 (2nd letter), Davidson Papers, vol. 11, f. 71; this paragraph is also cited in G.K.A. Bell, *Randall Davidson, Archbishop of Canterbury*, vol. 2 (London: Oxford University Press, 1935), p. 1251; Anselm Hughes, *The Rivers of the Flood* (London: Faith Press, 1961), p. 70; and Phillips, 'Elevation', p. 66.

17 Davidson's Journal, dictated 28.10.23.

18 Frere's objection, on the grounds that the telegram would be 'misunderstood' in Rome, earned him the undeserved mistrust of many fellow Anglo-Catholics. Hughes (*Rivers of the Flood*, p. 70) acknowledges that Frere's speech was 'courageous', but he implies that his protest earned Frere the offer of Truro, and he even alleges that Frere readily accepted: 'Too guileless in himself to suspect that this could possibly be a deliberate "move" on the part of the Archbishop, he accepted — it is said, perhaps untruly, on a post card.' Hughes sees this as the beginning of a deliberate policy to admit one, moderate, presumably pliable Anglo-Catholic to the Bench of Bishops. He quotes W.K. Lowther Clarke, that Frere, especially owing to his lack of sympathy for 'modern embellishments' in the liturgy, was 'not fitted to "represent" the rank and file of Anglo-Catholic parishes' (*Rivers*, p. 71). At the other extreme the Evangelical Bishop of Durham, Henley Henson, who regarded Frere's elevation to the episcopate as 'nothing less than the total collapse of Anglican discipline', considered that Frere's objection to the telegram 'can hardly outweigh the fact that he was there at all, still less that he was as fully committed as a man can be to the official programme'. See H.H. Henson, *Retrospect of an Unimportant Life*, vol. 2 (London: Oxford University Press, 1943), p. 139.

a representative was most particularly needed in the context of the ongoing progress towards Prayer Book revision, 'a juncture more critical in some respects than any which can be found in the last two centuries', where Frere's particular expertise as a liturgical scholar was felt to be needed 'in episcopal counsels and councils'.[19] Here again we note that it was as a bishop on the Bench and specifically as a member of the Upper House of Convocation, more than to undertake diocesan responsibilities, that Davidson sought to appoint Frere a diocesan bishop, and Frere partly objected on this basis. Within the rapidly developing central life of the Church of England, Frere argued, a body must be developed similar to the Roman Curia (a comparison to which Davidson objected, although he took the point) so that bishops could be relieved of provincial and national matters and concentrate on their dioceses. It was as such a 'curial' figure, and not as a diocesan bishop that Frere, at this stage, felt best able to use his gifts in the Church. His involvement in the nascent, as yet unofficial Malines Conversations was one particular area in which he felt it would be easier not to be involved as a bishop.[20]

It was the possibility of combining his episcopate with a continuing life in the Community, and even perhaps of using his episcopate to promote both the religious life and its values in the wider Church, as Davidson suggested,[21] that began to change Frere's mind, although he was always absolutely clear that for him this could not be on the basis of the Prelate Brother arrangement: 'I am incurably a community man ... for me it isn't links but life that are wanted.'[22] Here again, perhaps aware of the Community's early experience in the Wakefield Diocese,[23] he took a more cautious attitude than Davidson to the probable situation within the diocese, being especially aware of the way that the appointments system did not allow the diocese to express its mind. Would 'an English diocese [be] prepared to have a bishop break with 4 [sic] centuries of tradition to attempt the task' of living the religious life, and of modelling

---

19 Davidson to Frere, 28.8.23 (2nd).

20 Frere to Davidson, 1.9.23, Davidson Papers, vol. 11, f. 73; and Davidson's response of 4.9.23, Davidson Papers vol. 11, f. 74, where he argued, reasonably enough, that, since such a system would take time to develop, Frere should be made a diocesan bishop anyway to carry out this role.

21 Davidson to Frere, 28.8.23 (2nd).

22 Frere to Davidson, 1.9.23.

23 See Wilkinson, *Centenary History*.

his episcopate on this foundation? Another underlying concern was whether, given the 'prohibitive' distances involved and his advancing years, Frere would be able to balance diocesan duties with commitments not only in London but in Mirfield.[24] As we shall see, these were to become some of the defining questions of his time in Truro. Yet, once again, Davidson could not foresee any problem, and arguing that such an experiment only needed the right diocese in which to develop, Truro, because of its 'characteristic churchmanship', an ill-defined term, would certainly be appropriate, and the distance was immaterial.[25]

In the end, Frere's acceptance depended upon the approval of the Community Chapter. Given that brethren were scattered for the summer, this was relatively slow in coming and, although Frere wrote to Davidson that 'we have now I think all come round to it',[26] the Community's approval was not universal: Paul Bull appealed unsuccessfully to the Visitor that Frere's plan to remain a full member was unconstitutional and that being a bishop was not a Community work; and when the January 1924 General Chapter formally agreed that Frere should retain his vote and Truro should become a Community House for the duration of his episcopate, Bull registered his protest.[27] Nevertheless, Frere had his way, and however shakily, the foundations for a new model of episcopate in the Church of England had been laid.

The Monk Bishop: image and reality

The ordering of Frere's household at Lis Escop, the Bishop of Truro's official residence, has been regarded as 'the outward sign of the spirit of the episcopate'[28] by Hockley and others. It was only an outward sign, but

---

24 Frere to Davidson 1.9.23; see below for the toll that this balancing act eventually took on his health. Interestingly, a suffragan Bishop of St Germans in the 1980s, Michael Fisher SSF, who also took two of his community to live with him, notes in his memoirs the difficulties and strains of balancing commitments in London and Cornwall, even with the improved communications since Frere's day. See M. Fisher, *For the Time Being* (Leominster: Gracewing, 1993), pp. 185–95.

25 Davidson to Frere, 4.9.23.

26 Frere to Davidson, 13.9.23.

27 See Wilkinson, *Centenary History*, pp. 163–4, who also records the protests of some in the South African Chapter against sending Frere a gift and affectionate greetings.

28 Hockley and Johnson, 'Truro', p. 82.

certainly Frere's personal style as a bishop was radically different from that of most of his predecessors. Whereas the 'domestic background' of bishops of the Church of England since the Reformation, 'whether or not they were married men, [had] been that of the household of the upper class',[29] Frere, by contrast, 'carried his monastery with him wherever he went'. This meant in practice that at least two members of the Community lived with him, under the Rule,[30] and especially because of their pastoral and mission work in the Diocese (see below) they contributed many of the distinctive features of his time in office. Much has been made of the day-to-day routine of the Community house at Lis Escop: the small domestic staff and simple furnishings; the rumours around the diocese that the bishop cleaned his own boots, carried guests' bags and served at meals;[31] and the bishop's habitually shabby mode of dress. Even *Time* magazine particularly noted the latter when reporting to an American audience the novelty of a monk's admission to that curious British institution, the House of Lords, in September 1930.[32] Whilst to us these may seem to be minor domestic and personal details, they were clearly accorded more significance in a society and church where convention was more highly prized than in our own day.

Frere's personal style certainly attracted many, but baffled or irritated others. Dominic Whitnall CR, now in his nineties, has vivid memories of being confirmed by Bishop Frere in Truro Cathedral in 1927, after which the group were invited back to Lis Escop for tea. Having abandoned the drawing room, they sat round a large table in the hall and were deeply impressed that the Bishop himself brought in the food and waited on them. Perhaps the young, with a less ingrained sense of what was fitting for a bishop to do, responded more easily to the simple example of

---

29 Hockley and Johnson, 'Truro', p. 80.

30 William King, who acted as Frere's chaplain, and George Longridge both remained with him throughout his time in Truro. From 1925 they were joined by Bishop Rupert Mounsey CR, formerly a bishop in Borneo, who was officially appointed an Assistant Bishop in the Diocese in 1930, and greatly assisted Frere in his later years in office, when his health was declining.

31 See Wilkinson, *Centenary History*, p. 165, and also C.S. Phillips, 'Holiday Intermezzo: August at Lis Escop' (ch. 6), in Phillips, *Frere*, pp. 104 ff.

32 'Monk among Lords', article in *Time*, 15.9.1930: 'Habitually, this Lord Bishop of Truro dresses shabbily, in an old black cassock, a leathern girdle'; see www.time.com/printout/0,8816,788475,00.html, accessed on 17.2.2007.

Christian hospitality and service offered to them.[33] Frere's official portrait of 1933, commissioned and presented to him by the diocese in celebration of his tenth anniversary as bishop,[34] deliberately shows him not in pontificals but in his simple Mirfield cassock. Yet even C.S. Phillips, in his celebratory memoir, is slightly uncomfortable with this aspect of his episcopate. He prefers to picture Frere in the 'gracious environment' of the Lis Escop dining room, furnished for him as a gift by friends: here one could best understand Frere within the tradition of a Bishop Andrewes or a Dean Church, 'one who so well embodied that combination of learning, culture and a refined, unostentatious spirituality which represents the Anglican ethos at its best'.[35] His 'propensity for shabby clothes and (on occasion) for squalid surroundings',[36] considered by some not entirely fitting in a bishop,[37] could best be put down to an eccentric 'monkish austerity'.[38]

Yet, 'monkish' or not, this austerity, and even asceticism, combined with his celibacy, could make him appear distant, at least in contrast with his predecessor. After his departure, Bishop Guy Warman was praised by letters in the *Truro Diocesan Gazette* particularly for his gifts of 'approachableness' [*sic*] and his ability to make himself 'at home' in any surroundings. On Frere's retirement there were written requests to the Archbishop of Canterbury that the next bishop should be more like Warman.[39] Warman had begun each edition of the monthly *Gazette* with a friendly letter, beginning along the lines of, 'My dear friends' and ending, 'Your affectionate friend and Bishop'. The opening of Frere's first letter in January 1924 must, in contrast, have appeared formal and rather stiff: 'Walter, by divine permission Bishop of Truro, to all the faithful people in

---

33 The author interviewed Dominic Whitnall about his memories of Frere on 10.1.08. See the comment below by A.L. Rowse for another young opinion of Frere.

34 See Hockley and Johnson, 'Truro' p. 101 ff., where, as Archdeacon of Cornwall, Hockley's own speech of thanks and praise to Frere is reprinted at length.

35 Phillips, 'Intermezzo', p. 106.

36 Phillips, 'Intermezzo', p. 106.

37 'Much has been made of an overheard comment by a dignified guest: 'What an extraordinary establishment!' See Phillips, 'Intermezzo', p. 107 and Wilkinson, *Centenary History*, p. 165.

38 Phillips, 'Intermezzo', p. 105.

39 See Lang Papers, vol. 139, ff. 66–7, Lambeth Palace Library.

the diocese, an affectionate greeting in Christ our common Saviour, and good wishes for the coming year.'

He immediately went on to consider the ongoing crisis at home and abroad, and ended with an exhortation to prayer.[40] Thereafter, Frere would write such letters only intermittently, always beginning in the same way, and often his occasional official Pastoral Letter read to Sunday congregations would be published: Pastorals for the beginning of Lent feature prominently, as do those written for major events in the life of the diocese, such as its Jubilee in 1927 (see below). Frere's official tone, especially in printed material, could certainly appear aloof and detached, but this was perhaps because he held a different vision from Warman of what a bishop should be, and how he should relate to his people. Rather than addressing himself as one intimate friend to another, one report of his addresses at his enthronement described them as 'the words of a shepherd to his flock, and a father to his children: simple, straight forward, personal, spiritual'.[41] Moreover, from the start, Frere evidently made a particular effort to be accessible to his diocese in spite of his busy schedule. In his first month, December 1923, it was announced in the *Gazette* that he would be in his vestry in the Cathedral 'for chance interview' for two hours on two dates, including Christmas Eve, and this became a regular pattern over several years.[42] The historian A.L. Rowse's assessment, although clearly written by an Anglo-Catholic admirer, for whom 'Frere ... was my ideal bishop in every way', attempts to sum up the apparent paradox of one who was deeply aware of the gravity and dignity of his office, perhaps more than many Anglican bishops, but who yet wore that dignity lightly and humbly:

a scholar, an artist, a saint, a prince of the Church but very unaffected and easy to talk to; a monk but also a man of the world, who knew Europe from one end to the other, who knew Russian; a musician, an ascetic who appreciated the good things in life; a man who looked even

---

40 *Truro Diocesan Gazette* (*TDG*), January 1924, p. 2.

41 *TDG*, December 1923, p. 3; inclusion in the *Diocesan Gazette* indicates that the opinion has been vetted to some extent. Note how 'austerity' and 'simplicity' may represent differing perceptions of the same quality.

42 *TDG*, December 1923, p. 2.

more the part than Stubbs had done ... Frere was unpopular with the people who didn't know him.[43]

Re-imagining the episcopate: ecumenical and liturgical matters

Whether or not Hockley and Johnson are right to describe Frere's episcopate as the '*realization* of an ideal of a chief pastor's office in the Church',[44] Frere himself certainly had a strong and articulate sense of what the role of a bishop must be, even if he had not previously envisaged this role for himself. As we have seen, this vision found its most obvious expression in his style of living and leadership, but it was much more deeply rooted than all this. It was grounded in years of exhaustive theological and historical study, and was shaped by his own experience of living the religious life. Frere's breadth and depth as a scholar made him confident and versatile enough to adopt and adapt models of episcopacy very different from those normal in the Church of England in the early twentieth century.

As bishop, Frere is not known to have written any reflections on how the patterns of Eastern Orthodoxy, where the norm is for all bishops to be drawn from the religious orders, might influence his own situation as a 'monk bishop' in the Church of England. However, as he was one of Anglicanism's leading experts on the subject, the parallels must have influenced him. Soon after his visit to Russia to lecture in 1914, he had discussed with Archbishop Davidson the possibility of bringing a group of Russian prelates to England, possibly as official guests of some of the bishops.[45] Plans for such a visit had to be postponed because of the Great War and the ensuing crisis of the Russian Revolution, but, in 1925, Frere did succeed in bringing a group of Russian bishops to the Truro Diocese, a 'fresh and further indication of the tide ... flowing towards Christian Reunion',[46] and presumably also a chance for the Diocese to learn

---

43 A.L. Rowse, *A Cornish Childhood* (London: J. Cape, 1942, repr. Truro: Truran, 2003), p. 136; Rowse summed up Warman as 'kind but unimpressive and regrettably Low Church'. See below for an assessment of Frere's handling of controversy.

44 My italics, see above, note 2.

45 See the correspondence between Frere and Davidson, January to April 1914, on Frere's visit to Russia; Davidson Papers vol. 192, ff. 37–45.

46 Frere in *TDG*, August 1925; the July 1926 *TDG* also contains an article drawing attention to a forthcoming appeal to support persecuted Russian Christians.

something of a very different model of episcopacy. Frere's 1918 study, *Some Links in the Chain of Russian Church History*, describes how, from the earliest days of Christianity in Russia, the expectation grew that bishops would be celibate; and how the preference for monastics developed in Russia earlier than in Greece, given the high status of the monasteries as centres of evangelism and education 'as well as through the monastic piety so dear to the Russian soul'.[47] Clearly Frere was impressed by a church where the status and functions of the monasteries were so clearly established, and idea of a monastic bishop was not an embarrassment but a basic expectation. In discussing the contemporary Russian Church, which, as he was writing, was about to be brutally crushed, Frere expressed his admiration for the division of the clergy. On the one hand, the so-called 'white' clergy were, he argued, close to the people, and provided an example of domestic Christian living. They also provided a continuity of clerical life in the parishes, since they were always married and their sons often became priests. On the other hand, the 'black' clergy lived apart in community, with special facilities for learning and upholding an ascetic model, providing a cadre of bishops to govern and lead the church.[48] The parallels between the 'black' clergy and the way his own household would come to be ordered in Truro are obvious.

Frere's wider expertise in church history was also directly relevant to the way he understood and carried out his new role. A common feature of the *Diocesan Gazette* during his time are articles on a range of theological, historical and liturgical subjects, normally by the bishop himself, relevant either to issues in the Diocese or, especially in case of the Prayer Book question, to the wider Church.[49] In 1927, in preparation for a visitation connected to the diocesan Jubilee, a two-part article on the history of visitation appeared.[50] This was a distillation of the lengthy

---

47 W.H. Frere, *Some Links in the Chain of Russian Church History* (London: Faith Press, 1918), p. 18.

48 Frere, *Russian Church History*, p. 134. The preface to this work, expressing the hope that the Revolution might bring a new freedom to the Russian Church, is dated 'Mirfield, October 1917'.

49 A selection of the liturgical papers published in *TDG*, normally pithy and aimed at a general audience, is found in J.H. Arnold and E.G.P. Wyatt (eds), *Walter Howard Frere: A Collection of his Papers on Liturgical and Historical Subjects*, (Alcuin Club. London: Oxford University Press, 1940).

50 *TDG*, April and May 1927.

'Historical Introduction' to Frere's 1910 edition of visitation articles from the Reformation period, one of his major works of Reformation scholarship,[51] which provides an effective and thorough historical summary of the way in which bishops had administered their sees, as well an insight into Frere's own theory of the episcopate. Writing on the role of the bishop in the early patristic period, he commented that 'without him all was incomplete: there was not only no perpetuity, for lack of ordination, but also according to the custom of the earliest ages, no opportunity of celebrating the Eucharist'.[52] Where the bishop was, there the church was gathered around him, and as this church grew so the bishop's first duty, 'the supervision of the flock ... as his very name *episkopos* implies',[53] became more complex. The introduction traces, from the patristic period in Europe to the end of the Middle Ages in England, the developing practice of visitation as the primary expression of this duty; both of the diocese, by its bishop; and of the province by its metropolitan. Frere considers the varying approaches to practical questions, such as the developing roles of archdeacon and, to a lesser extent, suffragan bishop, or the subdivision of dioceses, to aid the bishop in his task: a yearly visitation of the whole diocese being a long established ideal. He considers the types of pastoral, administrative and judicial work done by the bishop at a visitation:[54] the celebration of Confirmation; the supervision of church fabrics, ornaments and liturgical practices; the settlement of disputes, in conjunction with the developing church courts, in his role as judge. He also lays special emphasis on the connection of visitation with the holding of synods, the gathering of clergy around their diocesan bishop for consultation in synod: 'The gathering of the clergy to one centre and the journey of the bishop round the different centres were each the parallel of the other.'[55]

Frere's particular enthusiasm for expressions of synodical government illustrates that he was not merely writing out of scholarly or antiquarian interest. The backdrop to his work both as an Anglo-Catholic scholar and

---

51 W.H. Frere, *Visitation Articles and Injunctions of the Period of the Reformation*, vol. 1 'Historical Introduction and Index' (London: Longmans, 1910); see Chapter 5, below, for an assessment of Frere as a Reformation historian.

52 Frere, *Visitation Articles*, p. 10.

53 Frere, *Visitation Articles*, p. 9.

54 Frere, *Visitation Articles*, e.g. p. 27.

55 Frere, *Visitation Articles*, p. 29.

as a bishop is what Arthur Burns has called the 'Diocesan Revival' in the Church of England.[56] Burns highlights that, from as early as the beginning of the nineteenth century, the bishops took the initiative in removing abuses and reinvigorating diocesan life, principally through more frequent and more thorough visitation by both bishops and archdeacons; the revival of the office of rural dean and the ruridecanal chapter; encouragement of the activities of national societies for overseas mission, education, church building and catechesis; and notably, after 1850, the revival of clergy synods and conferences of clergy and lay people.[57] These local reforms ran prior and parallel to those initiated by the government, particularly of church endowments, under the aegis of the Ecclesiastical Commissioners from the 1830s; the creation of new dioceses; and the revival of Convocation, all of which are better publicized. Burns's study covers the period (1800–1870) before Frere was active either as a scholar or as a bishop, but these ongoing issues of church government were of particular interest to Frere, whose keen understanding of the theological questions and historical precedents involved was sought out by those who addressed the issues, especially after his admission to the Lower House of Convocation representing the Wakefield Diocese in 1914.

His published pamphlets and unpublished memoranda from this period lay out a systematic understanding of how the Church should be governed. At the centre of the system is the bishop within his diocese:

> to him belongs the task of the government of the diocese and he therefore is responsible for the order and well-being of all the different spheres that lie within his area ... but he has no inherent authorization to exercise his episcopal authority elsewhere.[58]

---

56 A. Burns, *The Diocesan Revival in the Church of England, c.1800–1870* (Oxford: Oxford University Press, 1999). See especially the Introduction, pp. 1 ff., and Conclusion, pp. 260 ff.

57 Note that the first such synod, claimed by some to be illegal, was convened in 1851 in the Diocese of Exeter by Bishop Henry Phillpotts in response to and protest against the Gorham Judgement. See Burns, *Diocesan Revival*, pp. 223 ff.

58 W.H. Frere, *The Christian Ministry* (National Mission Paper no. 280. London: SPCK, undated), in Frere Papers, 1.5/4, Mirfield Deposit, Borthwick Institute for Archives, University of York.

For the bishop to exercise his authority responsibly he must be assisted by his clergy, who represent him in the parishes, and whom he should summon together in synod. A 1920 Report of the Wakefield Diocesan Conference, of which Frere was a member, on the question of establishing diocesan synods, noted the historical precedent that, 'In the ancient synods the bishop simply herd [sic] what the clergy desired to say, but they did not decide upon any question, the decision resting with the bishop alone.' This was precisely the conclusion reached in Frere's personal notes on diocesan synods, presumably briefing himself for the same discussion, where he stressed the synod's consultative rather than legislative role, 'for bishops are the real legislators of the Church'.[59] In fact he returned again and again to the importance of the diocesan synod at the centre of a healthy church government. Even in his writing on the Russian Church he deplored the demise of the diocesan synod, along with that of the Patriarchate, as evidence of how the Church had been subjected to the control of the Tsarist State.[60] Later, as a well-established bishop, working between 1932 and 1934 on the Oath of Canonical Obedience Committee for both Canterbury and York Convocations, he noted that a recovery of discipline must entail the restoration of diocesan synods, 'as the natural way by which the bishop takes the mind or secures the approbation of his clergy and is himself guided in the exercise of the less defined or less regulated authority which belongs to him'. True canonical obedience is not simply a literal adherence to a certain set of canons but 'the reverent obedience to superiors and the following of the godly admonitions'.[61] In this understanding of obedience we see most clearly how the leadership style of the monastic superior impinged upon that of the diocesan bishop. Yet ultimately Frere was not in favour of an absolute episcopal monarchy, but rather a system of checks and balances. In a 1915 memorandum on Church Unity, he argued that, whilst the diocese is the principal unit of the Church and any larger coalescence is merely a matter of convenience, the federation of dioceses into provinces was part of the Church's 'ancient constitution' and highly desirable both to enable the bishops to meet together to legislate and to enable a

---

59 Both documents are together in the Frere Papers, 1.5/18.

60 Frere, *Russian Church History*, pp. 132 ff.

61 'Some Notes on the Canonical Obedience by the Bishop of Truro' for the reference of members of the Committee, in Frere Papers 1.5/2.

metropolitan to supervise the bishops.[62] At the other end of the spectrum, he was strongly convinced of the need for a greater role for the laity, 'as much the members of Christ's body as anyone'.[63] Typically he saw this as restoring an ancient balance to Church government lost through the meddling of secular rulers from Constantine onwards and through medieval clericalism.[64] He recognized that their role must be strengthened within diocesan conferences, and most pressingly within the proposed new Church Council or Assembly to work alongside the Convocations.[65]

Leading an actual diocese

Frere's existing historical and polemical interests, then, serve to illustrate the areas that would become priorities once he found himself, on the brink of old age, thrust into the episcopate, a role of which he already had a deeply rooted understanding. These interests and priorities had been worked out against the background of the ongoing revival of diocesan life; a revival we must note, not a revolution, which encouraged bishops to do what they had always done, but to do it with more diligence and care. Happily for Frere, the Diocese of Truro, one of the youngest dioceses of the Church of England, had been founded as an expression of this revival and Frere certainly saw himself as inheriting and building upon that legacy. Bishop Henry Phillpotts of Exeter, through whose initiative the idea of a Cornish See was revived and financed, he described as 'that wonderful restorer of episcopal and diocesan efficiency'; and to Edward Benson, the first Bishop, he attributed 'that great diocesan organization laid out on the most modern lines'.[66] Truro also had a reputation for being

---

62 W.H. Frere, 'Memorandum on Church Unity', March 1915, Frere Papers, 1.5/8. Note that he contrasts this 'Federal' model with the Papal, and warns strongly against the dangers of over-centralization, above the level of a province, even within one nation.

63 *The Laity and the Church Council* (Church Self Government Association Paper. London: SPCK, undated), in Frere Papers, 1.5/4.

64 *The Laity and the Church Council*: whilst he strongly advocates the laity's right to participate and applauds their expertise, he is less definite about the powers that would be given them in the Church Council.

65 See also *Convocation and the Proposed Church Council* (Church Self Government Association Papers. London: SPCK, undated), Frere Papers 1.5/4.

66 See Frere's Pastoral Letter on the occasion of the Diocesan Jubilee, 25 April 1927, printed alongside the April 1927 *TDG*.

a 'High Church' diocese, which was certainly true for its central institutions;[67] a view which Hockley and Johnson support in their account, although which, perhaps in the light of some of the controversies that beset Frere, was a convenient simplification.[68]

The *Diocesan Gazette*, as the official press organ of the diocese, not only provides an account of the developments in the diocese during Frere's time, but really constitutes a manifesto and an apologia for the changes that he and his staff introduced,[69] and must be read as such. As we have already seen, Frere took an active interest in the *Gazette*'s content. In addition to the frequent scholarly articles often outlining historical precedent as a justification for a change, Warman's friendly introductory letter was quickly replaced[70] by an often extensive 'Bishop's Notes' on events in the life of the Church or the Church's response to matters of current national or international concern, and often a set of 'Diocesan Notes' and 'Cathedral Notes'. The Bishop's engagements calendar remained a prominent feature as in Warman's day. Many of the priorities were predictable: to an already busy programme of regular Deanery Conferences and an annual Diocesan Conference, alongside the unusual Truro diocesan institution from its foundation of a regular Devotional Conference for clergy,[71] Frere added the pattern of an annual synod of the clergy, immediately before the Diocesan Conference. The first, in June 1924, was summoned 'to discuss a difficult matter connected with clergy discipline'.[72] There is no further reference to this synod, but the 1925 synod at the same time of year, on the more controversial question of Holy Unction and the best expressions of the Church's healing ministry, clearly aroused more debate about the questions the synod should be

---

67 Calendars in the *TDG*, even in Warman's time, include even the dates of All Souls and Corpus Christi; and the Community of the Epiphany was well established with the Bishop as its Visitor.

68 Hockley and Johnson, 'Truro', p. 78 and see below.

69 Hence a substantial increase in length from the four pages of Warman's day.

70 *TDG*, January 1924, contains the first example, with notes on the difficulties in the Church in Japan (this was later extended into a separate section of Missionary Notes), the Bishop's programme of confirmations, and an extended essay attempting to familiarize the diocese with the two possible variations in the Consecration Prayer then being debated in the Church Assembly, and their relative merits.

71 The 'centenary', i.e. the hundredth of the six-monthly Devotional Conferences, was celebrated with the Jubilee in 1927.

72 *TDG*, June 1924.

asking and what the synod's role should be, and here the *Gazette* was very clearly used as a means of expressing the episcopal mind. A slightly exasperated note, presumably from the bishop, in the April edition[73] explained that wider questions surrounding spiritual healing were not up for discussion but only the question as to whether there should be public healing missions: the synod was 'not a debating society'. This was followed in May by extensive notes 'contributed at the request of the bishop' on the wider question of spiritual healing.[74] After the discussion at synod proved 'disappointing' from the bishop's point of view, even though he was heartened both by the 'fellowship' and the use of 'ancient synodical procedure',[75] the August edition contained an anonymous 'Plea for Unction' as something owing to the sick by right.[76] By 1927 the clergy synod had evidently become an established fixture and the laity had their own separate meeting for the first time;[77] but when, more controversially, Frere used a synod to gain his clergy's assent to the use of the rejected 1928 Prayer Book in the diocese, there were evidently more questions raised about the authority for such synods and their use in liturgical or doctrinal matters, which Frere strongly rebutted in the December *Gazette*.[78]

As we have already noted, and in line with Frere's most basic understanding of his role, Frere undertook a general visitation of his diocese in connection with the Diocesan Jubilee in 1927, again after careful preparation through the *Gazette*. In February 1927, the dates for the visitation for each deanery were issued, and it was noted that there had been only four visitations since the foundation of the diocese, the last in 1910:[79] Frere evidently felt that this was a duty long overdue. In March, the Bishop's Notes outlined the visitation plan whereby the

---

73 *TDG*, April 1925.

74 *TDG*, May 1925.

75 See *TDG*, July 1925, and consider the comments about 'fellowship' in the light of Burns's understanding of 'diocesan consciousness'.

76 See *TDG*, August 1925, the private celebration of the sacrament had been affirmed but there was much opposition to the idea of healing missions.

77 See *TDG*, August 1927.

78 See 'A Note on Synods', again appealing to historical precedent, in *TDG*, December 1928. He had already gained the assent of the laity at that year's Diocesan Conference, and gave approval in an Ad Clerum in March 1929 (see *TDG*, March 1929) but the controversy continued.

79 *TDG*, February 1927.

visitation business would take place in the afternoon and a Jubilee service in the evening. April and May saw the two historical articles on visitation, the second of which concluded that whereas, in one sense, with enhanced communications visitation was now going on all the time through the bishop's continual touring of the diocese for meetings or interviews, 'a special visitation every three years enables the Diocese to take stock of itself'.[80]

The programme for the Jubilee celebrations offers an insight into some other major priorities of Frere's episcopate. Hockley and Johnson make much of the invitation to the parishes to come in groups on a day pilgrimage to the Cathedral where they participated in its worship, were given tours and shown its treasures, and effort was made to distinguish the particular connection between that group of parishes and the Cathedral.[81] Their account identifies the major developments in the Cathedral in Frere's episcopate as first the issuing of blue cloaks to be worn by members of the Chapter, and secondly the erection of a nave altar. In fact, Frere's interest in the role of the Cathedral, of which by the foundation statues of the diocese he was also the Dean, was much wider than this. Burns[82] argues that the growth of a 'diocesan consciousness' was as important a part of the revival as the institutional changes, and the establishment of the Truro Cathedral as a centre of pilgrimage and focus of unity as the Mother Church of the diocese was an ongoing priority in Frere's time, as the arrangements for the Jubilee demonstrated. There are frequent references in the 'Cathedral Notes' section to the ongoing ornamentation of the building and the growing association of different groups with the various chapels and corners, women and children prominent among them.[83] Most importantly, it was in his Cathedral that Frere devoted much loving care to the liturgical expression of the priorities of his episcopate, notably through his ordering of the ceremonial at ordinations;[84] although the liturgy of

---

80 *TDG*, May 1927.

81 See Hockley and Johnson, 'Truro', p. 98.

82 Burns, *Diocesan Revival*, pp. 131 ff.

83 See e.g. *TDG*, January 1925.

84 In the Cornwall County Record Office are two heavily amended versions of an Order for an Ordination (AD1600/4/1 and AD1600/4/2) in Frere's hand, where he takes much care especially over the manner in which the candidates would be vested, and that he himself should always sing the 'special suffrage in the liturgy'.

the Cathedral was also a major point of high profile controversy.[85]

The Bishop's Pastoral Letter for the Jubilee in April 1927[86] first of all encouraged 'heartiest thanksgiving to God' throughout the whole year[87] for all that had been achieved on the foundations laid first by Phillpotts and Benson; for the growth in crucial areas such as numbers of services, churches, lay readers and especially confirmation candidates; but it also encouraged a note of penitence 'like a drone under a jubilant melody'[88] because though 'the level of parochial efficiency is higher now, the standard of evangelistic effort and response is lower'.[89] It is vital to recognize that though a major priority in the diocesan revival was administrative efficiency, for Frere, as no doubt for others, this was only a tool to encourage the ongoing mission of the church. Especially in his early years in Truro, what we would now term 'mission and evangelism' was made an ongoing priority at home and abroad. We have already noted how the *Gazette* was increasingly used to keep readers informed of the progress and setbacks in overseas missions, especially in recently converted areas. May 1927 saw a Diocesan Missionary Exhibition at Truro City Hall, postponed from 1926 owing to the General Strike,[90] the programme for which is reminiscent, on a smaller scale, of the 1925 Empire Exhibition at Wembley, with stands presenting an impression of the life of the Church in every continent. Evidently Frere himself felt a strong sense of urgency with regard to the world mission situation, as his Lenten Pastoral for 1926 calling for a year of 'Missionary advance overseas' to respond to the paralysing 'spirit of doubt and denial' manifest especially in the spread of Communism, and to 'direct aright' the growing

---

85 The authorization of the 1928 book in Truro Cathedral occasioned a protest by Protestant activists of the National Church League which culminated in an attempt to storm Lis Escop itself, although as Whitnall recalls (see note 33 above) Fr. Longridge CR charmed them away by asking if they had come to see his rhododendrons. See Frere's obituary in the *Yorkshire Post*, 4.4.1938 where the order to remove the hanging pyx in the Cathedral is also recalled.

86 See note 66 above.

87 As the year progressed it was suggested that the celebrations should be extended over three years, *TDG*, December 1927.

88 *TDG*, December 1927.

89 *TDG*, December 1927.

90 See *TDG*, April 1927, the programme for which was issued along with the *TDG* in May.

aspirations for education and political freedom throughout the world'.[91] At home, Frere's concern for the ongoing evangelization of his diocese was particularly expressed in the setting up of a yearly itinerant mission in remoter and poorer parts of the diocese, following the models already in use by CR and, in at least its first year, employing CR brethren as missioners, under the supervision of the Diocesan Missioner and Evangelistic Council.[92]

All these institutional initiatives were, most importantly, underpinned by Frere's ongoing emphasis on the necessity of personal conversion and response to the divine call, which lies at the heart of all his pastoral teaching, and which could occasionally be expressed in deeply unsettling tones. His Lenten Pastoral for 1925 railed against spiritual and moral indifference, arguing that 'As the stifled or starved soul is a prey to infection and disease, so health is bound up with the fresh air of community with God in prayer and the nourishment of communion with the Body and Blood of Christ.'[93] This commitment to personal conversion and vocation showed itself especially in Frere's dedication to the formation of ordinands, a task for which he must have been better qualified than most bishops, through the activities of their Guild of St John the Forerunner and its support fund which he set up in 1926.[94] It was expressed too in his concern for the right use of the Sacrament of Penance: as early as 1925, Fr William King CR was hearing confessions in the Cathedral on a weekly basis, an arrangement which, apparently on demand, then continued indefinitely;[95] and almost Frere's last act as Bishop in January 1935 was to issue a detailed and stringent 'Memorandum for the Guidance of Diocesan Counsellors [senior clergy, to whom difficult cases might be referred anonymously] and other Confessors'.[96] Most prominently, this imperative was expressed in the prominence he accorded to the Sacrament of Confirmation a 'most trusty weapon in the

---

91 Reprinted in *TDG*, February 1926; the 'Pastoral on the World Call' reprinted in October *TDG* is in a similar vein.

92 The first, in June 1927 was at Roseland (see *TDG*, February 1927, and the report in *TDG*, August 1927).

93 Reprinted in *TDG*, March 1925.

94 See his report on the first meeting, in *TDG*, November 1926.

95 See *TDG*, March and May 1925.

96 In CCRO, AD1600/4/14.

spiritual armour',[97] the candidates at which, as he noted at the Jubilee,[98] had steadily increased in spite of a declining population; and the administration of which occupied a substantial proportion of the Bishop's monthly calendar: frequently he would be touring to confirm on several days in a row, and sometimes twice a day. In late 1926 and early 1927, six articles on the essentials of confirmation preparation appeared in the *Gazette*, the last of which by Frere himself stressed that the 'decisive matter' when considering a candidate's readiness 'is not a question of age or learning but of conversion ... Confirmation and the gift of the Holy Spirit should come to the candidate as the divine seal upon a real conversion of heart to God.'[99] 'The recovery of the solemnity of the service',[100] which Frere himself had initiated in the diocese by encouraging the arrangement of the confirmation rite after mattins and the litany and immediately before the Eucharist, would help to persuade the sceptic that confirmation was not a 'pure formality'.[101] Here perhaps more than anywhere, Frere's care for detail and his personal fatherly attention to the candidates, as Whitnall records, had the deepest impression.[102]

Underpinning all Frere's initiatives was absolute commitment to the life of prayer, both for himself and for his flock, clergy and laity, whom he constantly encouraged to lay aside time for retreat, regularly offering his own home at Lis Escop for this purpose to both clergy and laity.[103] His very first message to the diocese, before his arrival immediately after his consecration, was an exhortation to mutual prayer, 'to lay the right foundation for the personal intercourse that is to follow'.[104] With many bishops this might seem a purely conventional encouragement, but not so with Frere. In the archive at Mirfield is his personal copy of his 1898 handbook of intercession (with A.L. Illingworth), *Sursum Corda*,[105]

---

97 See his comments in the 'Bishop's Notes', *TDG*, April 1925.

98 See above note 88.

99 *TDG*, March 1927.

100 *TDG*, March 1927.

101 *TDG*, March 1927; and see the article 'A Country Confirmation' in *TDG*, July 1926.

102 See above and *TDG*, December 1924, where Frere suggested that the previous year's candidates should be invited back to the Confirmation to sit behind the current year to support them, wearing the badges that Frere had given them.

103 See, e.g., *TDG*, January 1926.

104 'A Word from the New Bishop', *TDG*, November 1923.

105 Uncatalogued and until very recently presumed lost volume in the CR archive at Mirfield.

complete with his own annotated additions: a calendar of those to pray for on their year's mind, lists of fellow religious and fellow bishops, Truro Cathedral clergy, musicians and lay readers; and intricate beautifully drawn maps of each of the deaneries in the Diocese, showing all the parish boundaries and the location of the churches, and the name of the parish priest for whom to pray. For Frere, the monk bishop, prayer was a living, sustaining reality.

Controversies, endings

The previous section has considered the priorities and the successes of Frere's episcopate, which were considerable. The difficulties and controversies must also be considered, one of which was the complaint recorded by Wilkinson that he was often away from his diocese.[106] We noted in the opening section the potential difficulties of balancing responsibilities in Truro, London and Mirfield, particularly given that the demands of General Chapter normally kept Frere in the north for much of January and July, and also given that his expertise was much in demand on the bench of Bishops, as Davidson had hoped. But the evidence of the previous section should show that, in spite of the demands on him and even perhaps counter to Davidson's assumptions, Frere made his diocesan responsibilities a real priority. There is no space here to assess his contribution in the Upper House of Convocation, which in the case of Prayer Book reform can be traced in Chapter 8. But we should note the breadth of his contribution to convocation committees, on the Oath of Canonical Obedience, Ecclesiastical Courts, an abortive Union with the Free Churches, the Permanent Diaconate, the regulation of Religious Communities, to name a few.[107] The quality of his contribution to Convocation debates must also be recorded: hidden away in the copy of the Convocation Reports in the Community library at Mirfield is a slip of paper in Frere's own hand, a copy of a suggested collect for the Making of Deaconesses which he had effortlessly adapted from the Leonine

---

106 Wilkinson, *Centenary History,* p. 165.

107 These can be traced in the *Chronicle of Convocation* (Upper House of Canterbury) Reports for the relevant years (London: SPCK), and much of the paperwork for the first three of these together with his notebooks on the intermittent conversations with the Free Churches are in the Frere Papers (Borthwick) at 1.5/2, 1.5/3, 1.5/1 and 1.5/5 respectively.

Sacramentary in response to a request from the Bishop of Chester.[108] By as early as 1930, putting his all into his hugely varied and demanding commitments had clearly taken a great toll on his health.[109]

Hockley and Johnson refused to assess the greatest controversy of the period, that from 1932 surrounding the practices and ornaments at the Church of St Hilary, Mazarion, which culminated in the desecration of the church, as 'disfiguring' their account. When news of Frere's impending resignation was learned, in late 1934, the Archbishop of Canterbury received a stream of letters from laity and clergy[110] associated with Cornwall, requesting or even demanding that Frere's successor should not have Frere's perceived faults. Whilst the criticisms made of his leadership cannot be taken as representative,[111] they must nevertheless be assessed and valued. One such letter, from a Viscount Edgecombe, is fairly typical, purporting to represent the views of 'many thousands in Cornwall' who were opposed to the 'very strong high church views' of Frere, because of the strong presence of Nonconformity and the moderate position of most Church people. It was frequently alleged that Frere had sanctioned illegal forms of worship, or, as in this letter, that through his patronage of livings both as Bishop and as Dean he had appointed to parishes men of his own views who were frequently 'an utter failure'.[112] Many had been apparently driven into the arms of Nonconformity as a result. One letter describes him as 'not the man for Cornwall'[113] because its bishop needed to be looked up to by both Anglicans and Nonconformists. Quite a few writers tempered their criticism of Frere with

---

108 Both the collect, the letter of request of 30.11.23 and Frere's reply of 16.12.23 are hidden away in the *Chronicle of Convocation* for 1924. In the debate (see ibid., pp. 271 ff.) Frere was anxious to establish liturgically the theological differences between the Making of Deacons and that of Deaconesses. It is frequently wrongly assumed that since his liturgical views were not Romanist, Frere was in favour of the ordination of women to the priesthood: in fact a handwritten memo in the Borthwick strongly outlines all his theological objections to the innovation, Frere Papers, 1.5/16.

109 In 1930, he was forced to leave his only Lambeth Conference early on account of his health. See Phillips, 'Elevation' p. 70, and below.

110 See Lang Papers, vol. 139, ff. 51–77 *passim*.

111 On 18.12.34, C.J. Bex at the Church Union wrote to Lang warning that many of the clergy who were shortly to petition him demanding a Protestant successor were in fact Nonconformists, Lang Papers, vol. 139, f. 75.

112 Edgecombe to Cosmo Gordon Lang, 11.12.34, Lang Papers, vol. 139, ff. 66–67.

113 See Lang Papers, vol. 139, ff. 71–72.

admiration for his personal qualities,[114] which may well be more than a politeness, but all were united in their determination to have a 'moderate' bishop who would bring an end to the 'controversial atmosphere' which the MP for West Cornwall saw as 'deplorable'.[115]

It is certainly true that Frere, despite his enthusiasm for the rigours of visitation, had not thought it right to curb the ritualist practices at St Hilary which, whatever their merits, certainly exceeded the provisions of even the 1928 Prayer Book which he had introduced into his diocese so carefully.[116] In June 1934 one Ann King, apparently a parishioner of St Hilary, had petitioned the Archbishop of Canterbury to discipline Frere for his failure to act against Bernard Walke and his curates Frederick Carr and Ernest Gill for a long list of offences and apparently 'heretical' doctrines including the practices of Reservation and Benediction, processions of the Blessed Sacrament,[117] devotions to Our Lady, and prayers for 'Pius, Our Pope and Walter, Our Bishop'.[118] Lang himself was clearly not inclined to take the protests seriously, noting to his commissary that Miss King was probably being put up by an extreme Protestant faction, probably those who had made trouble for Frere in the past,[119] and replying to her that he had no jurisdiction in the matter.[120] When Lang put pressure on Frere to do something just so that she would no longer 'plague' him with letters,[121] Frere replied from Chapter at Mirfield, that having contacted both King and Walke, he was considering forming a committee to look at the question, but further steps could probably wait until his return to Cornwall in August, when he would see Walke and until after the Archbishop's holiday.[122] Lang agreed. Evidently Frere was disinclined to intervene in the situation. This may be put down to partiality to the Anglo-Catholic cause, to whose excesses he was

---

114 See, e.g., Lang Papers, vol. 139, f. 68.

115 W. Runciman to Lang, 30.11.34, Lang Papers, vol. 139, f. 51.

116 See note 78 above.

117 This was not the beginning of the matter: the Lang Papers contain correspondence as to whether a ruling by the Consistory Court in the Diocese for the removal of some of the church's ornaments should be enforced by the civil courts. See vol. 110, ff. 241–52.

118 King's petitions to Lang, and Frere, the list of unlawful practices, and her covering letter, are in Lang Papers vol. 139, ff. 128–135.

119 Lang Papers, vol. 139, f. 140, 2.6.34.

120 Lang to King, 16.6.34, Lang Papers, vol. 139, f. 148.

121 Lang to Frere, 7.7.34, Lang Papers, vol. 139, f. 156.

122 Lang Papers, vol. 139, f. 158 10.7.34, and f. 159, 11.7.34.

prepared to turn a blind eye. Whitnall[123] recalls Frere visiting Walke (who prepared Whitnall for confirmation) on a Sunday afternoon and saying something on the lines of 'Well, Bernard, perhaps you ought to be going for Benediction, or perhaps not.' In the CCRO is an example of a written approval (dated 29.8.1930) for Reservation in the Parish Church of St Erth, presumably on the conditions in the 1928 Prayer Book, but with a handwritten addendum from Frere that 'The customary place need not be changed.'[124] Walke seems to have become a friend of Frere's. But more importantly, even though their liturgical tastes must have differed, Walke was respected by him for the work he was doing at St Hilary which he was reluctant to disrupt. As Whitnall recalls, Frere had even taken part in Walke's broadcast nativity play, where Frere had given a blessing at the end in Cornish.[125] As one observer put it after Frere's death, he 'found there a spiritual genius capable of unique appeal and doing a work far beyond the parochial range; and he would not repeat the error which had ostracised Wesley'.[126] That at least was how Frere saw it. He was already known for his loyalty to his clergy in any controversy: when two thousand people had petitioned him to discipline Jack Bucknall, Curate at Delabole, for his strong Socialist preaching in the year of the General Strike, Frere had replied to the Secretary of the 'Emergency Committee' that its letter and petition was 'full of misrepresentations' and that he considered it 'a slanderous and libellous document'; a correspondence which he published in full in the *Gazette*.[127] Perhaps in the St Hilary case, Frere's declining health also contributed; nevertheless, the fact that controversy was unresolved evidently caused much ill-feeling. As to the other allegation, that Frere misused his patronage, an allegation which Hockley and Johnson deny perhaps too vehemently, in the one example of correspondence on an appointments question in the CCRO, concerning the benefice of St Crantock, Frere shows a great deference to the wishes of the incumbent concerning his own future and that of the parish.[128]

---

123 See above, note 33.

124 CCRO Ad1600/3/6/1 (a collection of documents on the issue of Reservation), reference for this document is p. 59.2.23.

125 See note 33 above: one parishioner, when asked which part he had liked best replied: 'that 'ere bishop, 'e was 'ansome'.

126 'Walterus Truron: By a Priest of the Diocese of Truro', *The Church Times*, 8.4.38.

127 See *TDG*, December 1926.

128 CCRO, AD 772/107–119.

The question of his relationship with the people of Cornwall is a more complex one. Clearly, Davidson had felt that, in Benson's diocese, a monk-bishop would be a generally acceptable innovation and, as we have seen, he was largely proved right. Those who objected that he was not the man for Cornwall did so on the grounds that an Anglo-Catholic bishop was a natural stumbling block in a diocese with such a strong Methodist presence. Yet the years of effort that Frere put into ecumenical conversation and questions of reunion with the Free Churches must not be forgotten,[129] together with a tribute in the press from a local Methodist leader, distancing Methodism from the position of the National Church League and praising Frere's work with the local Methodist Synod.[130] In discussing Frere's successor, Lang acknowledged 'as both Benson and George Wilkinson did' that 'sympathetic leadership' might harness 'the great latent force of personal religion in Cornwall',[131] with the implication that perhaps Frere had not done so; and the choice of the evangelical Cornishman, Hunkin, to achieve this, seemed to mark a deliberate change of tactics. Yet, as we have seen, Frere himself had huge and impressive forces of personal religion even if these were not expressed in the established evangelical manner,[132] and he also developed a deep appreciation of the county. His passion for Cornish church history found ample expression in his own exhaustive tours of historical sights,[133] his ongoing support, amply expressed in a huge variety of articles in the *Gazette*,[134] for Cornish historical scholarship; and his institution of the outdoor pilgrimage mass and lecture at the shrine of a different Cornish saint each August.[135] On his retirement he wrote simply and movingly that Cornwall had 'stolen half my heart'[136]

---

129 See above, note 107.

130 'A Nonconformist Tribute', *The Western Morning News*, 5.12.34.

131 Lang to Runciman, 30.11.34, Lang Papers, vol. 139, f. 53.

132 Whitnall (see note 33 above) recalls criticism of Frere's preaching in Yorkshire which might also be applied to Cornwall: 'I don't think much to Frere, he doesn't sweat enough!'

133 See Phillips, 'Holiday Intermezzo'.

134 See especially the note advertising the publication of the comprehensive *Cornish Church Guide* to the Duchy's parish churches, *TDG*, February 1926.

135 The first in 1924 was to the Oratory of St Pirran (see the account in *TDG*, September 1924), the success of which led to the creation of an annual event, sponsored by the English Church Union.

136 *TDG*, February 1935.

and this surely must refer not first to its history or landscape, but to its people.

The correspondence from the last few months of Frere's episcopate, between Lang, Hockley as Archdeacon and Frere himself over the rapidly declining state of his health following a dizzy spell at Lambeth in October 1934,[137] makes sad reading, especially considering Frere's blunder in allowing the *Daily Mail* to learn of his plans before Downing Street[138] and his considerable distress, shared vicariously by Lang, at the embarrassment which this caused to all involved.[139] When this is set alongside the letters of criticism that Lang received it is easy to gain the impression of an old and ill man who had lost his way; an impression which the Petition from all the clergy of the East Wivelshire Deanery to Lang goes some way to remedy. It attempts to counter some of the more negative opinions by stressing all that they felt Frere had brought to the diocese: 'steady growth in corporate church life', the development of a 'strong spirit of unity and fellowship' and an 'affectionate and impartial rule'.[140] Many other tributes in a similar vein would be made both at Frere's retirement, and just a few years later at his death in 1938; but had his episcopate truly seen the 'realization of an ideal of a chief pastor's office in the Church'? Whether or not Truro had proved the right diocese for such an experiment, as Davidson had hoped in 1923, is questionable, although, as an obituary in the *Church Times* noted, his model of an episcopate combined with life in Community set 'a great and inspiring example and a profound witness to that stability for which Frere himself cared above all things'.[141] What is certain is that in all his actions as bishop, Frere, ascetic though he may have been, was motivated by a great but simple passion for the faith; by a passion for all that he believed in most dearly; by a monastic's sense of the demands and joys of a personal vocation, which in his case had led him to seek to restore community life from his earliest adulthood, and had led him by twisting ways eventually to be made Bishop of Truro. Yet

---

137 See, e.g., Hockley to Lang, 28.10.34, on Frere's gruelling personal work regime and his 'highly strung constitution' (Lang Papers, vol. 139, f. 32) and a Memo (12.10.34) from Frere to Lang on his giddy spell (Lang Papers, vol. 139, f. 28).

138 See Frere to Lang, 29.11.34, Lang Papers, vol. 139, f. 48.

139 Lang to Frere, 1.12.34, Lang Papers, vol. 139, f. 56.

140 See Lang Papers, vol. 139, f. 81.

141 *Church Times*, 8.4.38.

this passion was combined with a scholar's breadth of vision and a saint's humility to make room for those with whom he disagreed[142] 'for we all need all the help we can get', as he put it memorably in an 'evangelical' sermon in support of Reservation in Truro Cathedral, 1928.[143] It was surely this generosity, vision and care which led one observer among many to note on his death that 'the Bishop before all presented himself as shepherd of souls',[144] surely the way he would most desire to be remembered.

---

142 One Evangelical, Barker Lumb, writing to the *Illustrated London News* (5.4.38) on Frere's death, recalled his 'kindly simplicity' in addressing Confirmation candidates and his humility in vesting in the same manner as the vicar, much to the satisfaction of the congregation: 'a true and sympathetic friend to all his clergy alike'.

143 CCRO, AD 1600/3/6/1: a handwritten note on the transcript of this sermon by one who heard it reads, 'God be praised that I have lived to hear an English Bishop give such instruction in his Cathedral.'

144 'Walterus Truron', *Church Times* 8.4.38.

5

A Son of the Reformation? Walter Frere's historical scholarship reviewed[1]

ALEXANDER FALUDY

Introduction: saints and sinners in historiography

Writing on historiography, especially its Reformation branch, tends to privilege the historical profession's awkward squad, either those angular personalities who, because of ideological bias, egregiously 'pushed their dogmas beyond the point of moderation',[2] and (one might add) factual sustainability, or those admirable figures credited with unsettling a complacent consensus, usually to the irritation of their 'elders and betters'. William Cobbett is a classic nineteenth-century example of the former class; Christopher Haigh, some would argue, a contemporary one of the latter.[3] Either way, the end result entails the marginalization in academic consciousness of industrious and honest, but uncontroversial, scholars, who research with diligence and write with 'good sense and charisma'.[4]

---

1 This chapter is dedicated with affection to the memory of my late friend Arnourt de Waal, and was delivered in draft form as a paper at the University of London Institute for Historical Research seminar, 'Religious History of Britain 1500–1800', in April 2009. I am grateful to the colleagues present for their helpful suggestions for its revision and likewise to the Revd Drs Hannah Cleugh and Gordon Jeanes. Thanks also go to my students in the Mirfield and Leeds University Church History classes for 2006–7. Any remaining errors are entirely my own.

2 A.G. Dickens and J.M. Tonkin, *The Reformation in Historical Thought* (Oxford: Basil Blackwell, 1985), p. 350.

3 For an analysis of Cobbett's social polemic in *A History of the Protestant Reformation in England and Ireland* (London, 1824–7), see R. O'Day, *The Debate on the English Reformation* (London: Methuen, 1986), pp. 71–4. On Haigh, see n. 7 below.

4 Dickens and Tonkin, *The Reformation in Historical Thought*, p. 350.

This essay argues that Frere's Reformation scholarship manifests this class's virtues but does not deserve to share in its obscurity.[5]

Frere's trustworthiness tends to be assumed rather than discussed or critiqued by non-revisionist historians.[6] His name may not occur as a foil amid their narrative arguments but his books, especially his editions of primary sources, are omnipresent in their footnotes and bibliographies.[7] On the other hand, their revisionist colleagues make equal technical use of him, but also like to wheel him out occasionally as a bogeyman to provide a sound-bite example of Anglo-Catholic attitudes to the Reformation. Most often cited is his stern judgement on the Edwardian Church – 'the lowest depth to which English Christianity ever sank'[8] – or on Archbishop Grindal's spirited defiance of Elizabeth as 'a particularly unfortunate piece of Puritan crankiness'.[9] The contention of this essay, however, will be that such uses obscure both the achievements and the complexity of Frere's endeavours and attitudes.

Frere, it will be argued, is an interesting and worthy object of study for, as we shall see, he wrote at an important, though historiographically neglected, time of transition for both Anglo-Catholicism and Reformation studies. At that time new trends were emerging but a new paradigm had yet to crystallize, a circumstance which encourages us to read his work with a particular sensitivity to nuance and context.

---

5 See, e.g., O'Day, *The Debate on the English Reformation*; Dickens and Tonkin, *The Reformation in Historical Thought*, accords him a brief 'honourable mention' (p. 339) for his part in making documents of the Elizabethan Puritan movement available in print.

6 Here 'non-' or 'post-' revisionist refers to scholars who have treated the prevalent 'Reformed Consensus' model of the Elizabethan with caution (allowing, for instance, for some Lutheran-Reformed tension), without wishing to revert to older high-church models of the processes involved. See, e.g., Judith Maltby, *Prayer Book and People in Elizabethan and Early Stuart England* (Cambridge: Cambridge University Press, 1998).

7 On which see below and C. Haigh (ed.), *The English Reformation Revised* (Cambridge: Cambridge University Press, 1987), E. Duffy, *The Stripping of the Altars* (New Haven: Yale University Press, 1992), D. MacCulloch, *Tudor Church Militant: Edward VI and the Protestant Reformation* (London: Allen Lane, 2000). For some comments on Frere's editing see P. Ayris, 'The Challenge of Interpretation: Using Documents of the Early English Reformation Period', *Reformation & Renaissance Review*, vol. 6.2 (2004), pp. 203–30 at pp. 203–4.

8 *Articles and Injunctions*, vol. 1, p. 143.

9 *The English Church in the Reigns of Elizabeth and James I* (London: Macmillan, 1904), p. 192. Cited in P. Collinson, *The Elizabethan Puritan Movement* (London: Jonathan Cape, 1967), p. 196.

The purpose of this chapter is to stimulate interest in and further research on, Frere's achievements as a Reformation historian and is thus suggestive rather than comprehensive. It takes as its focus a selective cross-section of historical issues relating to the sixteenth-century Church of England. Much more can (and should) be written about Frere's work on other aspects of that period and indeed the seventeenth century, but the constraints of space and focus delimit us here. Instead, I will address the essential preliminary for such work: introducing contemporary readers to the range of Frere's scholarship, teasing out his relationship with the interpretative approach which present thinking labels 'The Myth of the English Reformation', and also to divergent trends within post-Tractarian thinking.[10] Finally, the essay will pause to consider how our investigation of Frere might cause us to reconsider some of the challenges created for the writing of Reformation history by confessional bias in the historian.

Frere the Historian

Frere's academic interests were famously diverse: spanning liturgy and musicology as well as Reformation studies. They are, however, united in the approach he took to them: even when dealing with subjects not taught in a history department, his work is in both texture and orientation fundamentally historical, concentrated on the analytical description of known developments rather than the posting and debate of abstract norms. This is perhaps unsurprising when we take into account the place of historical work (more strictly understood) as both the preface and 'spine' for all his other activities: he read the whole of Gibbon's *Decline and Fall of the Roman Empire* by way of preparation for theological studies at Cambridge, his earliest published works were explicitly historical, and he continued to bring forth new work of this sort in every decade of his life.[11]

His initial endeavours were focused on local history: namely that of his title parish in Stepney (whose Tudor and Stuart vestry minutes he

---

10 D. MacCulloch, 'The Myth of the English Reformation', *The Journal of British Studies*, vol. 30.1 (1991), pp. 1–19, and N. Tyacke, 'Lancelot Andrewes and the Myth of Anglicanism', in P. Lake and M. Questier (eds), *Conformity and Orthodoxy in the English Church c.1560–1660* (Woodbridge: Boydell & Brewer, 2000), pp. 5–33.

11 See C.S. Phillips, 'Family and Training', in Phillips et al., *Walter Howard Frere, Bishop of Truro* (London: Faber & Faber, 1947), pp. 13–31 at p. 27, and A. Hamilton Thompson, 'The Historian', in Phillips, pp. 147–57 at p. 147.

published with a critical introduction in 1890 as *Memorials of Stepney Parish*) and of the parish of Barley in Hertfordshire whose *Parochial History* appeared in the same year. Over time his writings expanded massively in both scope and scale. He continued the work of publishing primary sources right up to his closing years (the multi-volume *Registrum Matthei Parker* appeared between 1928 and 35) but also published broad narrative history (*The English Church in the Reigns of Elizabeth and James I*, 1904), and highly technical examinations of particular problems (*The Marian Reaction in its Relation to the English Clergy*, 1896). His apologetic and ecumenical work (such as *English Church Ways*, 1917) also frequently contained presentation of and reflection on the events of the Reformation and will be drawn into the discussion below.

Contemporary opinion tended to treat *The English Church* as his 'chief contribution to history', the one on which his reputation as an historian must principally rest because of its clarity in presenting complex material and considerable toning down (if not elimination) of the partisan rhetoric that had tended to characterize writing on the period; in relation to this, his editorial productions stood as subsidiary *pièces justificatives*.[12] Later judgement has tended to reverse this estimate: according to Brett Usher, although *The English Church* does indeed represent a step forward in detachment – 'anti puritan but never tub thumping'[13] – it was rapidly superseded and is seen now as no more than a 'holding operation and an interim account pending a longer and more considered study',[14] although it was reprinted as late as the 1960s by AMS Press. Rather, it is for the close work on documents, both in presentation and analysis, that posterity has true reason for gratitude; he was a pioneer of administrative history and the integration of local records into the national picture. His works relevant to these concerns will be surveyed here briefly and in chronological order.

In *The Marian Reaction in its Relation to the English Clergy* (1896), Frere

---

12 Thompson, 'The Historian', pp. 150 and 153.

13 Usher to Faludy, personal communication, 10 April 2008. Much of the following analysis of Frere's technical utility is indebted to the same source. See also F. Heal and R. O'Day (eds), *Continuity and Change: Personnel and Administration of the Church in England 1500–1642* (Leicester: Leicester University Press, 1976), p. 12.

14 Usher, pers. comm. Frere's revision of Procter's *History of the Book of Common Prayer* likewise enjoyed an extended publication afterlife (into the 1960s); F. Procter and W. H. Frere, *A New History of the Book of Common Prayer* [1901] (London: Macmillan, 1961).

set about a very specific task at the request of the Church Historical Society: searching the episcopal registers for evidence which would shed light on the Marian view of orders conferred under the Edwardian ordinal; a key point in contemporary controversy with Rome (although his publication narrowly pre-dated *Apostolicae Curae*).[15] Despite the circumstances of the project's genesis, later scholars have found the methodology flawless, 'a model of forensic excellence … packed with a wealth of previously unpublished facts' (especially as regards ordination lists).[16] As far as the evidence would permit, Frere persuasively argued that Marian deprivations of Edwardine clergy had been for marriage *not* invalidity. Both this point and the other data drawn in support of it have been of lasting benefit to investigators working on the prosopography of Edwardian clerics and bishops, the mechanics of ecclesiastical separation, and, more recently, the social history of clergy marriage. Frere's transcriptions both here and elsewhere are agreed to be technically flawless, a remarkable achievement in a period when palaeographical expertise frequently caused his contemporaries, Henry Gee, for example, to make painful errors in such work, meaning that later scholars had to go back to the original manuscripts for themselves. *Puritan Manifestoes* (1907), reproducing the *Admonition to Parliament* and related documents (last reprinted in 1972), was pronounced 'indispensible'[17] by the great Tudor historian Conyers Read in 1959, and has remained so.

Frere and Kennedy's joint effort, *Visitation Articles and Injunctions of the Period of the Reformation* (1911), is a landmark work in the field, 'a monumental achievement by any scholarly standard',[18] collating information from a formidable number of sources. Together with Kennedy's own later work, *Elizabethan Episcopal Administration*, it changed the direction of later scholarship, forcing historians to examine what bishops actually *did* in their dioceses, once installed. It is significant testimony to the special arduousness of their labours that no scholar set about producing similar work on the Jacobean period for another eight decades.[19] The later

---

15 Hamilton Thompson, 'The Historian', pp. 148–9.

16 Usher, pers. comm.

17 In C. Read, *Bibliography of British History: Tudor Period* (2nd edn, Oxford: Clarendon Press, 1959).

18 Usher, pers. comm.

19 K. Fincham (ed.), *Visitation Articles and Injunctions of the Early Stuart Church* (2 vols., Woodbridge: Boydell Press, 1994–8).

but similarly scaled *Registrum Matthei Parker* is singular, both in being an early modern cuckoo within the nest of the Canterbury and York Society's otherwise exclusively medieval publications and (like the *Visitation Articles*) not having been replicated by anyone else with regard to the Archbishop's immediate successors.

The sort of meticulous scholarship Frere undertook required enormous patience and the willingness to plug away at projects in tiny increments over time: 'his kind of scholarship required the equability which allows you at the end of the day to leave a library feeling disappointed that you haven't achieved more and yet in the last analysis confident that you will finish the wearisome task'.[20]

The close acquaintance with primary sources that Frere exhibited still has lessons to teach today's researchers, and a case in point is that of the *Wanley Part Books*.[21] These are manuscripts (lodged in the Bodleian Library, Oxford) of musical settings for elements of an early draft of a revised communion rite which overlap substantially with the 1549 Book of Common Prayer but which also contain some fascinating instances of divergence. Frere unearthed the MSS and published on them in a *Journal of Theological Studies* article in 1900.[22] Both the manuscripts and Frere's article about them entirely fell out of the scholarly citation trail and the former had been assumed lost, together with all other examples of its experimental class.[23] As well as highlighting interesting technical features divergent from the first Prayer Book,[24] Frere points to the novel use of the Apostolic in place of the Nicene Creed in the Eucharist and the existence of a post-communion collect discarded in the later authorized liturgy. To modern eyes the former suggests interesting parallels with Lutheran liturgical practice but it is the latter which is of greater

---

20 Usher, pers. comm.

21 Oxford, Bodleian Library, Ms. Mus. Sch. e.420–22.

22 W.H. Frere, 'Edwardian Vernacular Services before the First Prayer Book', *Journal of Theological Studies* 1 (1900), pp. 229–46.

23 This was the case for liturgists and church historians. See D. MacCulloch, *Thomas Cranmer: A Life* (New Haven: Yale University Press, 1996), p. 396, and G.P. Jeanes, *Signs of God's Promise: Thomas Cranmer's Sacramental Theology and the Book of Common Prayer* (Edinburgh: Continuum, 2008), p. 99. Musicologists, however, remained alert to their existence: see J. Wrightson, *The 'Wanley' Manuscripts: A Critical Commentary* (New York: Garland, 1989).

24 That is, experimentation with the Gloria, 'Christ Our Paschal Lamb' text and post-communion sentences.

significance. Gordon Jeanes's recent investigations (prompted by a re-reading of Frere's article) have shown that the collect subtly but significantly adapts an earlier prayer from the relatively cautious Cologne liturgy (*The Consultation*) revised by Martin Bucer and Phillip Melanchthon for the city's Archbishop Hermann von Wied in 1543.The effect of the alteration is to render the prayer's doctrine compatible with the Reformed theological position known as Symbolic Parallelism, a position to the left of Calvin and associated with Heinrich Bullinger and the other Zurich theologians.[25]

This piece of evidence is very important in strengthening the arguments advanced by scholars in recent decades for dating Cranmer's move to a Reformed position on the Eucharist (to a date anterior to the 1549 Prayer Book's final compilation, let alone publication), perhaps indeed as early as late 1547. Needless to say this is contra the old high church argument championed by Frere that this change of sympathies occurred sometime between the two Prayer Books.[26] Indeed the *Part Books* not only confirm but advance the claims of the modern consensus: until now the earliest securely identifiable first-hand statements by Cranmer affirming his new outlook have been those found in the third edition of his *Catechism*, published some time late in 1548, and the record of his speech to the House of Lords in the debate on eucharistic doctrine in December that year.[27] The evidence of the *Part Books*, however, suggests Cranmer either authored or at the very least authorized Reformed-Parallelist language in relation to the sacrament during the 'experimental' phase, which began in the earliest months of the year in those places where local church authorities 'were sympathetic or could be bullied by

---

25 A Reformed position, originating in the thought of Heinrich Bullinger, which sees the union of Christ's body and blood with the believer as articulated by rather than brought about through the reception of the eucharistic elements. Cf. Calvin's far stronger 'Instrumentalist' or 'Virtualist' position which was espoused by many 'High' Anglicans until the nineteenth century.

26 For a perceptive critique of both the Wanley Texts and Frere's unhelpfully obscure presentation of these materials, see G.P. Jeanes, 'Early Steps in the English Liturgy: The Witness of the Wanley Part Books', paper delivered to the Society for Reformation Studies Conference at Westminster College, Cambridge, in April 2010 (publication forthcoming). I am most grateful to Dr Jeanes for allowing me to see this piece in draft form.

27 On these sources and the complex debates surrounding the dating and authorship of several other documents, see Jeanes, *Signs of God's Promise*, pp. 114–35, and MacCulloch, *Thomas Cranmer*, ch. 9 *passim*.

the government into compliance'.[28] The very latest *terminus ad quem* for the Archbishop's change of heart is thus pushed back considerably further than verifiable hitherto: in fact to the very earliest months of 1548. The conclusions drawn here are inimical to Frere's own writings on the subject, but they would be quite impossible without them.

The Revisionist paradigm: views on history and historiography

The Myth of the English Reformation is that it did not happen, or that it happened by accident rather than design, or that it was half hearted and sought a middle way between Catholic and Protestant; the point at issue is the identity of the Church of England.[29]

In order to assess Frere's place in the history of Reformation scholarship, it is first requisite to introduce the general reader to what researchers have said both about the English Reformation and the history of its interpretation by scholars. Revisionism,[30] the academic movement that has dominated scholarship on the English Reformation since the 1980s, has banished the use of the term 'Anglican' from the historical lexicon of the pre-restoration Church of England as being both misleading and anachronistic. The understanding (still popular at large) of the Elizabethan settlement as either a synthetic *via media*, harmonizing Catholic and Protestant values, or the creation of an environment in which they could co-exist more or less peacefully, has been vigorously attacked.

According to the new orthodoxy, the late sixteenth-century English church was certainly peculiar but for quite other reasons than traditionally supposed. Lutheran influence on the English Reformers

---

28 MacCulloch, *Thomas Cranmer*, p. 395. Second-hand reports of Cranmer's move from a Lutheran to a Reformed position prior to 1549 (rather than, as many later Anglo-Catholics argued, between 1549 and 1552) date back to Ridley's statement to that effect at his trial in 1555 and a preface (attributed to Sir Thomas Cheke) to an edition of Cranmer's works printed at Emden in 1557.

29 MacCulloch, 'Myth of the English Reformation', p. 1.

30 In another direction revisionism has also (with considerable success) challenged older notions about the 'decay' of the late medieval church and the 'popularity' of the Reformation; see Haigh, *The English Reformation Revised*. In pursuit of a rhetorical foil it has, though, been felt by some to have unfairly misrepresented its opponents, especially A.G. Dickens. See N. Tyacke, 'Rethinking the Reformation', in N. Tyacke (ed.), *England's Long Reformation 1500–1800* (London: Taylor & Francis), p. 4.

waned terminally in the 1530s and thereafter the intellectual cue was taken from the Swiss Reformed:[31] when the Reformers were able to show their hand under Edward they moved inexorably, if at first slowly, in that direction but were cut short by the King's early death in 1553.[32] Whatever Elizabeth's opaque private views, she set out to restore her brother's Church, but her approach was idiosyncratic: she wanted not the Church that was emerging in 1553, rapidly heading for conformity with continental models, but a 'snap shot' of the Church as it had seemed at the time of the promulgation of the second Prayer Book in 1552: with a liturgy still more conservatively styled than (though not in essence theologically divergent from) that of Zurich or Geneva and episcopal government and much traditional canon law still firmly in place. Additionally Elizabeth, principally for reasons of expediency in foreign policy, threw the Lutherans 'a few theological scraps'[33] on ceremonial and sacramental issues via the ornaments rubric and tweaks to the Prayer Book and Articles. The Marian Bishops, excepting the pliable Kitchen of Llandaff, being deposed, successors had to be found from among the Reformed. These latter were included, many well disposed to pressing reform further, but were respectful of the doctrine of the 'Godly Prince' and generally (with the notable exception of Archbishop Grindal) acquiesced in her policy, despite the opposition of their Puritan co-religionists at home from whom they were separated, not by doctrine, but by 'the degree of regret that they felt about the situation';[34] equally, full communion (including interchangeable ordination) with the continental Presbyterians was to be maintained for another century.

In this perspective 'Anglicanism', if it can be said to have existed at all, was a later development. Only in the 1580s did doubts about Calvinist predestination begin to surface and not until the 1590s did the ancient

---

31 The term 'Reformed' is used throughout this article in preference to 'Calvinist'. Calvin represented only one stream of thinking in what became the Churches loyal to the Helvetic and allied confessions, and ideas often labelled 'Calvinist' by historians, especially touching the Eucharist, are not ones he would own. See note 25 above and B.D. Spinks, *Sacraments, Ceremonies and the Stuart Divines* (Aldershot: Ashgate, 2002), *passim*.

32 The classic expression of this view is provided by MacCulloch in *Thomas Cranmer* and *Tudor Church Militant*, especially in his discussion of Prayer Book reform.

33 D. MacCulloch, 'The Church of England 1533–1603', in S. Platten (ed.), *Anglicanism and the Western Christian Tradition* (Norwich: Canterbury Press, 2003), pp. 18–41 at p. 29.

34 MacCulloch, 'Myth of the English Reformation', p. 15.

church structure 'begin to reassert its fascination',[35] allowing a positive (rather than expedient) regard for both episcopacy and liturgy to begin to reassert itself as a sort of *ex post facto* rationalization of the peculiar Catholic fossils left behind by Elizabeth's settlement; survivals which had heretofore been frozen 'like the mosquito blood in the amber of Jurassic Park'.[36] The seeds of 'Laudianism' and indeed the Civil War were thus sown but were to take many more years to germinate. Puritans were not 'deviants from an Anglican norm', rather it was the new high churchmen of the 1590s and onwards who 'were popularly seen as promoting an ecclesiastical and theological revolution';[37] before the 1590s their ideas had probably been unthinkable and at any rate 'unsayable'.[38] To suppose otherwise is 'wishful thinking'.[39] Some important modifications to this picture have recently been proposed, but it remains normative.[40]

Allegations of 'wishful thinking' against Anglo-Catholics are indeed among the favourite rhetorical *topoi* of the revisionist approach. The flip side to this historical argument has been a scathing historiographic critique of pre-1960s (and some later) English Reformation scholarship.

It has been argued, with some force by Diarmaid MacCulloch and

---

35 D. MacCulloch, *The Later Reformation in England, 1547–1603* (2nd edn, Basingstoke: Palgrave, 2001), p. 78.

36 E. Duffy, 'The Shock of Change: Continuity and Discontinuity in the Elizabethan Church of England', in Platten, *Anglicanism and the Western Christian Tradition*, pp. 42–64 at p. 63.

37 MacCulloch, 'Myth of the English Reformation', p. 18.

38 P. Lake, 'The "Anglican Moment"? Richard Hooker and the Ideological Watershed of the 1590s', in Platten, *Anglicanism*, pp. 90–121 at p. 108.

39 MacCulloch, 'Myth of the English Reformation', p. 10.

40 Recently a 'new', 'post-revisionist', interpretation has begun to emerge which (leaving aside recusants and separatists) argues for a subtler three-shade spectrum within the Elizabethan Church: 'two parties' inheriting respectively the (smaller) Lutheran and the larger (Reformed) streams of Edwardian Protestantism, and a third in much closer synch with Reformed sentiment as it had continued to develop abroad. See R. Bowers, 'The Chapel Royal, the First Edwardian Prayer Book and the Elizabethan Settlement of Religion 1559', *The Historical Journal* 43.2 (2000), pp. 317–344, esp. pp. 320–1 and 333–4; S. Dorran, 'Elizabeth I's Religion: The Evidence of Her Letters', *Journal of Ecclesiastical History* 51.4 (2000), pp. 699–720, and N. Tyacke and K. Fincham, *Altars Restored: The Changing Face of English Religious Worship 1547–c.1700* (Oxford: Oxford University Press, 2007), pp. 31–5. Aspects of this interpretation were foreshadowed by W.P. Haugaard and O. Chadwick in the 1960s. See Haugaard, *Elizabeth and the English Reformation* (Cambridge: Cambridge University Press, 1968), and Chadwick, *The Reformation* (3rd edn, London: Pelican, 1972), pp. 211–32.

others, that the Anglo-Catholic 'Myth of the English Reformation' was born out of 'the rewriting of English church history, pioneered by John Keble and John Henry Newman in the 1830s' and carried on by a 'troupe of historians too clever for their own good',[41] among whom members of the Community of the Resurrection played a special role.[42] They dominated the university scene into living memory.[43]

These writers were, it is claimed, heirs to the Laudians ('the same party revived')[44] and re-invigorated an earlier historiographical tradition established by the likes of Peter Heylin and Jeremy Collier in the late seventeenth/early eighteenth century.[45] The tradition rested on a skilful interlocking of several mutually supporting historical arguments which we may here summarize under four heads. First, an excessive focus on the early, politically driven and personally shadier facets of the English Reformation (especially its Henrician phase) entails an unwonted reduction of the importance of theology as a determinative factor in the story.[46] Emphasizing domestic politics at the cost of doctrinal disputes prepares the way for the second line of argument: unjustifiable assertion of the independence of the English from the continental Reformers' 'thought world'[47] and, in consequence (thirdly), a distortion of the perceived relationship of later Conformists and 'Geneva-phile Puritans': artificially magnifying the gap between the centre and circumference of Elizabethan Church life.[48] Silence, though, could be as powerful as distortion: unpalatable data like the iconoclasm of the Edwardian Church was left out of the story.[49] Fourth (and finally), historical perspective was

---

41 D. MacCulloch, 'Putting the English Reformation on the Map', *Transactions of the Royal Historical Society* 15 (2005), pp. 75–95 at p. 76.

42 MacCulloch, *Tudor Church Militant*, pp. 105 and 157, also 'Myth of the English Reformation', p. 7, n. 7.

43 Duffy, 'The Shock of Change', p. 43.

44 MacCulloch, 'Myth of the English Reformation', p. 1.

45 MacCulloch, 'Myth of the English Reformation', p. 4.

46 O'Day, *The Debate on the English Reformation*, chs. 2–4, *passim* and Tyacke, 'Rethinking the Reformation', pp. 4–32, esp. pp. 1 , 24 and 25.

47 For a summary, see D. MacCulloch, 'Can the English Think for Themselves? The Roots of English Protestantism', *Harvard Divinity Bulletin* 30 (spring, 2001), pp. 17–20.

48 See MacCulloch, 'The Myth of the English Reformation', pp. 5–7, and P. Lake, 'The "Anglican Moment"? Richard Hooker and the Ideological Watershed of the 1590s', in Platten, *Anglicanism and the Western Christian Tradition*, pp. 90–121.

49 MacCulloch, 'Myth of the English Reformation', p. 12.

foreshortened in relation to the Edwardian and early Elizabethan Church so as to elide the discontinuities between the conformist churchmanship of the writer's and the subject's periods.[50] How does Frere's work fit into this pattern?

Frere and 'The Myth' compared

Though the early Reformation's internal characteristics and place within the whole were not the main focus of his attention, Frere's handling of them does him great credit:

> political causes are mainly important as offering the occasions for the outbursts of the movement and in some degree shaping its overt course. The real causes lie further away. The politicians emerge steering their boats on a strong current, independent of them in its origin, which has long and secretly been accumulating its course ... Henry's breach with Rome is far from being the whole or even the chief part of the English Reformation.[51]

Frere was perceptive in upholding (contra James Gardiner) continuities between Lollardy and 'the controversial ground of the sixteenth century'.[52] He did not shirk from discussion of uncomfortable features of the Edwardian Reformation, however much he disliked them: 'the disgraceful iconoclasm which wrecked the churches is a conspicuous and familiar example'.[53] His 'lowest depth' remark was predicated on recognizing how far the Edwardian Church stood from his own values. More positively, the discerning and appreciative use he made of Foxe and Strype as sources runs strongly counter to their polemical knocking by S.R. Maitland et al.[54] He also transcended earlier partisanship in his appreciative reliance on the Parker Society volumes, a library of English

---

50 MacCulloch, 'Myth of the English Reformation', pp. 5–7 and 15.

51 W.H. Frere, 'Lollardy and the Reformation' [review article] in *Church Quarterly Review* 1910 (January), pp. 426–39 at pp. 427 and 431; see also p. 439.

52 Frere, 'Lollardy and the Reformation', p. 436.

53 Frere, 'Lollardy and the Reformation', p. 439.

54 See the Preface to *The English Church*, p. ix, also the notes to *Marian Reaction*, *passim*. On Maitland, see O'Day, *The Debate on the English Reformation*, pp. 87 ff.

Reformation texts produced mid-century by evangelical opponents of the Tractarians.[55]

Much less consistent and assured, however, was his handling of the English Reformation's relationship with its European context. Despite his well-attested enjoyment of European travel, Frere does, like the later C. W. Dugmore, have an unfortunate tendency to write 'as if every theological breeze which crossed the sea from Germany or Switzerland brought some kind of strange spirit to the pure air of English Religious thought'.[56] His presentation of the process of Prayer Book revision is perhaps a useful index.

Although Frere is agnostic regarding the identity of the architect of the first (1549) Edwardian Prayer Book, it is obliquely made to seem the product of the sort of '"New Learning" which was soundly catholic at heart' while the second (1552) was compromised by the interference of Bucer and Vermigli – 'a further disturbing element in the situation'.[57] Frere seems to want to acknowledge the influence of foreign divines on Cranmer's redactional activity but to exclude any direct interpolation of texts from foreign Protestant liturgies: verbal similarities, where they could be found, were explained away. 'The family likeness, such as it is, is collateral not lineal',[58] a weak argument which has come in for considerable criticism from later scholars, especially with regard to Frere's overlooking of Cranmer's borrowings from early Lutheran rites.[59]

---

55 See. P. Nockles, 'Survivals or New Arrivals? The Oxford Movement and the Nineteenth Century Historical Construction of Anglicanism', in Platten, *Anglicanism and the Western Christian Tradition,* pp. 144–191 at p. 159.

56 Haugaard, *Elizabeth and the English Reformation,* p. 233.

57 Frere, *The Modern History of the Church of England* (London: SPCK, 1925), p. 4, and Procter and Frere, *History of the BCP,* p. 71. Modern studies have convincingly demonstrated the unity of authorship (Cranmer's) and established the Archbishop's personal conversion to Reformed eucharistic theology as predating the issue of the first book. See MacCulloch, *Thomas Cranmer,* chs. 9–11, also Jeanes, *Signs of God's Promise,* pp. 4–5. Jeanes's work is the most accomplished modern study of Cranmer's development as a liturgist.

58 Procter and Frere, *History of the BCP,* p. 90. He makes an exception for Luther's litany and the Cologne *Consultation* (1543). Although he acknowledges Bucer as lead author (p. 28), he consistently associates the text instead with the (more acceptable?) name of its authorizer Archbishop Hermann in all subsequent references.

59 See, e.g., B. Hall, 'The Early Rise and Gradual Decline of Lutheranism in England (1520–1600)', in D. Baker (ed.), *Reform and Reformation: England and the Continent c.1500–1750* (Oxford: Blackwell, 1979), pp. 103–31 at pp. 121–2. Also Jeanes, *Signs of God's Promise,* ch. 5 *passim.*

A similar tension is at work in his depiction of Cranmer's personal response to the foreign divines. Thus, in the space of a few pages within his update of Francis Procter's *History of the Book of Common Prayer,* we encounter strangely varied portraits of Cranmer, both eagerly pressing forward with the course of Reform in partnership with Vermigli and Bucer, and being unwillingly forced thence under some peculiar form of psychological duress. On p. 77, Frere writes of Cranmer voluntarily pledging himself to reform and on p. 79 of the 1551 convocation 'the opportunity for which Cranmer and the reforming bishops had been waiting, was now come'; however, by p. 84 (and late 1552):

> The Archbishop had apparently at last reached the end of his tether. He had been pushed on and on by foreign influence, by Bucer first and after Bucer's death by more extreme men from abroad: but he would go no further.

Predictably he exhibits great distress on the subject of the black rubric (which insisted that no veneration of corporeal presence in the sacrament was to be taken as implied by the act of kneeling at communion): 'Thus against the Archbishop's will and without the consent of the Church, English religion reached its low water mark and the ill-starred book of 1552 began its brief career.'[60]

Gordon Jeanes has argued cogently that his depiction (which nearly reverses the more measured account offered in Procter's original) is, like his reticent analysis of the draft 1548 liturgies, thoroughly propagandist in intent:

> At stake for Frere was the future revision of the Book of Common Prayer and his project for the reconstruction of the Church of England's Eucharistic liturgy using traditional Prayer Book material but looking to the shape of ancient Eucharistic prayers. In this

---

60 Procter and Frere, *History of the BCP*, p. 85. For Cranmer, the kneeling posture signified not adoration of a corporeal presence in the host but that the communicant was a beggar after grace. The black rubric (so called because its late insertion into the Prayer Book meant it was not coloured red like other rubrical notes) enshrined this teaching contra the objections raised against the posture by John Knox but was misunderstood by posterity as a setback for the Archbishop. See MacCulloch, *Thomas Cranmer*, pp. 525–30.

endeavour the 1549 Canon was an essential link, and its credentials as a 'catholic' liturgy all important. In effect, the reconstruction of catholic Anglicanism depended largely on the 1549 Prayer Book being an authentic English expression of catholic Christendom.[61]

Does this (clearly strained) attempt to insulate the early English from the continental Reformers translate readily into a distortion of the relationship between Conformist and Puritan in the Elizabethan Church and of the former to later high churchmanship? The answer is not straightforward. Again we seem to be dealing with a case of 'two voices'.

On the one hand Frere is certainly keen to maintain the Channel's insulating function. He speaks with some relief of the fact that the Marian loss of Calais meant that, by Parker's archiepiscopate, 'fortunately England was by that time cut off from the continent'.[62] Similarly the admission (without re-ordination) of foreign Reformed ministers to work in the Church of England is explained on the basis of a distinction between posts 'with cure of souls' and those without: claiming that those with Presbyterian orders could only hold the latter 'on the same terms as laymen and according to a custom which was fast being discredited and abolished by the bishops',[63] a bald statement which does justice to neither the complexity nor the balance of the surviving evidence, as Norman Sykes showed long ago.[64]

The divide is, though, held to be temperamental as well as structural. Frere's lack of first-hand acquaintance with the works of the magisterial reformers (and their depth of patristic citation) tells embarrassingly when he asserts that 'the main body of English Reformers',[65] who remained at home under Mary, believed in reform on the basis of a return to the

---

61 Jeanes, 'Early Steps in English Liturgy', p. 12.

62 W.H. Frere (ed.), *Registrum Matthei Parker Diocesis Cantuarensis, A.D. 1559–75*; transcr. E.M. Thompson (3 vols., Oxford: Oxford University Press, 1928–33), vol. 1, p. 27.

63 Frere, *The English Church*, p.126, also p. 201.

64 N. Sykes, *Old Priest and New Presbyter: Episcopacy and Presbyterianism since the Reformation with Especial Reference to the Churches of England and Scotland* (Cambridge: Cambridge University Press, 1956), ch. 4. Despite the increasingly high view of episcopacy taken by English conformists from the 1590s, interchangeability of orders with the continental Reformed churches ceased only with the 1662 Act of Uniformity.

65 C.E. Douglas and W.H. Frere, *Puritan Manifestoes* (London: SPCK, 1907), p. xii.

Fathers, whereas foreign Protestants were intent on 'giving up the creeds'[66] and infected those English exiles who became puritans with 'a crudely biblical method'[67] in theology. Matthew Parker the scholarly Archbishop 'and catholic-minded reformer'[68] par excellence, is cast heroically (his close ties to Martin Bucer oddly forgotten)[69] and the story of the Elizabethan Church and the struggles within the 1563 convocation misleadingly introduced, as a battle between "The Reformers Anglican and Genevan".[70] If distance across space (England and the Continent) has been unduly magnified, distance across time seem to have been unfortunately contracted. Frere opines that 'the formulation of the Anglo-Catholic position had made great progress through the learning and piety first of Hooker and then of the new generation of whom Bishop Andrewes was the leader'.[71] The claim is curious given that, for all their positive appreciation of ceremonial and episcopacy, both Hooker and Andrewes held an 'Instrumental' view of eucharistic presence akin to Calvin's and declined to unchurch foreign Protestants for their want of the tactile apostolic succession, the *locus classicus* of both Tractarian and later Anglo-Catholic thinking.[72]

On the whole, so far, one might say, so flawed. However we have already noted that the depiction of the Henrician Reformation is not of a piece

66 Frere, *English Church Ways, Described to Russian Friends in Four Lectures Delivered at St Petersburg in March 1914* (London: John Murray, 1914), p. 17.

67 Frere, *The English Church in the Reigns of Elizabeth and James I*, p. 272. Also Frere, *Lancelot Andrewes as a Representative of Anglican Principles* (London: SPCK, 1898), pp. 7–10. On the uses of the Fathers within Reformation theology, see A.E. McGrath, *Reformation Thought: An Introduction* (3rd edn, Oxford: Blackwell, 1999), pp. 154–7 and, on the continuing normative status of the creed, pp. 241–44.

68 Frere, *English Church*, p. 71.

69 See D.J. Crankshaw and A. Gillespie, 'Matthew Parker (1504–1575)', in *Oxford Dictionary of National Biography* (Oxford: Oxford University Press, 2004), pp. 707–28.

70 Frere, *English Church*, p. 94. The key modern corrective to this picture is to be found in Haugaard, *Elizabeth and the English Reformation*, ch. 2, though for some important supplements cf. also D. Crankshaw, 'Preparations for the Canterbury Provincial Convocation of 1562–63: A Question of Attribution', in S. Wabuda and C. Litzenberger (eds), *Belief and Practice in Reformation England* (Aldershot: Ashgate, 1998), pp. 60–93, and Tyacke and Fincham, *Altars Restored* pp. 41–4.

71 Frere, *Modern History*, p. 15.

72 On the Eucharist, see Spinks, *Sacraments, Ceremonies and the Stuart Divines*, pp. 19–24 and 45–7 and on ecclesiology Paul Avis, *Anglicanism and the Christian Church* (Edinburgh: T&T Clark, 2002), pp. 57–8 and 132–3.

with the 'Myth' trajectory and in other spheres too the reader is taken aback by the impression of an entirely contrary interpretation operating underneath the surface, and, indeed, occasionally breaking out in open revolt. Frere's warning in *The English Church* about the dangers of anachronism would not be out of place in a much later piece of scholarship:

> when the eye of the student of the period has looked forward and grasped that division which was ultimately to emerge, the next thing is for him to look back and see how inchoate and ill-defined the whole of the actual position of things still was; the left comprised many gradations of reforming zeal still barely distinguishable from one another, the right was hardly less complex; and the centre was only gradually forming itself round the middle policy which at first seemed only to be the dubious policy of a temporising government.[73]

His dissection of the *early* character of Puritanism and its theological common ground with conformity is also acute. In his local history work of the 1890s, Frere writes in full awareness of how integral 'Puritan' values were to the life of the established Church in the Elizabethan period, and that alienation from it was a facet of the changing circumstances of the Stuart period: 'By 1579 when the [vestry] minutes open Puritanism, using the word in its Elizabethan sense, was firmly established in Stepney, though there still lay before it a gradual development into the more distinct Puritanism of the Commonwealth.'[74]

Concomitantly in his *The English Church*, minority Presbyterianism is carefully differentiated, as in recent historiography, from a more widely diffused 'moderate Puritanism': 'It would, however, be entirely misleading to judge Puritanism by its extreme men. The best of the composite body comprehended under that term were not spoilt by ... violence or bitterness.' They were rather 'high-souled men of piety who had the fear of God and a pure ideal before their eyes ... who could exalt the ministry of preaching without depreciating the ministry of sacraments or the

---

73 Frere, *English Church*, p. 71.

74 G.W. Hill and W.H. Frere (eds), *Memorials of Stepney Parish Church* (Guildford: Billing, 1890–91).

orderliness of fixed worship.'[75] Moreover, before being pushed leftwards, and eventually out, by the repeated trial of the conformity campaigns, these ministers accepted episcopacy as a 'given' if not cherished fact, as indeed was the case of the Northamptonshire connection who, as late as 1571, made successful endeavours to 'secure approval from their bishop'[76] for their adaptations to liturgy and discipline.

The qualities of Conformity as both protean and initially Reformed come across too: between the bishops and their opponents in the 1560s' vestiarian controversy, 'doctrinal difference at present there was none to be seen',[77] and even the later complexity of Whitgift's stance is honoured ('he was decidedly in sympathy with the Calvinists in his doctrinal standpoint'). He is also under no illusions about ceremonial: 'the ornaments rubric was from the first set aside'.[78] Frere saw clearly, as recent scholarship has, the importance of the fellow feelings generated by a common exile which acted both as a polemical check on the hierarchy (for most of whom episcopacy was 'a mere matter of policy'[79]) and upon dissenting moderates until the 1590s.[80] From then onwards he claims a new generation argued for episcopacy assertively on theological principle rather than out of the 'hollowness' of 'civil delegation'.[81] Unsurprisingly, as Peter Nockles has further commented:

> The idea of 'Anglicanism' slowly emerging in the 17th Century [not the 16th] was explicit in both Richard Church and Walter Frere's studies of Lancelot Andrewes ... Frere [though] held that it was not only Andrewes but Laud and the Restoration divines who finally worked out Reformation principles.[82]

Frere it would seem had tendencies both to perpetuate 'the myth of the

---

75 Frere, *English Church*, p. 184; see also p. 126.
76 Frere, *English Church*, p. 168.
77 Frere, *English Church*, p. 114.
78 Procter and Frere, *History of the BCP*, p. 110.
79 Frere, *English Church*, p. 224.
80 Frere, *English Church*, p. 155.
81 Frere, *English Church*, p. 276.
82 P.B. Nockles, 'A Disputed Legacy: Anglican Historiographies of the Reformation from the Era of the Caroline Divines to that of the Oxford Movement', *Bulletin of the John Rylands University Library of Manchester*, vol. 83.1 (2001), pp. 121–67 at p. 150.

English Reformation' and fundamentally to undermine it. His relation-ship with it was clearly patchy and unstable. How are we to account for this?

Conflicting influences: Old High Churchmanship Tractarianism, and the contemporary scene

To understand the profound tensions within Frere's historical writing, we need to turn our search for guidance away from the historiographic models used by today's Reformation historians and towards those used by scholars like George Herring and Peter Nockles, investigating nineteenth-century religion. Both have maintained that the scandal of Tractarianism (as manifested in characters like Newman and Froude) lay in its departure from established high-church norms, especially as regards attitudes to the Reformation inheritance. According to this perspective, it had indeed been the concern of old fashioned, High and Dry 'Two Bottle Orthodoxy' to show that 'high churchmen and Arminians, rather than evangelicals and Calvinists, were the heirs of the English Reformers': they were indeed adherents to the 'Myth of the English Reformation'.[83] However, the concern of the new generation (with the exception of Pusey) shifted, particularly in Froude's *Remains* and Newman's *Tract XC*. The Tractarians, contrary to MacCulloch's assertions, manifestly 'did not rewrite the history of the Church of England by leaving out its more protestant elements, but rather by confronting and rejecting those elements as illegitimate and extraneous'.[84] This manifested itself in

a) Recognizing and reacting in horror to the violence and Protest-antism of the Reformation process ('a limb badly set'),[85] and the deficient

---

83 Nockles, 'Survivals or New Arrivals?', p. 154. See also G. Herring, *What Was the Oxford Movement?* (London: Continuum, 2002), *passim* but esp. pp. 34–7.

84 Nockles, 'Disputed Legacy', p. 161, see also J.M. Cameron, 'Editor's Introduction' to Newman's *Essay on the Development of Christian Doctrine* (Harmondsworth: Penguin, 1974), p. 13. Confusingly, MacCulloch cites Nockles's article in support of his thesis even though it flatly and specifically contradicts the former's view of the subject as articulated in an earlier publication: see MacCulloch, 'Putting the English Reformation on the Map', p. 76, n.

85 R.H. Froude, *The Remains of the Late Reverend Richard Hurrell Froude*, J. Keble and J.H. Newman (eds.) (4 vols., London and Derby, 1838–9), vol. 1, p. 251, cited in P. Nockles, 'Survivals or New Arrivals?' pp. 150–1.

moral ethos of the Reformers, including Elizabethan churchmen like John Jewel (a hero to old high churchmen), characters who, Hurrell Froude told Keble, he 'would most have despised and hated if he had known them'.[86]

b) Asserting the legitimacy of a thoroughgoing appeal against its tenets to what they understood to be a patristic standard of doctrine.[87]

Since both Homilies and Articles appeal to the Fathers and Catholic antiquity, let it be considered whether, in interpreting them by these, we are not going to the very authority to which they profess to submit themselves ... *we owe no duty to the framers*.[88]

In contradiction of the revisionist viewpoint, and also the old high-church position, it would seem the Tractarian approach to the Reformation (including the Elizabethan Church) was a hermeneutical and ecclesiological, *not* an historical one. Moreover its attitude was one not of distortion but of dismay and critical distancing; 'the Tractarians largely abandoned the old high church defence of the reformation as a conservative orderly settlement'.[89] Their appeal to intellectual ancestors was not to Tudor theologians but to the seventeenth-century Caroline divines, using the latter either directly, where their views coincided, to *correct* the reformer, or indirectly, where correspondence was weaker, as a methodological precedent for going 'beyond and behind the Reformation' to the 'undivided church'.[90] Their view of the Reformed character of the Elizabethan Church was realistic and surprisingly close to that of modern scholarship. Both Newman's *Essay on the Via Media*

---

86 Froude, *Remains*, vol. 1, pp. 434–5, cited in William J. Baker, 'Hurrell Froude and the Reformers', *Journal of Ecclesiastical History* 21 (1970), pp. 243–59 at p. 248. See also the more recent work of James Perriro, '*Ethos' and the Oxford Movement: At the Heart of Tractarianism* (Oxford: Oxford University Press, 2008), esp. ch. 5.

87 See P. Nockles, *The Oxford Movement in Context: Anglican High Churchmanship 1760–1857* (Cambridge: Cambridge University Press, 1994), pp. 122–7, esp. p. 123, and 166; Baker, 'Hurrell Froude and the Reformers'; J.H. Newman, *Tract XC: On Certain Passages in the XXXIX Articles* (London: A.D. Innes and Co., 1893) *passim* but esp. p. 83; Herring, *What Was the Oxford Movement?*

88 Newman, *Tract XC*. Emphasis mine.

89 Nockles, 'Survivals or New Arrivals?', p. 183.

90 Nockles, 'Survivals or New Arrivals?', p. 150, see also pp. 177 and 184.

and Charles Gore's *Roman Catholic Claims* have been cited (by MacCulloch) as examples of historical 'special pleading': the ascription is inaccurate and somewhat puzzling, as on first-hand examination they both turn out to be emphatic examples of the more radical, more intellectually respectable, *hermeneutical* approach.[91]

Frere may indeed have been, as another contributor to this volume has put it, 'like Pusey, a once born high churchman': old high churchmanship, and with it an idiosyncratic view of the Reformation, was the context of his family life and university education; it is to pre-Tractarian, high-church sources and attitudes that his presentation refers in its weaker places.[92] However, the characters among whom he later moved in CR (especially Charles Gore) owed far more to the broadly hostile 'critical distance' approach to the Tudor churchmen pioneered by Newman and Froude. The tensions within Frere's *English Church* and other historical works are testimony to the complexity of the continuing interaction within Anglo-Catholicism (and sometimes within a single person) between the values of old high churchmanship and new Tractarianism in the decades after *Tract XC*, and to the interaction of these values with the presenting facts themselves.[93]

---

91 Cf. MacCulloch, 'Myth of the English Reformation', pp. 2 and 7, n. 7, respectively. Newman brackets his identification of an Anglican *via media* between 'Protestantism' and 'Popery' with indications of its applicability to Caroline and Modern times but *not* the *Magisterial* Protestant period, see J.H. Newman, *The Via Media of the Anglican Church* (2nd edn, 2 vols., London, 1877), esp. pp. 20–2, but also pp. 26, 33, 34 and 39. Similarly Gore cautions 'we do not think catholic minded people can be in any idolatrous attitude towards the English Reformation or indeed that we can take an optimistic view of the process', *Roman Catholic Claims* (11th edn, London: Longmans, 1920), p. 172, see also 170–2 and 179–80.

92 See, e.g., his remarks on the subject of the Prayer Book's supposed hostility to Reformed understandings of sin which rely on Richard Laurence's 1804 Bampton Lectures on the 39 Articles. Cf. Procter and Frere, *History of the BCP*, p. 368 and cf. P. Lake, *Moderate Puritans and the Elizabethan Church* (Cambridge: Cambridge University Press, 1982), pp. 161–2.

93 Dix, 'The Liturgist', in Phillips, *Frere*, suggests a characterization along these lines but is mistaken in contrasting Frere with Pusey who like him tried, albeit with difficulty, to stay loyal to old high-church historiography. See Avis, *Anglicanism*, pp. 224–235. An interesting comparison might here be made with R.W. Dixon, *History of the Church of England* (6 vols., London: Routledge, 1878–1902), the work of a Tractarian-influenced high churchman which shows both insight and commendable detachment; see esp. vol. 6., p. xxxvi and following. For more on the continuing interaction between the two approaches, see Nockles, 'Survivals or New Arrivals?', p. 189.

Frere's attitude to the Reformation is, however, characterized by change as much as by tension. Looking at the development of his work from the 1890s to the 1930s, one gets the impression of a slow movement towards acceptance of Reformation values on their *own* (not a re-envisioned) set of terms, albeit within a broader historical perspective. The overall feel of early work is grudging in the credit given to the more definitely Swiss-style facets of the process. 'The English churchman as he looks back on this troubled period, so full of gain and full too of loss' and those within the Church loyal to Reformed principles down to the present 'remained in a false position, attempting to subvert the system to which they nominally conformed'.[94] However even in such writings there are hints of something different (for instance his early and profound admiration of the Clapham Sect), the seeds of a more positive estimation. By the time of 'Lollardy and Reformation' (1910), the rhetoric is near reversed so that in contemplating the violence of the break-off effected by the Reformation 'we need not so much reckon up our losses as ... dwell on our inalienable gains'.[95] In later years he published, in turn, appreciative remarks on the subjects of present-day Nonconformity (which he saw as internally maturing and becoming a fitting object for reunion), Richard Baxter's piety, and the vital importance of the evangelical revival in shaping the Oxford Movement.[96] In places one suspects a paradoxical echo of Newman's views on the development of doctrine:[97] Protestant theological movements are valued according to their ultimate *teleology*, their long-term effects as needed (if flawed) correctives to abuses rather than in relation to their original presenting characteristics.[98] Over the

---

94 Procter and Frere, *History of the BCP*, p. 677.

95 'Lollardy and Reformation', p. 439. On early respect for the Clapham sect, see Frere, *Lancelot Andrewes*, p. 28, and Procter and Frere, *History of the BCP*, p. 678.

96 See *English Church Ways*, p. 8, Sykes, *Old Priest and New Presbyter*, p. 258, Frere's preface to A.R. Ladell, *Richard Baxter: Puritan and Mystic* (London: SPCK, 1925), Frere, 'The Debt Owed by the Church of England to the Evangelical Revival', in *Report of the Oxford Movement Centenary Congress* (London and Oxford: Anglo Catholic Congress Committee, 1933), pp. 167–77. On Frere and reunion with the Free Churches, see Sykes, *Old Priest and New Presbyter*, p. 258.

97 Archetypically expressed in J.H. Newman, *An Essay on the Development of Christian Doctrine* (1845), repr. with an Introduction by J.M. Cameron (Harmondsworth: Penguin, 1974).

98 Avis, *Anglicanism and the Christian Church*, pp. 250–256, cf. Frere 'Evangelical Revival', pp. 167–8.

decades his *Via Media* comes slowly to be less like Newman's ('a unique Anglicanism ... a determined exclusivity')[99] and more like that of Maurice and Gore: a forum for the fruitful and dynamic interaction of parties.[100] Puritanism, Methodism and even Evangelicalism all develop in his writing away from a mainly negative classification as dangers to Catholicity and towards recognition as a historically important element in preserving the Catholicity of the Church by recalling it to biblical fidelity and vital renewal when imperilled by unwholesome developments or by spiritual torpor.[101] Catholicity itself even shows tentative signs of becoming for Frere less a quality to be defended, and more a future state to be looked forward to with hope.[102]

It is perhaps instructive to compare Frere with Hurrell Froude. Among the latter's most famously controversial claims was that with growing acquaintance he became 'a less and less loyal son of the reformation';[103] by contrast Frere's affection for it seems to have increased with familiarity and years. Frere's *metanoia* was slow burning but profound – to the point where a number of his own party felt unsure of him. Positively, the change doubtless reflects his personal contact with the learning and pastoral zeal of Free Church leaders and Anglican evangelicals in his ecumenical and episcopal ministry. However, it was also negatively a reaction to the increasing power and hubris of Anglo-Papalism, whose medievalist/ baroque exuberance he distrusted (like the Tractarians, his own standards were patristic).[104] In such circumstances he could see that a vigorous but

---

99 Nockles, 'Survivals or New Arrivals?', p. 162.

100 See Frere, *Modern History*, pp. 30–31 and 'Evangelical Revival', pp. 174–7. Cf. J.N. Morris, 'Newman and Maurice on the Via Media of the Anglican Church: Contrasts and Affinities', *Anglican Theological Review*, vol. 85.4 (2003), pp. 623–640 and C. Gore, *Roman Catholic Claims*, pp. 3–6.

101 See Thompson, 'The Historian', p.151, and 'Evangelical Revival' *passim*.

102 Cf., e.g., the relative stress in relation to Catholicity on 'antiquity' in *Marian Reaction* (*passim*) and 'future' in *Modern History*, p. 9, respectively.

103 Froude, *Remains,* vol. 1, p. 336, cited in Herring, *What Was The Oxford Movement?*, p. 36.

104 See M. Yelton, *Anglican Papalism 1900–1960* (Norwich: Canterbury Press, 2005), *passim*. On tension between patristic and medieval sympathies in Anglo-Catholicism, see A. Chandler, *A Dream of Order: The Medieval Idea in 19th Century English Literature* (London: Routledge, 1970), cited in J. Livesley, 'John Mason Neale and the Anglo-Catholic Idea of History' (unpublished Oxford History Faculty M.St thesis, 2003), pp. 10–11. On Frere's own views see, for example, his relative evaluation of patristic and medieval forms in Part II of his *History of the BCP*, *passim*.

'churched' evangelicalism was needed as a counter weight to keep the Church of England steady.

Conclusion

Walter Frere emerges from the above pages as a supple and interesting historian: one who wrote with attractive clarity and who, through his close work in documentary editing and analysis, helped to channel out the courses for much later and more detailed scholarship. What, though, in the last analysis, are we to make of his trustworthiness not only as a technician but as an exegete?

It is clear that at times Frere's ideological context was complicated and that at times it obscured his interpretative judgement, but this needs to be set in context: as we have seen, today's historians have themselves (in their misrepresentation of the Tractarians) at times taken polemical short cuts which do not bear close scrutiny of sources. Frere's generation was quite wrong to assimilate positive enthusiasm for the Elizabethan settlement to a patriotically isolated strain of patristic Catholicity, rather than discerning the enduring influence of Martin Bucer and Phillip Melanchthon, but historians are now suggesting that revisionism's mistake was to deny its existence.[105]

All historical achievements are relative: even the most professional scholars can usually look at the past only indirectly through the haze of others' understandings, and as E.H. Carr put it 'history *means* interpretation'.[106] Today's Reformation scholars have good reason to be grateful that Walter Frere looked so hard and for so long.

---

105 See the works of Maltby, Tyacke and Fincham cited above.
106 E.H. Carr, *What is History* (Harmondsworth: Penguin 1964), p. 23. My emphasis.

6

The Malines Conversations

BERNARD BARLOW OSM

On Monday 5 December 1921, Walter Frere found himself in the company of Charles Lindley Wood, the 2nd Viscount Halifax, and J. Armitage Robinson, the Dean of Wells, journeying to Belgium to begin 'informal' conversations with a group of Roman Catholics headed by Cardinal Désiré-Joseph Mercier, the Archbishop of the Malines-Brussels. This project had been conceived and prepared by Lord Halifax and his friend the French Lazarist priest, Abbé Fernand Portal.

These two friends had dedicated most of their lives to the cause of Christian unity, particularly that of union between the Roman Catholic and Anglican Churches. Their first attempt at a reconsideration of the validity of Anglican Orders by both sides had been sidetracked into a solely Roman Commission that ended in the publication in 1896 by Pope Leo XIII of *Apostolicae Curae*, declaring Anglican Orders null and void. After this, both Halifax and Portal redirected their efforts, each within his own communion, to work for a better understanding of the other Christian groups.

In 1920, having passed through the horrors of the First World War, the Anglican bishops, gathered at the Conference at Lambeth, issued a document entitled 'An Appeal to All Christian Peoples'. In this Appeal, the bishops announced that they would be willing, in the cause of reunion of the Christian Churches, to accept a form of commissioning from the authorities of other Churches in order that the ministry of the Anglican clergy might be recognized by others.[1] In fact, this statement was intended

---

1 'An Appeal to All Christian Peoples', *Conference of Bishops of the Anglican Communion, Holden at Lambeth Palace July 5 to August 7, 1920* (London: SPCK, 1920), Section V, Report No. 8 of Committee on Reunion, pp. 132–61.

principally for the non-episcopalian Churches, because the statement then went on to address those communions that did not possess episcopal structures.

Following the publication of the Lambeth Conference Appeal, the person who picked up the possible broader application of the Appeal to the Roman Catholic Church was Walter Frere himself. Even Abbé Portal, who in the intervening years had continued to work actively in affairs of reunion through a new publication, *Revue catholique des Églises*, was not struck immediately by this possibility. In fact it was Walter Frere who pointed it out to Portal in a letter of 3 December 1920. Frere himself had become intimately involved in matters of reunion, having been one of the instigators and founders of the Anglo-Catholic Congress (eventually to be united in 1933 with the English Church Union), and it was he who seems to have brought paragraph 8 of the Appeal to Portal's attention.

It was also Walter Frere who saw in the terms of the Appeal the possibility of surmounting the great difficulty that had arisen because of the declaration of *Apostolicae Curae* on the invalidity of Anglican Orders. But did the Anglican bishops in their statement really mean that they were ready to accept conditional 're-ordination' from the Church of Rome? It was in this context that Portal decided to write to Cardinal Mercier of Belgium, pointing out the importance of the Lambeth Appeal, and to try to relaunch some kind of dialogue between the Church of England and the Church of Rome.[2] The answer to Portal's niggling question of the application of the Lambeth Appeal to the Roman Church only came in a letter from his old friend Canon T.A. Lacey some two months later, in which Lacey revealed that he had been involved in the drafting of the Appeal for the Lambeth Conference, and he assured Portal that the mind of the Anglican bishops was that, if the cause of reunion required it, 'they would not shrink from "re-ordination"'.[3]

The problem of setting up such 'informal conversations' was that each side had to ensure that their official authorities not only knew of them, but should give some recognition that they were taking place and at least tolerate them. The Archbishop of Canterbury, Randall Davidson, was conscious that the Anglican representatives were reflective of only one part of the Church of England, and he insisted that other theological

---

2 Letter of Portal to Mercier, 24 January 1921, Archief Kardinaal Mercier (1851–1926).
3 Letter of Lacey to Portal, 6 March 1921, Portal Papers, Paris.

opinions be represented at the later meeting at Malines. In fact, he makes quite clearly the point that Lord Halifax 'does not go in any sense as an ambassador or formal representative of the Church of England'.[4] Cardinal Mercier had informed Pope Benedict XV of his wish to hold ecumenical meetings at Malines, but received no reply from the Vatican.[5]

Before proceeding to Belgium, Lord Halifax had drawn up a Memorandum for the first meeting as a general basis for discussion. The Memorandum was based on those elements that were common to the Anglicans and Roman Catholics and were considered essential by both the Thirty-Nine Articles and the Decrees of the Council of Trent. In this Memorandum, Halifax recalls that Dr Pusey had postulated that these two sources were compatible, and, if he were indeed right, here was a promising point of departure. The Memorandum could consequently be divided roughly into two distinct parts, the first dealing with the constitution of the Church and the nature of the sacraments – baptism, Eucharist, and the necessity of episcopal ordination – and the second dealing with the Lambeth Appeal. In proposing to deal with the 'constitution' of the Church, Halifax was trying to avoid walking immediately into the thorny issue of the nature of the Church in which both sides had clear and often opposing views. In many ways, this first conversation was to have an exploratory perspective, and was to see whether there was a case for the holding of conferences between Romans and Anglicans, with some real, though at first informal, encouragement from the highest authorities on both sides.

Frere himself described the first encounter in his own small book of recollections.

> On Monday, December 5, 1921, we set out for Malines under the care of James, Lord Halifax's admirable valet. He became quite a part, an inseparable part indeed, of the conferences, being excellent company on the journey, very capable of seeing us and our luggage into the right places: and very acceptable also when we got to Malines, for he had already friends there who had been refugees at Hickleton in the days of the war. Arriving late the same evening at Malines, we were greeted

---

4 Letter of Davidson to Mercier, 19 October 1921, Archief Kardinaal Mercier.

5 Memorandum of Mercier to Benedict XV, 21 December 1920, Archief Kardinaal Mercier, File 1.

with a voice that it seemed almost impossible to believe was not an English voice; it came from Canon Dessain, the Cardinal's Chaplain and an old member of Christ Church at Oxford. From that moment his help and companionship was a very marked feature of Malines. That welcome was the first episode that I remember.

The second was of a different nature. As the Dean emerged from our carriage, a grand silhouette in the dark station with his decanal hat and gaiters, a man waiting on the platform, having some suspicion of what was going on, supposed that this great figure must be the Cardinal himself, and knelt for his blessing, helped perhaps by the glint of the decanal ring upon the figure's finger. The Dean was a little puzzled at first to know exactly what was happening; but when it was explained to him, he rose to the occasion: and the good man did not go away unblessed.[6]

During the meetings, which began the following day, Frere was given the task of producing minutes of the meeting, based on the notes that he had tried to take, and he and Portal were asked to prepare both an English and French copy. Frere was not terribly happy with this task as he felt that his notes were necessarily incomplete and somewhat disconnected, owing to the necessity of taking part in the discussions themselves.[7]

At the end of the series of meetings that composed this 'First Conversation', the group agreed to certain conditions that they thought necessary to maintain the good atmosphere of the meetings. It was agreed that the Minutes (*Compte Rendue*) should be confidential and shared only as necessary, that discretion towards the press should be guarded, and that the names of the participants would not be announced.

There is no doubt concerning the positive and enthusiastic impression that all the participants experienced at this first Conversation. The charity and breadth of vision of the Cardinal impressed all the Anglicans, and the piety and sincerity of the Anglicans deeply touched the Cardinal and the other Roman Catholic members. Dr Robinson had an interview with

6 Walter Frere, *Recollections of Malines* (London: Centenary Press, 1935), pp. 20–1.

7 For a more detailed description of the contents of the conversations, see B. Barlow, *A Brother Knocking at the Door: The Malines Conversations 1921–1925* (Norwich: Canterbury Press, 1996).

the Archbishop of Canterbury on his return to England, and he reported to Lord Halifax in a letter of 12 December:

> I gave your message to the Archbishop, who went through with the keenest interest so much of the English summary as Dr Frere had got ready in time. He was much impressed and confident that our gathering was both of importance and true service.[8]

Frere's assessment was similar, expressing the view that there were great hopes for peace if this modest beginning was kept discreetly quiet and not widely discussed. Both sides seemed to be very pleased with the outcome of the Conversation, and particularly with the friendships that had begun to be established. Dean Robinson wrote a personal letter to Cardinal Mercier, thanking him for his hospitality.

Events now took an unexpected turn. At the end of January 1921, six weeks after the first meeting at Malines, Pope Benedict XV died. Cardinal Mercier, together with his fellow Cardinals, headed for Rome to participate in the conclave to elect a new Pope. Archbishop Davidson, the Archbishop of Canterbury, mused in a letter to Walter Frere on 4 February, 'What a strange thing it would be if your Cardinal host were to remain in the Vatican. I do not imagine that it is probable; but I have heard it suggested as not quite improbable.'[9]

In the event, it was Achille Ratti, Archbishop of Milan, who was elected Pope on 6 February 1921, and he took the name Pius XI. The new Pope was a personal friend of Mercier, and the day after the election he met with him in private. In the Cardinal's notes in Malines, it is clear that Mercier spoke to the Pope about the private meeting he had held at Malines with the Anglican theologians, and he notes the Pope's response as 'I can see nothing but good from these meetings.'

Despite the agreement of the participants at Malines to keep their meetings as discreet as possible, in September 1922 the whole affair was brought to the notice of the public by the publication by Lord Halifax of a pamphlet entitled *A Call to Reunion, by Viscount Halifax, Arising out of*

---

8 Letter of Dr Robinson to Lord Halifax, 12th December 1921, Malines Papers, Lord Halifax File A4 271, Box 1.

9 Letter of Archbishop Davidson to Walter Frere, 4 February 1922, Lambeth Palace Archives, box 186, File 1.

Discussions with Cardinal Mercier, to which is Appended a Translation of the Cardinal's Pastoral Letter to his Diocese. Originally this was intended as a response to a request from the Cardinal for the publication of an English translation of his Pastoral Letter to his diocese. Mercier's Pastoral was principally concerned with the institution of the papacy, highlighted by the recent election of Pius XI, and the rights of the successors of St Peter. But Halifax was not at all keen to publish it unadorned, as he considered some phrases and expressions would not be acceptable to the ears of the English public. Once started on the project, however, the Viscount warmed to his subject and, together with a foreword, included also an account of the First Conversation and the text of the Memorandum that had been discussed. Because of the agreement to keep the Conversations private, Halifax had to obtain the consent of the other participants, and, although not all agreed on the wisdom of his project, Halifax went ahead with publication.

Although Archbishop Davidson tried to distance himself from any involvement with the publication, and insisted that the Malines meetings were a private affair of Lord Halifax, there was, nevertheless, pressure on him to give some kind of official or semi-official backing to the meetings with the Roman Catholics at Malines. Halifax also wrote to Cardinal Mercier urging him to obtain some kind of recognition from the Vatican. Although Mercier had received some personal encouragement from Rome, he now felt obliged to write asking for a more official approval, which he could show to the Anglicans as proof that Rome really did approve and support the meetings. A reply came very quickly from the Secretary of State, Cardinal Gasparri, stating that 'the Holy See approved and encouraged the Conversations and [he] prayed with all his heart that God would bless them'.[10]

In his own memoir, Walter Frere describes all this frantic negotiation in his normal calm way:

A year passed; this was full of discussion as to future continuance of the Conversations thus begun: filled by correspondence with the Authorities, here in England, by mutual visits between Hickleton and Mirfield, and by correspondence with the Cardinal, in which, besides

---

10 Letter of Gasparri to Mercier, 25 November 1922, Archdiocese of Malines Archives, Cardinal Mercier files, B1.

Lord Halifax, the Archbishop of Canterbury took some part ... Soon the question arose as to the members who should take part in any future continuance, their number, and the amount of authority that they should have; it was felt on both sides that there should be more recognition of what was going on, though still not any authoritative approval.

Before the year was out, the Cardinal wrote saying that he had reason to believe that the Conversations were being followed with approval in Rome, and that their continuance would be well regarded. This led to the same question being more distinctly raised on the English side, and some little skirmishing as to the amount of authority and responsibility that either party would take. In the end, a happy solution was reached. The same people were to go to the Conferences as before; they would go with the approval of their Authorities; but they would make their own programme, would be responsible for their own statements, and would not be in any sense official representatives of either side.[11]

Once again it was the Anglicans who prepared the Memorandum, more precisely Halifax and Frere, who spent two days drawing up the points for discussion. This agenda for the second Conversation was principally on practical aspects of reunion. How could the Roman Church deal with issues like the Anglican communion, the validation of Orders, the autonomy of local dioceses, and, indeed, what would happen to the existing Roman Catholic hierarchy?

Frere explains that, whereas the first meeting had dealt with establishing points of agreement, this second meeting attempted to deal with some of the more controversial issues. He states:

In this set of Conversations there was a much further approach made to the hot points of controversy; the previous set had aimed at establishing the points where agreement could fairly easily be found. This one raised some of the thorniest questions, those on which any sort of agreement was much more unlikely. It would not have been possible to have carried it on with the frankness and good temper

---

11 Frere, *Recollections of Malines*, pp. 30–1.

which prevailed, unless already the group that was gathered round the table had achieved a very close friendship, mutual respect and unity of heart.[12]

On returning to England, Frere and Dr Robinson reported to the Archbishop of Canterbury on 16 March 1923, and brought him the minutes of the Conversations, in both English and French. The participants at the meeting had countersigned the minutes to signify that they were accurate, but Davidson thought the signatures meant agreement, and he was not at all happy. Frere noted that even 'the breathing of the word *pallium* caused shudders in Lambeth and elsewhere'.

The Archbishop was becoming increasingly concerned that practical issues were being discussed without the fundamental dogmatic issues having been addressed, and hence he began to push for additional participants for the Malines meetings who would present more forcefully the Anglican position, especially on the topic of papal primacy. This was a delicate matter as he did not wish to be seen to be sending 'representatives', but a little public controversy between Bishop Charles Gore of Oxford and Mgr Pierre Batiffol, a French Catholic theologian, helped with the suggestion that they argue around the Cardinal's table rather than in public. Another two figures were added to the participants at the third Conversation, Dr Kidd of Keble College, Oxford, and Père Hippolyte Hemmer, a well-known French church historian. Walter Frere notes that this seemed to be a suitable framework for renewed meetings.

Thus we begin the second phase of the Conversations, which, while retaining the ground won at the exploratory conferences in the way of friendly and mutual understanding, was able to go more into details and use more formal kind of discussion. The increase in the numbers necessarily made the discussion a little more formal; but also a great deal more was done this time in the way of preparation of papers and replies to papers.[13]

Another helpful event was a colloquy held at Lambeth in October 1923

---

12 Frere, *Recollections of Malines*, p. 32.
13 Frere, *Recollections of Malines*, p. 38.

and attended by representatives of many different phases of English Church life. This colloquy did a great deal of good, as it brought many into contact with the real facts, and was able to allay many suspicions. The Archbishop of Canterbury introduced the topic himself, expressing his view of the situation, explaining what had been done already, and what was in contemplation. Frere notes that the Archbishop put the matter before the whole body, and an important and helpful discussion ensued.

The third group of Conversations began on 7 November 1923, and many important papers were read by the participants, particularly on the papacy and its place in the primitive Church. Frere recalls his own impression that the biblical points put forward by the Anglicans had not really been faced: 'Apparently one or two texts concerning St Peter had hypnotized the Roman Catholics in their outlook, to the exclusion of the scriptural description of the Church itself. The differences revealed were wide.'[14] At the end of the meetings it was agreed that very encouraging results had come from the present series of Conversations, but that the doctrine underlying the papal claim needed fuller examination later on.

Apart from the participants at the Conversations and the few people in the know, there was, as time went on, a growing leakage of information and misinformation about what was happening at Malines. Following this third Conversation, the Archbishop of Canterbury determined to issue a circular letter to the bishops and Metropolitans of the Anglican Communion. It was framed as a report on the consequences to the Lambeth Appeal, which the bishops had issued in 1920, but it also gave him the opportunity to give an account of what was happening at Malines. Frere reports on its effect as follows:

> The immediate effect of the Letter, as might be supposed, was to cause a somewhat violent reaction in two opposite camps; the English Roman Catholics were greatly upset to know what had been going on, and there was a considerable agitation caused in Protestant circles in England, both inside and outside the Church, accompanied by something like protest and dismay.[15]

---

14 Frere, *Recollections of Malines*, p. 43.
15 Frere, *Recollections of Malines*, p. 48.

On the other side of the Channel, Cardinal Mercier came under attack for his hosting of the Conversations, with particular blasts of disapproval from his co-religionists on the English side of the Channel. The Cardinal decided to reply by means of a letter to his clergy of 18 January 1924, which was devoted to an explanation and justification of the Conversations at Malines.

The time before the next meeting was dragged out because of difficulties in coordinating timetables and the recuperation of the Dean of Wells from an accident. But the time was used fruitfully in informal meetings both in England and in Malines in preparing memoranda for the next Conversations. Walter Frere speaks warmly of his work sessions in the Cardinal's palace at Malines:

> in the Cardinal's house too there was the added warmth of pure friendship. I remember several details of the conversation round his table of a very friendly character, with plenty of chaff and fun between the meetings. The Frenchmen generally led the way in this, Portal with a rich but very quiet humour, Batiffol very sparkling and brilliant. I remember going out with Bishop Gore for a short walk before our morning meeting; as we got outside we found a Rogationtide procession on its way through the parish, so we joined in and followed for some time until it was time to get back to our gathering.

> At déjeuner subsequently Batiffol said to the Cardinal, 'Eminence, do you know that there were two Anglican Bishops following in the Rogationtide procession this morning?'
> The Cardinal in his grave way said, 'Then indeed we are coming nearer to unity.'
> 'Yes', said Batiffol, 'but does your Eminence know that they didn't follow the procession the whole way?'
> 'Ah?' said the Cardinal.
> 'No, they left just before the prayer for the Pope.' This scandalous misstatement was drowned in roars of laughter; in fact we had left in the middle of the invocation of Virgin Martyrs.[16]

---

16 Frere, *Recollections of Malines*, pp. 52–3.

The fourth Conversation at Malines was eventually held on 19 and 20 May 1925. There were no new members of the groups, and so the representatives were the same as those of the third meeting, namely, Cardinal Mercier; Dr Walter Frere, Bishop of Truro; Dr Charles Gore, former Bishop of Oxford; Dr Armitage Robinson, Dean of Wells; Dr Beresford Kidd, Warden of Keble College, Oxford; Mgr Van Roey, Vicar-General of Malines; M. Fernand Portal, Congregation of the Mission; Mgr Pierre Batiffol, Canon of Notre-Dame at Paris; M. Hemmer, Parish Priest of La Sainte-Trinité at Paris.

The theme for these meetings was principally the papacy and the relationship between bishops and the Pope, and the first day was taken up with theological and historical papers, and vigorous discussions. On the second day, Cardinal Mercier presented a paper which he said was in response to a question he had put to a canonist, namely, 'Is it possible that the English Church could be re-united without being absorbed in the Roman Church?' The Cardinal presented this paper on his own private responsibility, and he said he would report this personal initiative to Rome. Frere noted that:

> the document consists of an introduction, an historical consideration, a description of the existing Uniate plans, and finally an application of considerations of this sort to the case of England, before leading up to practical conclusions.

> All this took our breath away, especially as it seemed to lead up to a proposal for a Canterbury patriarchate.[17]

Frere stated that, without having the document in hand, it was impossible to discuss the contents properly, and so, after some short discussion, the meeting moved on to the prepared texts.

The topics chosen as the subject for these meetings, centring as they did on the Roman claims to papal primacy, elicited frank discussions and not a few points of disagreement. At the conclusion of the meeting, it was decided that in the minutes they should concentrate on the points of agreement rather than magnifying those of disagreement.

---

17 Frere, *Recollections of Malines*, p. 56.

This meeting proved to be the last of the Conversations held under the presidency of Cardinal Mercier. It had been hoped that not too long would elapse until the next meeting and much correspondence ensued to this end. It was hoped also that some kind of report could be prepared for publication which would summarize what had been done. The Cardinal fell ill, however, and all hopes for a speedy resumption faded. In July of 1925, Lord Halifax accepted the invitation to give a speech at the Anglo-Catholic Congress at the Albert Hall in London, and he incorporated into his speech the theme that Cardinal Mercier had spoken about in his Memorandum. Reunion, he claimed, was not a case of absorption of the Church of England, but rather the union of the two Churches under the primacy of the successor of St Peter, the Bishop of Rome.

In the audience that evening was a Jesuit priest, Fr Francis Woodlock, who himself was engaged in various ecumenical efforts. Fr Woodlock took exception to that part of Halifax's speech wherein he claimed the merits of the historic claims of Canterbury. Woodlock wrote to Halifax protesting this claim, and he proceeded to publish his objections in the press both in England and in France. It soon became clear that English bishops in England and in Rome were putting pressure on the Vatican to bring a swift end to these Conversations at Malines.

The fifth Conversation was scheduled eventually for January 1926, but in December it became clear that Cardinal Mercier's cancer was terminal. He wrote to Halifax saying that the meetings would take place under the chairmanship of Van Roey. In a series of letters to Abbé Portal, Halifax expressed his increasing concern for the Belgian prelate, and asked Portal to join him in visiting their dying friend and to seek his benediction. In the same letters of 18 January, he told Portal that he wanted to ask Cardinal Mercier if he would write to the Archbishop of Canterbury, to the Pope and to Cardinal Bourne urging them to continue the work which he had begun for the cause of reunion.

It was at this last encounter that Cardinal Mercier gave Halifax his episcopal ring as a memento, and after Halifax and the others had departed, Cardinal Mercier dictated his final letter to the Archbishop of Canterbury. There is no indication of letters to either the Pope or Cardinal Bourne, which were probably never written. Two days later the Cardinal died.

There was also a certain amount of anxiety on the part of Frere and Halifax about the French language report of the Conversations as Batiffol, who was responsible for them, seemed to be dragging his feet. Walter Frere notes his concern in his laconic manner as follows:

> I think I detect also a certain tendency to regard everything that is said on our side as a kind of 'supplica', addressed to the authorities by the wandering sheep and that inclines them to think, probably unconsciously, that the right thing is that we should do all the documenting, and they at the proper moment should give a suitable reply to our petitions.

> I believe they are shaped like this, and I can't help feeling that that is what is inbred in them and it may add to their slowness about putting anything down.But in any case, do stir up the Abbé to get something done.[18]

The fifth Conversation was now rescheduled for the end of June 1926, when Abbé Portal became ill and died in that month. Lord Halifax was so devastated that he had neither the energy nor the will to attend his friend's funeral.

When the fifth Conversation was eventually arranged for 11 and 12 October 1926, it turned out to be a very cursory affair, its main objective being to draw up a report of all the previous meetings. It was proposed that there be two reports, one from each of the participating sides, with the Roman report placing more emphasis on the positive aspects of points of agreement from the meetings, but complementary to the Anglican report. The first day was spent drawing up the Anglican report and the second on the Roman report, both sides agreeing to the contents. It was also agreed that both reports should be published in their original language.

In preparation for the fifth meeting at Malines, Halifax had drawn up a Memorandum of how he had seen the meetings progress, and a copy in the Frere archives shows how heavily edited it had been by Frere. With the risk of offending his old friend, Frere felt obliged to state clearly his objections. In a letter of 18 September 1926, Frere wrote:

---

18 Letter of Frere to Halifax, 1 April 1926, Borthwick Institute, York, Mirfield Deposit, W.H. Frere, 1.6/1.

Thank you for your letter and the copy of yours to the Archbishop with its appendices. I think it would be a gain in view of it to have a further talk before we go to Malines: and it would be best at Lambeth with the Archbishop if he would have us.

We could then discuss and if necessary amend the three passages in the Draft Memorandum and so have it more fully ready for discussion with our R.C. colleagues. But until we meet them much is uncertain. They unfortunately did not set to work to do their Report when we did ours: and all has been confusion since out of which all that we know is a general approval of the Memorandum from Batiffol and some details of criticism from Portal. In particular we do not know the new archbishop's mind: nor what he would say to Portal's criticism of his paper. That however is surely very important. However these details can't be dealt with finally till Malines and after.

As to your notes I cannot agree to their publication along with our Joint Memorandum. I ought to explain why. They would create an impression I think that what in fact were preliminaries intended to lead up to serious discussion, were <u>results</u> acquired after serious discussion. Such an impression would mislead I fear, and do great harm to the cause. My reasons then why I could not agree to your Notes being published with our memorandum are (a) they are out of proportion – the porch is made bigger than the house: and (b) they give a misleading importance to a preliminary exploration of the ground to be covered and present as results things that were only preliminaries. It is I suppose open to you to publish them without the consent of any of the rest of us: well, but if so, you must be prepared for others to do the same and repudiate what you say. And then what a pretty result of an attempt after Union for the enemy to jeer about!

I have no authority to speak for others but in friendship and love I ought to tell you what is in my own mind. Hitherto I have kept silence with difficulty when you have said in pamphlet and in speech things which seemed to me not tenable and have so connected them with the Malines Conversations, as to my mind to create a danger of the Conversations being misinterpreted.

You have said (I know) that you spoke only for yourself, that in a way exonerates me; but it also challenges me to speak for myself when the time comes. I am very unwilling that it should come; and I hope it will not: but it must if you continue the policy of individual action apart from others.

I hate to have to write thus. But we have come to a point at which it would not be loyal or honest if I didn't.

There is my big objection to the Notes. I don't therefore stop over any points of detail in criticism of them.

I am as I have always said in favour of making such additions of a hopeful kind as we can agree to make to the Memorandum. But I think we shall do this best at Malines and on our return.

Meanwhile we must recover our confidence in one another and our mutual understanding. That I think and hope may be done by meeting for a few days before we start and especially if the archbishop will help us himself.[19]

Even when they returned to England, Halifax lobbied the other Anglican participants to agree to a supplement to the Anglican Report. The supplement requested by Halifax read as follows:

It may be convenient to add a few words to the Report, partly of summary, and partly of anticipation. The Conversations have touched upon questions both of doctrines and discipline.

On the first two occasions the main object was to ascertain that in both of these spheres there was sufficient agreement to justify a further and more detailed examination of the main points at issue.

The first Conversation shewed that a considerable number of dogmatic questions, which had been subjects of contention in the past, need not

---

19 Letter of 18 September 1926, Mirfield Deposit, W.H. Frere, 1.6/1.

be so in the future at all, or at any rate not in the same degree. The second revealed new possibilities with regard to organisation. Then the more detailed examination began with the third Conversation, at which the membership of the conference was increased from 6 to 10. On that occasion the crucial question of the papacy occupied the whole time; and this subject was continued during the greater part of the fourth Conversation. Some space however was given then to further proposals on the subject of organisation put forward from the Roman Catholic side.

The fifth meeting (Oct 11, 12, 1926) with its numbers reduced on the one side by the irreparable loss of Cardinal Mercier and the Abbé Portal and on the other by the absence of Bishop Gore and the Dean of Wells, was concerned only with the drawing up of the Reports.

The net gain of this series of Conversations may be described as the elimination of several subjects which have ceased to be causes of difference, and the elucidation of others that still remain. As regards other dogmatic points, including those that were handled briefly in the first Conversation, there is an opening for further discussions which, we think, would be profitable, and would lead not only to a better understanding but also to a greater measure of general agreement upon the matters in question.[20]

The one objective that now remained to Lord Halifax was to see to the completion and publication of the two reports. Halifax expected that they would be in print within a reasonable time, and certainly before Christmas of that year. The two reports were to be published together as, at least in Halifax's mind, 'the French document, with its greater emphasis upon what had been agreed, put the English document into a better perspective'.[21] He could not have foreseen the difficulties that began to emerge.

In England, Archbishop Davidson began to show even greater reluctance to involve himself in the publication of anything connected

---

20 Loose page notes, Mirfield Deposit, W.H. Frere, 1.3/6.2.

21 J.G. Lockhart, *Charles Lindley, Viscount Halifax* (London: Centenary Press, 1935), vol. 2, p. 333.

with Malines, and was uncomfortable about the reports finding their way into the public forum. At this time there was an ongoing controversy about the Revised Prayer Book and its passage through Parliament. Although this was entirely unconnected with the happenings at Malines, many of the more Protestant-inclined members of the Church of England were linking the revision of the Prayer Book with the Conversations at Malines. Halifax himself then fell ill, and was unable to take up the cause of publication again until April 1927.

It was then that Halifax heard from Gore that there were difficulties on the Roman side as to the publication of the reports. Bishop Gore wrote that he had met both Hemmer and Batiffol in Paris, and they informed him that since Cardinal Mercier's death the Pope's sympathy with the Conversations was gone, and that Cardinal Bourne's influence was now in the ascendancy. Gore told Halifax that Batiffol was clearly nervous about the publication of the Malines Reports, and wanted only the English edition printed without any preface from the Archbishop of Canterbury.

Walter Frere had also been busy trying to convince Archbishop Davidson to hasten with the publication of the Report, but without success. Frere reported to Halifax on 7 June 1927 that he was thinking of going to Paris to visit Batiffol and Hemmer and 'see what was the matter'. Frere told Halifax that this impressed the Archbishop more than all the correspondence he had received. About Hemmer and Batiffol, Frere stated that 'they have been got at by the English Romans and are being tempted to hold the whole thing up'.[22]

In the end it was not Frere who went to Paris, but the 88-year-old Halifax. He met with Hemmer and Batiffol, and wrote to Archbishop Davidson on 25 July 1927, reporting that:

I have given up going to Wells, have given up asking the Dean of Wells to take the steps I had had in my mind, and which our French Friends, in view of nothing better, had advocated and agreed to; and have thought of another step which will, I think, if successful, be more effectual and which involves no one but myself, and can expose no one, other than myself, should there be any, to blame. I am remembering

---

22 Letter of Frere to Halifax, 7 June 1927, Mirfield Deposit, W.H. Frere, box 1.6/1.

what your Grace said about 'not committing me' and can assure your Grace that is the last thing I wish or have in my mind.

The situation at Rome, owing to Cardinal Bourne and Cardinal Gasquet's actions (I should say intrigues) is that the Pope's mind has been changed and that a message has been sent to Archbishop Van Roey that the Conversations at Malines must cease and that those (the Frenchmen) who took part in them must not publish their report as had been agreed to at our last meeting at Malines and which, if there had not been all these delays, would have been in the hands of the public by now.

The French, Hemmer (who is most friendly – and much annoyed) wished both accounts, theirs and our, to appear together as had been agreed, said quite clearly they could publish nothing themselves. Privately, I think Hemmer for one would not be sorry if someone took the bull by the horns and published what they are forbidden to do.

I saw him and Mgr Batiffol several times. Batiffol had seen and had a long conversation with the Pope, but as your Grace knows, Portal did not trust Batiffol as he did Hemmer. The other Frenchmen I saw were all most sympathetic and did not conceal their annoyance at and dislike of the action at Rome.

... Therefore, if anything has to be done it must be done here – in England – with an eye to France.[23]

It was after this trip to France that Halifax decided to publish the reports himself. He knew that it was not what officialdom wanted, and he regretted that he could not conform to the wishes of the Archbishop of Canterbury, and states that this is a matter of 'deep regret'. However, it was obvious that both the Anglican and Roman Church authorities had vested interests in delaying the publication, and, in the case of the Roman Church, of not proceeding at all.

---

23 Letter of Halifax to Davidson, 25 July 1927, Malines Papers of Lord Halifax, A4 271, Box 9.

On 15 December 1927, the House of Commons rejected the Revised Prayer Book, and Halifax now felt free to proceed. He sent advance copies to all the participants of the Conversations, and despite the protests and hesitations of almost all of them, the reports became public in January 1928 under the title 'The Conversations at Malines'. In the same month appeared the Papal Encyclical *Mortalium Animos* of Pius XI, in which the pontiff condemned certain unnamed movements involved in the efforts for Christian unity, and in which he also reiterated in strong terminology the doctrine of Papal Supremacy.

Halifax maintained that the Encyclical was directed at the World Conference on Faith and Order which had met the previous year, but there were certainly parts of the Encyclical which could be aimed at Malines. In January 1928, the *Osservatore Romano* announced that there were to be no further Conversations.

Although the Conversations looked like a failure at the time, they set the groundwork for future initiatives such as the ARCIC talks, but they had to wait until the Roman Catholic Church had undergone the cataclysmic renewal that was Vatican II. But it was the faith and perseverance of strong personalities that prepared the ground for sowing, among whom Walter Frere was one. His ability to be at ease with everyone, his modesty, his humour and the equilibrium he brought to the other participants, in particular Lord Halifax, contributed in a major way to the fact that the meetings took place at all.

7

Between the Devil and the deep blue sea: Prayer Book revision and beyond

PHILIP CORBETT

Rather than examine the minutiae of the Prayer Book revision crisis and repeat what other authors have said,[1] in this chapter I intend to investigate what part the opinions and actions of Walter Frere played in the failure of the 1928 Revision to be ratified. I will also consider Frere's role in the revision of Prayer Books around the Anglican Communion and his imprint on the liturgies of the Communion. The 1928 Prayer Book and Frere's contribution to it have influenced all subsequent Anglican liturgies. That the Prayer Book is still held in high regard is shown by the 2008 edition, designed for public worship and private devotion. Indeed, very often when a church describes itself as 'Prayer Book' the liturgy found there is the 1928 Prayer Book. Whilst many of the proponents of Prayer Book revision may have felt that they had failed in securing a permanent change, the effects of the work carried out by those pressing for revision has lasted.

Frere was always interested in liturgical reform. He had a strong interest in the Book of Common Prayer, had studied it in detail, and had revised and rewritten Procter's *History of the Book of Common Prayer* (Frere's edition was first published in 1901). He was a great liturgical scholar with a great zeal for reform, but by the end of his life he would find himself tired by the struggle. After the 1928 revisions failed to go through, he

---

1 Most recently by Donald Gray, *The 1927–28 Prayer Book Crisis* (2 vols., Alcuin Club. Norwich: SCM-Canterbury Press, 2005–6).

wrote to the Bishop of Pretoria that 'the spirit of generosity has faded and has been replaced by a general desire to tie up everyone who is regarded as tiresome; that is to say Anglo-Catholics'.[2] Frere partly included himself in this; he realized that liturgical reform stirred up in people powerful and conflicting passions, which he described in terms of eruptions and earthquakes.[3] Frere was one for calm study and reflection, as is shown in his first major work in this area: *Some Principles of Liturgical Reform*.[4] In this book, he stressed that reform was long overdue but that it was a process that needed to include the whole Church, not just the Church of England, and that could not and should not be rushed. Frere argued that in the revision process ancient texts should be studied and explored so as to better understand the shape of the liturgy. He also stressed that what was needed was not simply a tinkering with the Prayer Book but an entire overhaul. Frere believed that the 1662 Book was out of touch with the people. They needed to be engaged with – in the Catholic context this would include the expansion of ritual and of devotions to the saints, etc., and also the issue of Reservation of the Sacrament. Frere feared that if there was not a complete overhaul of the texts there would be unauthorized local revisions, such as those carried out by many more ritually advanced Anglo-Catholic clergy. He hoped that revision would help to enforce more uniformity, and that this would be done on more Catholic lines, with the 1662 Book remaining for more conservative churchmen. In 1912 the Archbishop of Canterbury proposed that there should be an Advisory Committee on Liturgical Affairs; Frere would sit on this Committee as would fellow Alcuin Club member Percy Dearmer. The two would work together, allocating questions to the one better suited to answer.

It is interesting that Frere should write so passionately about making the liturgy more accessible to the people, especially when it came to the service of Holy Communion. In the 1890s, whilst at St Faith's Church in Stepney, Frere was one of the pioneers of what would become the Parish Communion Movement, which sought to establish the main service on

---

2 Letter from Frere to Neville Talbot CR, Bishop of Pretoria, in R.C.D. Jasper (ed.), *Walter Howard Frere: His Correspondence on Liturgical Revision and Construction* (Alcuin Club. London: SPCK, 1954), p. 172.

3 Jasper, *Frere*, p. 179 ff.

4 W.H. Frere, *Some Principles of Liturgical Reform* (London: Murray, 1911).

Sunday as Holy Communion, ensuring that the Parish Eucharist was central to the weekly life of the Church. And thus revision of the rite of Holy Communion would be central to Frere's hopes for overall revision. He also hoped to encourage the laity to attend mattins and evensong. To this end, in 1925 he proposed a complete revision and reworking of the Psalter. This, he argued, should be rewritten in a more lyrical style to make it easier for congregations to sing, maintaining that often the psalms were unintelligible and that the laity received no spiritual nourishment from them. His proposals, however, which would have resulted in the omission of 14 psalms and 66 verses, were strongly opposed by evangelicals and generally fell on deaf ears. The proposals would not be discussed in the 1928 revision – although, in the decades following Frere's original suggestions, work would begin on revising the Psalter to make it easier to use. The 1980 Alternative Service Book Psalter and the *Common Worship* Psalter do allow for some verses to be omitted in reading, those verses being placed in brackets. Morning and Evening Prayer in the nineteenth and early twentieth century continued to be the preserve of the priest or parish clerk. Frere proposed that if 50 or more people were due to attend mattins or evensong and it was appropriate, a church might consider the use of solemn mattins (that is with acolytes and incense) and in such cases the laity should be used as readers and servers to encourage them to attend.

Frere might be described as a gentle Anglo-Catholic; liturgically he came from the 'English Use' branch of Anglo-Catholicism. He was not one who looked to Rome and he was far removed from Anglo-Papalism. His Catholicism was shared liturgically by the likes of Percy Dearmer and the Alcuin Club, of which Frere was the president. The Alcuin Club sought to show that the Prayer Book of 1662 was indeed a Catholic liturgy and saw the need for the revival of an English Catholic ceremonial along the lines of the Use of Sarum. Many of Frere's own papers relating to liturgy would be published by the Alcuin Club. Anglo-Catholicism has never been a monochrome grouping within the Church; it is far from monochrome today and it certainly was not at the turn of the century. These divides in Anglo-Catholicism would make Prayer Book revision almost impossible. Those who looked to the English liturgy would find themselves at loggerheads with those who sought to use Roman Catholic liturgical texts or the English Missal and its related texts. Indeed, by the 1920s there were several liturgical books that were used by more advanced clergy. These included *The Priest to the Altar*,[5] published at the end of the nineteenth century and containing various liturgical texts for use by priests. Many ritualist clergy would intersperse the Prayer Book Holy Communion with Latin texts or the canon from the Roman Catholic liturgy. One of the areas in which Prayer Book revision hoped to enforce some uniformity was over the use of unauthorized texts. In this hope Frere would come into conflict with many Anglo-Catholics. In many of the more 'extreme' churches he was viewed with some suspicion, although many saw him as a champion of the Catholic cause. This is illustrated in a short article from the January 1924 edition of the *Graham Street Quarterly*, the magazine of St Mary's, Bourne Street, an Anglo-Papalist bastion. The anonymous author writes that 'Dr Frere belongs to that element in the Catholic movement which is least in sympathy with us', and goes on to explain Frere's background as a bishop and member of the Community of the Resurrection, stating that he has had ample opportunity to gain a good grasp of the liturgy. The author then sets out his hopes and fears concerning Frere and the revision:

> Our one fear is that he may feel himself bound by his conscience to limit the development of the Catholic movement along the lines which he himself believes to be right ... we trust however that he will see the necessity in the present state of affairs of allowing a latitude in the practice of Catholic devotion which goes beyond what he himself would be inclined to desire.

Frere was to be faced with the great dilemma brought about by the various groups within the broad Catholic movement of which he was a part. Much of his work would be in managing their different desires and aspirations alongside his own conscience.

Frere's attitude to the more extreme Anglo-Papalist elements in Anglo-Catholicism can be illustrated through his views on the Reservation of the Blessed Sacrament. Frere believed in Reservation, but did so in the context of a very English Catholicism. In a letter of 8 November 1926 to the Bishop of Southwark, Frere indicates that, whilst he hopes that Reservation will be allowed in the revised Prayer Book, he also hopes that

---

5 *The Priest to the Altar* (3rd edn, London: Rivingtons, 1879).

the tabernacle will not be allowed. Rather he favours the more English hanging pyx, arguing that it is better to revert to an 'English custom and not adopt a foreign one'.[6] Without a tabernacle, Frere insists, people will be less likely to genuflect or do something in the particular direction of the Sacrament. It will, he suggests, also make life easier for clergy, and servers do not 'feel the same way constrained to pay respect and reverence' when the Sacrament is held in a hanging pyx as 'all is on a higher plane, and the Presence is pervaded rather than localised'.[7] Frere goes on to counter those who would seek to follow the practices of Rome by insisting that the Sacrament when reserved will be used only when the priest takes Communion to the sick and at no other time:

> We can't regulate the services in any complete sort of way, or prescribe what may be said or what may not. Someone reciting the ordinary Prayer Book Litany to the Sacrament may be doing exactly what we should not wish, but we can't prevent it; still less can we prevent the singing of such a hymn as 'Jesu, my Lord, my God, my All' with that intention. What I think can be prescribed is that the Sacrament should not be removed for any purpose except Communion.[8]

Here Frere is clearly arguing against any devotion to the Sacrament and certainly against the service of Benediction, which was used in many ritualist parishes in the 1920s.[9] There was for Frere to be no thought of prayer to the Sacrament; its reservation in a hanging pyx gave the sense of the presence of the divine but its use was strictly limited. He hoped that the custom of giving Communion to the sick would, once adopted, be used 'wherever there is the need, and by all sorts of churchmen'.[10] This move to regulate the use of the Reserved Sacrament would be opposed by many hard-line Anglo-Catholics; as Lord Halifax, the President of the English Church Union, pointed out:

---

6 A letter by Frere added as an appendix to D.L. Murray, *Reservation: Its Purpose and Method*, Alcuin Club Prayer Book Revision Pamphlets (2nd edn, 1953), p. 37.

7 Murray, *Reservation*, p. 38.

8 Murray, *Reservation*, p. 29.

9 For more details of Frere's response to ritualist practices, especially those at the Church of St Hilary, Mazarion, when Frere was Bishop of Truro, see Chapter 4.

10 Murray, *Reservation*, p. 40.

Do you think that those clergy, and there are many throughout the length and breadth of the country, who really believe, when they recite the Creed, in the Catholic Church and the Catholic heritage of the Church of England, and who have the support of a devoted band of laymen behind them, are likely to abstain from such adoration of our Blessed Lord in the Reserved Sacrament as they are accustomed to give Him in the celebration of Holy Communion? Do you imagine they will submit to the surrender of what has become their usual practice in celebrating divine service, and that not merely in England, but in South Africa and in the United States of America?[11]

The question of Reservation would be a bone of contention, with the Protestant clergy not wishing to countenance it at all, and the more Catholic feeling that any measure did not go far enough. There were the moderate English Use Catholics in the middle. The difficulty, as we have seen, is that they were too small a minority within the minority of Anglo-Catholicism to have any effect on the outcome of the votes in Parliament.[12] It is interesting to note that Frere was until his death the Visitor of the Benedictine Nashdom Community, which used only Roman Catholic liturgies, and often in Latin. Frere, it would seem, was happy not to interfere with the life of this Community when it came to liturgy, seeing his work as more pastoral.

Indeed some people, Lord Halifax for example, would have preferred that the 1549 Prayer Book be authorized for use in the Church of England. This was a view shared by many of the moderate members of the English Church Union who would eventually feel unable to support the Revised Prayer Book. The 1549 Book had allowed for the Reservation of the Sacrament for Communion of the Sick but this rubric had been removed in the 1552 Book. The 1928 proposals returned to the 1549 rubric but did not go far enough for many. In the end Randall Davidson, the Archbishop of Canterbury, would entrust Cyril Garbett with the task of revising the rubric on Reservation – a thankless task, as no one would

---

11 Speech by Lord Halifax to the House of Lords in 1927, quoted in Sidney Dark, *Lord Halifax* (Milwaukee: Morehouse, 1934).

12 It is interesting to note that in the Community Church at Mirfield a hanging pyx is still used for the reservation of the Sacrament. The pyx itself was originally used in Truro Cathedral when Frere was Bishop.

be happy. As Charles Smyth records in his biography of Garbett, the latter was a stickler for the rules. He was a high churchman and not an Anglo-Catholic. What he sought was uniformity, which would be difficult to achieve.[13] Writing about liturgical revision, Garbett himself would acknowledge the value of the 1928 revision which sought to deepen the Church of England's appreciation of the Communion of Saints. Garbett comments that until 1928 public worship had been noticeably weak in its expression of the Communion of Saints. He suggests that by revising the kalendar of the Prayer Book there has been a deepening of the devotion to the departed of all centuries and that this has led throughout the Church of England to bringing 'home the reality of Paradise and of the Communion of Saints'.[14]

Frere himself supported the Alcuin Club's proposals for revision which, in pamphlet form, became known as the 'Orange Books'. The English Church Union also published their proposals as the 'Green Book'. There were then two sets of proposals from the Anglo-Catholic wing of the Church. This would prove difficult. Whilst not all of the 'Orange Books' proposals would make the Deposited Book, they did greatly influence Frere's understanding of the revision process.

The Alcuin Club had been founded by four Anglican laymen in 1897, its stated aim to 'promote the study and history of the Book of Common Prayer'.[15] Frere would be a loyal member and would work for it in many ways; indeed, the Club would eventually publish his papers on liturgical matters. The 'Orange Books' were published from 1912 onwards and Frere was on the publishing committee (the founder of the Community of the Resurrection was at that time the Club's president). The 14 pamphlets covered a wide range of topics from Reservation to Eucharistic Prayers. The Club, however, sought to claim that it took 'no side in the discussion' as to whether revision was advisable.[16] This may seem a strange claim, given that by 1923 the Club felt its executive needed to meet on a fixed day

---

13 Charles Smyth, *Cyril Foster Garbett* (London: Hodder and Stoughton, 1959), pp. 146–7.

14 Cyril Garbett, *The Worship of the Church*, an extract first published in 1947. Reprinted as an extract in *Faith and Worship* No. 63 (Michaelmas 2008), p. 26.

15 George Timms, 'The History of the Alcuin Club', in Peter Jagger, *The Alcuin Club and its Publications 1897–1987* (2nd edn, Norwich: Hymns Ancient and Modern, 1986), p. 6.

16 Timms, 'History', p. 9.

of each month so as to keep abreast of the situation.[17] The pamphlets seem to reflect Frere's standpoint on revision, that it should be based on what might be described as the English Use tradition. Frere believed that there should be a number of options and that experimentation could be allowed on a broad basis rather than a narrow party basis. The Alcuin Club's difficulty was that, rather than coming out with firm proposals, it sought to nudge people along with suggestions of moderate high-church practice. The alternative was offered in the Catholic wing by the Church Union which put forward more strident demands for revision. Neither side would be satisfied with the outcome. Frere himself made the greatest contribution to the work of Prayer Book revision, yet he would in the end be forced to reject the final proposals. He did, however, authorize it for his own diocese and use it in his daily prayers. He was a moderate who believed that the liturgy should help in developing people's faith and lives. He was not popular among Anglo-Papalists who did not believe him to be a 'proper Catholic' (that is to say one who used the Latin rite of the Church). At one gathering of religious, a monk from Nashdom (a strongly Papalist community) commented 'That rogue Bishop Frere defiled our high altar by using English at it.'[18] His was to be very often a lonely stand for English liturgy.

Frere did have some success when it came to liturgical reform. He was known throughout the Anglican Communion as a leading liturgical scholar and reformer. He was consulted by many different Provinces with regard to the drawing up of liturgies for those Provinces that until the early twentieth century mainly used the 1662 Prayer Book. These revised liturgies reflected the strong influence of the Anglo-Catholic missionary societies: for example, the Church in South Africa and what was then Rhodesia were greatly influenced by Frere's own Community of the Resurrection, and their liturgies strongly reflect the liturgical style and theological position of that Community. Frere had hoped that the Church of England would have led the way in Prayer Book revision and that it would have set an example for Anglican churches overseas. When this process seemed to be slowing, and as the outcome was less than satisfactory, Frere decided to offer his advice independently of the work

---

17 Timms, 'History', p. 9.

18 Anselm Hughes, *The Rivers of the Flood* (London: Faith Press, 1961), quoted by Alan Wilkinson in 'Frere: Ecumenist, Feminist, Socialist', *Church Times*, 28 March 2008.

taking place in England. He must have found this a liberating experience, as the churches he helped were less constrained by assemblies and committees and there was less of a tendency towards Erastianism. He assisted in the reforms of the liturgies of the Church of Japan, the Church of Northern Rhodesia and the Church of Ceylon (1932), the Church of South Africa (1919) and the United Church of Southern India (1928). Working with these churches (especially in Africa) Frere developed ideas before work really began in England and before disappointment over the 1928 Prayer Book, which would hit him greatly. He believed that giving congregations and PCCs a choice over which Eucharistic Prayer to use was disrespectful not only to the clergy but to bishops as well. He was also never entirely happy with regulations regarding the Reservation of the Blessed Sacrament which left the decision firmly in the hands of diocesan bishops and which Frere believed would lead to an abuse of the regulations (either that they would be enforced too strictly or not at all). The English scene was far removed from the liberation of the churches of the Anglican Communion where Frere was able to offer assistance to churches in need of his liturgical expertise.

Frere's overriding concern in this area of his work was to ensure that the liturgy was of use to worshipping communities and that it reflected the adage *lex orandi, lex credendi* in each individual situation. One area where there was a clear pastoral need was in the churches that served 'Hebrew Christians'. This group of Jews who had converted to Christianity sought to retain some of their Jewish identity in their Christian worship. On 24 May 1924 Randall Davidson, the Archbishop of Canterbury, wrote to Frere concerning the translation of the Communion Service into Hebrew by one Dr Levertoff. Davidson was cautious about the translation, believing it to read like 'a Communion Office of a novel kind which has not been hitherto known in the Church of God'. Davidson's concerns had been further compounded on hearing that 'the Bishop of Truro approves of it'. In writing, the Archbishop seeks Frere's advice which he clearly holds in high regard. Frere was indeed in favour of the move, and for pastoral reasons. Agreeing that the liturgy would have to be carefully scrutinized and studied, Frere goes on to say, in a letter of 29 May, 'I would like to endorse the plea.' He argues that it is highly desirable to create a liturgy that would allow 'Hebrews to become Christians' without losing their 'own strong piety and liturgical tradition'. Frere urged that the liturgy should steer away from Latin or English traditions. Given current debates about the nature of Anglicanism Frere makes an interesting distinction here: he quite clearly wants the liturgy to be Anglican in its final conception but different and indeed unique when placed alongside other Anglican liturgies. For Frere, whilst this new book would have a clearly missionary aim, it would also have to be carefully based on Anglican doctrine and teaching. The final liturgy was entitled 'The Order of Service of the Meal of the Holy King' and was used at Holy Trinity, Shoreditch, where Levertoff was priest-in-charge. It has rarely been used in any other liturgical setting. Writing in *Liturgy and Worship*, W.K. Lowther Clarke comments that 'the beauty and impressiveness of the rite are beyond compare'. He was, however, less clear as to whether such a departure from liturgical tradition could ever be justified.[19] What is clear from Frere's involvement is that he believed that liturgy had both a missionary and a pastoral importance.

It was through his membership of the Community of the Resurrection that Frere might be said to have gained a deep understanding of what was required of liturgical revision for the Provinces of the Church in Africa. With a clear understanding of the needs of mission and pastoral care, Frere was well placed to revise these texts. The Liturgy of Northern Rhodesia was only ever provisional; it was, however, the only liturgy in the vernacular. English-speaking congregations in general used the South African Prayer Book, despite the comment by the Bishop of Northern Rhodesia in 1928 that 'our European congregations are the most conservative in the world; it is unlikely that they will ever willingly consent to anything but 1662 for use on Sundays'.[20] The Bishop did not see this as a problem as 'our own liturgy is never likely to be published in English'.[21] Thus it is interesting to note that the vernacular liturgies in Africa were often more Catholic than those used by the English-speaking congregations. And thus they contained provision for a Mass of the Catechumens and also for Eucharistic Prayers that more closely resemble Roman Catholic Eucharistic Prayers with a concern for the use of the

---

19 W.K. Lowther Clarke and C. Harris (eds), *Liturgy and Worship* (London: SPCK, 1932), pp. 815–6.

20 Letter from Dr Alston James Weller May, Bishop of Northern Rhodesia, to Frere, 21 December 1928, in Jasper, *Frere*, p. 242f.

214 Jasper, *Frere*, pp. 242f.

epiclesis. Frere argued that this was simply a return to the historic worship of England exemplified in the use of the Sarum Missal.

As with all his liturgical revision, Frere might be described as solidly Anglican with a clear understanding of the historical development of the liturgy and the fact the Anglican Church was both Catholic and Reformed. This becomes clear when we consider Frere's 1920 memorandum to the Liturgical Committee of the Lambeth Conference. At the request of the Bishop of Calcutta,[22] he was asked to consider liturgical reform in light of the missionary work of the Church, so that firm proposals might be brought before the Lambeth Conference. In all that he does Frere is quite flexible. He argues that the bishops of different provinces should have the right to authorize prayers for Holy Communion suitable for their particular mission field. For example, because of the difference in cultures, the prayers used in the mission field in India might be different from those used in China.[23] Frere points out that in France in the seventeenth and eighteenth centuries the Roman Breviary was adapted by the local church to make it more useful for priests, and thus the Anglican Communion had a precedent for adapting its liturgies to suit pastoral need or to respond to 'a desire for variety, freedom and enrichment'.[24] Frere does naturally believe that there must be some uniformity and that when devising liturgies the core of the faith must be maintained. Thus he is keen to suggest that each newly devised Holy Communion Service should have the following: 'the Mass of the Catechumens [important for teaching in a missionary context], the Prayers and Confession of Faith of the faithful, the Anaphora, which should include the recital of the words of institution and Thanksgiving'.[25] Thus for Frere 'rigid uniformity is not necessary across the Anglican Communion'.[26] Where disputes arose they were to be discussed by provincial bishops and if need be by the Lambeth Conference. The missionary zeal should not be stifled and pastoral concerns must be taken into account. The liberty for the use of liturgies whether, as Frere often

---

22 Letter from Dr Westcott, Bishop of Calcutta, to Frere 23 July 1920, in Jasper, *Frere*, p. 193.

23 Jasper, *Frere*, p. 194.

24 Jasper, *Frere*, p. 195.

25 Jasper, *Frere*, p. 196.

26 Jasper, *Frere*, p. 197.

advised, they came from Eastern or, more usually, Western sources was to be left up to the local bishop. What was important to Frere was that the faith was not lost. A great deal of care was needed (care sometimes lost today and that would have greatly distressed the liturgists like Frere who saw the liturgy as being an important declaration of faith and intent) over the content of the prayers. This was to ensure that

> the Scriptural and Catholic balance of Truth was maintained, that consideration should be given to the precedents of the Early Church, that due consideration was given to the guidance of higher synodical powers [i.e., Provincial Synods or the Lambeth Conference], and to remember with brotherly considerations the possible effect their action might have on other provinces ... of the Anglican Communion.[27]

In this we see the range of Frere's concerns, his looking to history and his belief in the brotherly ties of the Anglican Communion on which strain should not be placed. His ideals would be used to govern liturgical reform across the Anglican Communion for many decades. Finally Frere was keen to point out that the development of liturgy takes skill and knowledge which might not be available in all provinces. In such cases he urged bishops to seek guidance and assistance. We need to remember that Frere was writing mainly for a group of bishops who had been sent from England to serve native churches and who would have a similar education and a shared liturgical experience in the Church of England. This may have made his task of liturgical reform easier but his concern is always that the liturgical reform must be of use to the people and not just something dreamt up by the bishop of the diocese.

Frere was not afraid of taking issue with liturgical reform that he did not support. In the case of revisions to the liturgy of the Nippon Sei Ko Kai (Anglican Church in Japan), Frere was not entirely enthusiastic about attempts to join Morning Prayer with the office of Holy Communion and certainly he felt the order as presented to him by the Bishop of South Tokyo, Dr Boutflower, was long-winded and unnecessary. He objected, for example, to the use of the Lord's Prayer at the beginning of the combined service, as it could only possibly be used there as a form of

---

27 Jasper, *Frere*, p. 174.

private devotion. For Frere the combined service contains too much repetition of prayers and litanies, and he also objected to the use of the Grace and the Prayer of St Chrysostom together. What is clear is that he was very pleased that the order of the Communion Office was restored (something he tried to do in all his revisions); thus there was no break in the Eucharistic Prayer (unlike in the 1662 Book of Common Prayer) and the Lord's Prayer was prayed before receiving Communion. In the Japanese liturgy the correct order is restored as follows: 'Prayer of Humble Access, Sursum Corda, Proper Preface and Sanctus, The American Prayer of Consecration, The Lord's Prayer, Communion'.[28] For Frere this is the ancient order of things and certainly reflects the usage of Sarum. For him this order not only makes more sense but is more appealing liturgically. He also urged that there should be some sentence to encourage people to come and receive Holy Communion but this was his only criticism of the Communion part of the service. He could not praise the proposed order for Communion highly enough, declaring that he was 'delighted' and that he 'very much hope[d] that you will secure this'.[29]

In his revision of the South African Prayer Book, Frere would seek to put all this in place. The drawing up of the liturgy began in 1911 when a schedule of modifications to the 1662 Prayer Book was implemented. Frere's own work of revision began in 1918. This was a major work and in it Frere put in place all that he believed to be historically necessary and important to the Eucharistic Prayer and order. This included the restoration of the Benedictus following the Sanctus which in the past had been 'barbarously mutilated by its excision'. Frere also ensures that there is an epiclesis in the prayer before the words of institution as had appeared in earlier prayers. One point of interest comes after the Lord's Prayer where Frere places the Prayer of Humble Access, which he changes so as to resemble the *Libera* prayer found in the Roman Rite ('Deliver us Lord from every evil and grant us peace in our day'). Thus the new prayer begins 'Deliver us from all evil and preserve us in all good, for we do not presume to come to this thy table, O merciful Lord!' Thus here again the Prayer of Humble Access does not intrude on the Canon but continues to have an important use and is linked to the Lord's Prayer. In seeking all

---

28 Jasper, *Frere*, p. 200.

29 Letter from Frere to Dr Boutflower, Bishop in South Tokyo, 11 July 1912, in Jasper, *Frere*, p. 202.

these revisions, Frere hoped to ensure that the 'Province of South Africa is provided with a worthy Liturgy, and the Anglican Communion in general with a very valuable model'. Frere succeeded and was able to put into place three historical and liturgical norms that would come into use in liturgies across the Anglican Communion and would become bench marks for liturgical reform. These were, first, 'to recover the unity of the Canon or Anaphora'. This might be said to be the aim of all of Frere's liturgical reform: clean up the untidiness of the Reformation liturgy and to bring it into line with the liturgical precedence of the historic church. Secondly Frere sought

> to enrich the commemoration there made of Our Lord's work, first by introducing a definite reference to the Incarnation ('to take our nature upon him and to suffer death ...') before coming on to the event of Holy Week ... and by recovery of the Anamnesis of his Passion, Death and Resurrection, and Ascension by making reference to his coming again.[30]

Again here Frere seeks to deepen the faith of the people by enriching the prayers of the Church, especially in the prefaces and later in the Canon. He sees this as part of the ministry of teaching in the Church as well as a recovery of older traditions. Finally he sought 'to bring in some form of Invocation of the Holy Spirit'. In all three of these aims Frere succeeded. He was not without his critics or detractors but with his solid scholarship and pastoral care he was able to succeed in his reforms, giving to the Anglican Communion a fine example of Catholic eucharistic theology in an Anglican context.

In his dealing with the liturgy for the Church in Ceylon, Frere again displays a pastoral concern. In a memorandum published in 1932 he sets out some of the considerations for the revised liturgy. In it he indicates that the liturgy should seek to look eastward as well as westward and that any reform should tend towards the direction 'of some future and quite different liturgy which may be required for the Church of the Diocese'. Frere was keen that the liturgy should correspond in some way to 'the Eastern [church's] own nature and outlook'. Thus it was suggested that the

---

30 Jasper, *Frere*, p. 211.

Beatitudes might be used instead of the Ten Commandments, the General Intercession might take the form of a litany and the Prayer of Consecration might be enlarged not only with more prefaces but also with alternatives in the Eucharistic Canon. In choosing liturgical texts Frere sought to look to the Greek Church, indicating that at the Offertory there should be some music and ceremony relating to the Great Entry in the Eastern rite. Other pastoral concerns resulted in prayers being added for times of monsoon. Perhaps most interesting is Frere's proposal that the role of the permanent diaconate be revised and implemented. Whilst there is no indication that it was the case, it is possible that Frere saw this as a way of encouraging local men to take part in the ministry of the Church. In doing this Frere is also encouraging the High Mass as a norm for Sunday and festal celebrations. Frere was keen that the ancient role of the deacon should be encouraged as it was in the East and that in all things the liturgy in Ceylon should 'follow the East and not the West'. Frere extended his look to the East in liturgical reform in relation to the liturgy for the South Indian Church. In 1928 the Bishop of Bombay (Dr Edwin James Palmer) wrote to Frere to ask for his advice about the way in which the liturgy of the United Church of South India might be combined with that of the Anglican Church in South India. This was already a controversial situation and Palmer's concern was that the liturgy should be valid. He writes for confirmation of whether Frere believes that certain fixed words need to be included for the consecration prayer in the Eucharist to be valid. He recalls that Frank Weston, the Bishop of Zanzibar, had said that he would use any Eucharistic Prayer so long as it contained Our Lord's words of institution and the elements he used. Palmer's main concern was to discover what for Frere were indispensible elements of the liturgy 'that if they were absent you would have serious doubt whether the Service as conducted without them was really a Communion Service.' Frere replies with his usual care and concern for pastoral issues. He is, however, quite clear about the difficulties of bringing together liturgical and non-liturgical traditions as was happening in the South India union. Frere's advice again points to the oriental churches, urging that the intercessions, for example, should not be in the Anglican position but woven into the Eucharistic Prayer. Indeed, he urges an expanding of the English style of liturgy to encompass as much material suitable for the local setting as possible. His concern is that, in dealing with local congregations with different cultural norms to that of Western Christianity, the Church should 'want to leave them the fullest liberty to make their own sort of expansion of the sequence of ideas that must be common to all alike'. What Frere indicates is that there are indeed elements of the liturgy that are necessary and that are shared across different denominations but that different cultural settings may cause different developments in the liturgy. In the case of South India, Frere feels that the liturgy should be expanded to allow for a more devotional focus, with the scheme concentrating more on Eastern liturgies than Anglican ones as they seem to be better suited to what is required in South India. Frere here displays his dedication to and understanding of the Eastern Churches and his desire for unity with them as well as his clear understanding that the liturgy was for the people, the work of the people if you like.

After a career in liturgy and a life of worship, in his final book, *Anaphora*, Frere reflected that more study was needed of the liturgies of the Church before revision could take place, but he acknowledged that more revision would be carried out – as indeed it has, through Order I and II, the Alternative Service Book and *Common Worship*, as well as in other liturgies in the Anglican Communion. Writing in 1938, he commented that the Anglican Communion was more ready than it had ever been to study liturgy and to develop it 'whatever be our particular predilections or affiliations'.[31] It was these predilections and affiliations, especially from the Catholic wing of the Church of England, that would cause him the most pain and difficulty in his involvement with Prayer Book revision. After 1929, his last major work sought to set out the history of the Eucharistic Prayer. In this, and in his earlier work on revision in England and the Anglican Communion, he would continue to influence later liturgical scholars. In professing a moderate 'English Use' Catholicism, his hope was to return the worship of the Church of England to older forms, but also to make it more accessible to the laity. In doing all this he sought 'to remove such prejudices, ignorances, and other misfortunes as those that arose in 1927/28, and partly to prevent similar mistakes in the future'.[32] This is his lasting legacy.

By way of a footnote, with the announcement of Anglican Ordinariates

---

31 Walter Frere, *The Anaphora, or, Great Eucharistic Prayer* (London: SPCK, 1938), p. vi.

32 Frere, *Anaphora*, p. 205.

in Communion with Holy See it is possible that we will see more of Frere's liturgical legacy in use. His work on Prayer Books across the world, especially in South Africa and America, may form the basis of the worship of some in the Ordinariates.[33] Thus a fulfilment of the work for Christian Unity may indeed lead to a wider use and understanding and appreciation of Frere's liturgical genius.

---

33 Indeed, it should be noted that the 'Book of Divine Worship' used by the Anglican Use Roman Catholic Churches of the USA has elements of the 1929 Episcopal Prayer Book on which Frere gave advice. Those Continuing Churches (especially the Traditional Anglican Communion) seeking union with the Holy See often use a version of the South African Prayer Book, again a book on which Frere gave advice.

8

'A scholar's scholar'?:[1]
The intellectual context of Walter Frere's
contribution to Anglican liturgical reform

JOHN LIVESLEY

I think few even of the Bishops, as they sate [sic] round the table in Lambeth Palace engaged in the task of [Prayer Book] revision, escaped an uncomfortable feeling of unreality and misgiving when they listened to the earnest and learned pleas of those members of their body (they were not many) who spoke as recognizably expert in liturgical science.[2]

Walter Frere, Bishop of Truro 1923–1935, was a leader among those bishops whose liturgical expertise, according to one observer, became increasingly irrelevant in the later stages of Prayer Book revision before 1928.[3] The history of liturgical reform in the Church of England, from around 1890 until after Frere's death in 1938, has tended to focus on the causes and consequences of what has been called the 'debacle of 1928':[4] the debate surrounding the revision of the Book of Common Prayer and the final rejection of the revised book by Parliament in 1928. The fate of

---

1 H.B. Green, 'Frere, Walter Howard', in *Dictionary of National Biography*, www.oxforddnb.com.wam.leeds.ac.uk/articles/33/33274, par. 5, accessed 29/11/2005.

2 H. Henson, *Retrospect of an Unimportant Life*, vol. 2., pp. 152–3; cited in G.J. Cuming, *A History of Anglican Liturgy* (2nd edn, London: Macmillan, 1982), p. 165.

3 Yet, as Green ('Frere', par. 3) suggests, Archbishop Randall Davidson had pressed for Frere's appointment to Truro precisely because of his liturgical expertise and his identification with the movement for Prayer Book revision gathering pace in the wake of the First World War.

4 Cuming, *Anglican Liturgy*, p. 191.

proposals for liturgical reform in this period has been understood as primarily dependent upon ecclesiastical and national politics. Both Ronald Jasper and Geoffrey Cuming, laying out what might be termed the 'causes of 1928', focus on the controversial breakdown of liturgical discipline in the Church of England at the end of the nineteenth century, especially in the attempts of 'ritualist' priests, from as early as the 1840s,[5] to adapt and bend the rubrics of the Prayer Book in a more 'Catholic' and often explicitly Romanist direction; and in the high-profile attempts of Protestant pressure groups, particularly the Church Association, to stamp out such tendencies.[6]

The lengthy process of revision that produced the Deposited Book of 1927, agreed by the Convocations and Church Assembly, had been initiated by the 1906 Report of the Royal Commission on Ecclesiastical Discipline: an exhaustive account of the ways in which the rubrics of the 1662 Book of Common Prayer were commonly breached, concluding that 'The law of public worship in the Church of England is too narrow for the religious life of the present generation', and that 'the machinery of discipline has broken down'.[7] Thus, just as the revised Book was originally conceived to remedy chaos, the same chaos engulfed it in its final form, 22 years later. It was opposed by an increasingly assertive Anglo-Catholic party for whom the rubrics on Reservation and the new Eucharistic Canon were too restricted; and by Evangelicals who saw all deviation from the 1662 Book as a concession to Anglo-Catholicism (and, implicitly, to Rome),[8] and who were able to call on the support of Nonconformists and non-English members in the Commons to bring the measure down.

---

5 For one example of early ritualist controversy, see N. Yates, *The Oxford Movement and Parish Life: St Saviour's, Leeds, 1839–1929* (Borthwick Papers No. 48, York: St Anthony's Hall Publications, 1975).

6 R.C.D. Jasper, *The Development of the Anglican Liturgy, 1662–1980* (London: SPCK, 1989), pp. 61–79; and Cuming, *Anglican Liturgy*, pp. 157–64.

7 Cited in Jasper, *Development of the Anglican Liturgy*, pp. 77–8.

8 The Anglo-Catholic Congresses of 1920, 1923 and 1927 demonstrated an explicit and self-conscious preoccupation with the theme of 'Reunion'; the editors (F. Underhill and C.S. Gillett) of the *Report of the Second Anglo-Catholic Congress* referred to a message of respect to the Pope as 'the evidence ... the fruit' of a 'desire for the Reunion of Christendom ... more sanguine, more eagerly active and resolute amongst Anglo-Catholics than amongst any other Christian people in the world' (London: Society of Ss. Peter and Paul, 1923, pp. xiv–xv). The message had aroused hostile press attention.

Frere and the 'Debacle of 1928'

The complexities of what might be called the political history of the 1928 Prayer Book have consumed the attention of religious historians,[9] and consequently the role of liturgical scholars like Frere has been played down. Yet, Frere had been an active participant in the revision debates from the beginning. In 1911, following the publication of a series of lectures as *Some Principles of Liturgical Reform*, he had been appointed to the committee of liturgical experts, suggested by him[10] and convened by Archbishop Davidson to review and coordinate the various proposals for reform to be put forward by the Convocations. Subsequently, as the Church sought to respond to the spiritual crisis of the First World War, Frere took a leading role in the Archbishops' Committee on the Worship of the Church. This was one of five committees of investigation established following the 1916 National Mission of Repentance and Hope, which concluded in its report of 1918 that 'a refusal to reform [the Book of Common Prayer] has meant, and will mean, the alienation from the Christian religion of the important minority of men of all classes who are in some real degree mentally and spiritually alive'.[11] In 1923–24, newly consecrated bishop, Frere had been involved in compiling the so-called 'Orange Book', an attempt to harmonize the proposals of the 'pronouncedly' Anglo-Catholic[12] 'Green Book' of the English Church Union (1922) and the modernist and liberal 'Grey Book' of the Life and Liberty Movement (1923) with the proposals already agreed by the Convocations and the new Church Assembly.

Yet, in spite of this unswerving commitment to reform, following the rejection of the Deposited Book by the House of Commons and its further revision by the Church Assembly, Frere voted against the Book in its final form in the House of Lords in 1928.[13] To him the final Book

---

9 Cuming, *Anglican Liturgy*, pp. 170–2, offers a succinct account of the proceedings in the Church Assembly and in Parliament in 1927–28.

10 W.H. Frere, *Some Principles of Liturgical Reform* (London: Murray, 1911), p. 8.

11 Cited in A. Wilkinson, *The Church of England and the First World War* (London: SPCK, 1978), p. 83.

12 See Cuming, *Anglican Liturgy*, p. 169.

13 In March 1927, he had written to the Archbishop of Canterbury that the idea of voting against 'the result of our labours has never occurred to me', in spite of some misgivings about detail. See R.C.D. Jasper, *Walter Howard Frere: Correspondence on Liturgical Revision and Reconstruction* (London: SPCK, 1954), p. 127.

seemed 'to offer now no sufficient hope of settlement, but on the contrary, to lead up to acute trouble',[14] especially owing to the new authority vested in Parochial Church Councils as to the forms of worship adopted; and the rubric concerning Reservation of the Sacrament in which 'Unworthy influences such as suspicion and intolerance [had] led to excessive restriction.'[15] This was a protest vote, registering his disgust that, whereas his own contributions (notably the 'Orange Book'), though distinctively Catholic, had been offered in an irenic spirit, the interests of party in church and state had triumphed in the House of Commons.[16] His continued frustration that the fruit of almost 20 years' work had apparently been sabotaged is seen in his preface to his final work, *The Anaphora* (1938), where he fires an uncharacteristic parting shot at the 'determined obscurantist and retrograde movement, which poses noisily as catholic [i.e., the 'Romanist' party within the Church of England], but is really anarchist in method though medieval in outlook'.[17]

Perhaps his own sense of failure has limited Frere's impact. Some have seen him primarily as, in the words of Benedict Green, a 'scholar's scholar', whose 'most enduring work was in the production of *instrumenta studiorum*', rather than in any public role, distinguished by his academic qualities: a 'head for detail, wise critical judgement, beautifully clear miniscule handwriting, and the ability to sustain work on a variety of projects in spare moments over many years';[18] qualities similarly

---

14 Frere to Chancellor Cooper of Truro Cathedral, 10 March 1928, Jasper, *Frere: Correspondence*, p. 149.

15 Jasper, *Frere: Correspondence*, p. 150.

16 In the same letter, he protests at the lack of an alternative Eucharistic Canon for those with whom he disagreed on the necessity of an epiclesis: 'Peace and contented worship can hardly be secured while the desire of so large a class of worshippers is ignored or refused.'

17 W.H. Frere, *The Anaphora, or, Great Eucharistic Prayer* (London: SPCK, 1938), p. vi. This charge of being 'retrograde' and 'medieval' was precisely that which these advocates of the contemporary 'Roman Use', associated with *The English Missal* and the liturgical publications of the Society of Ss. Peter and Paul, had noisily levelled at the advocates of the revived medieval 'English Use' associated with Percy Dearmer and *The Parson's Handbook* of 1899.

18 Green, 'Frere', par. 5; he also provides a list of Frere's more important projects, historical, liturgical and musical, beginning in the 1890s, including his editions of the Hereford Breviary, Winchester Troper and Sarum Missal, and his three-volume *Studies in Early Roman Liturgy* (Alcuin Club. Oxford: Oxford University Press, 1930–1935).

eulogized by Gregory Dix in his memoir of Frere.[19] The implication is that as a scholar he maintained some detachment from worldly affairs; or that antiquarian liturgical scholarship provided an escape from the burdens of office for one who was at heart a monastic; an impression reinforced with great irony in the preface to his *Links in the Chain of Russian Church History* (1918), a work intended to familiarize English readers with the essentials of Russian Orthodoxy, but whose conclusions were already being overtaken by events.[20] Equally, because of his association with Percy Dearmer in producing *The English Liturgy* (1904), and subsequently through their common involvement in the Alcuin Club, Frere could be misrepresented as a mere partisan for the 'English Use', supported by his scholarly editions of the Sarum liturgy, in the narrow and often bitter arguments among Anglo-Catholics concerning liturgical style.[21]

The Liturgical Movement, Jungmann and Vatican II

More seriously, historians' concern with the political battles surrounding the 1928 Prayer Book has tended to isolate developments in England from those on the Continent. Cuming argues that whereas

> Throughout the first half of the twentieth century, the Roman Catholic Church in Europe was greatly renewed by the teaching and practice of the Liturgical Movement ... the movement reached this country too late to have any influence on the 1928 Book.[22]

He singles out A.G. Hebert's *Liturgy and Society* (1935) and *The Parish Communion* (1937) as the most influential works in terms of practice,

---

19 G. Dix, 'The Liturgist', in C.S. Phillips (ed.), *Walter Howard Frere: A Memoir* (London: Faber & Faber, 1947), pp. 121–4.

20 He notes that 'a great deal of change has been taking place while these proofs are going to press', and speculates that 'a new era has been opened by the Revolution, from which the Church has been the first to profit ... History shows how in Russia's earlier days the Church has been the rallying point and the saving of the State. May it be so again!' dated, 'Mirfield, October 1917'; W.H. Frere, *Some Links in the Chain of Russian Church History* (London: Faith Press, 1918), pp. v–vi.

21 See note 17.

22 Cuming, *Anglican Liturgy*, p. 193.

establishing the Eucharist as the main act of worship in most Anglican churches over the next 30 years. But Cuming suggests that in liturgical scholarship 'the new era' began in England only with Gregory Dix's *The Shape of the Liturgy* in 1945.[23] Yet, seven years earlier, in the preface to *The Anaphora*, Frere had suggested that 'the moment [had] come for some revaluation of the principles that govern the form and structure of the Eucharistic Anaphora' precisely because 'in the Latin West a strong and realistic *Liturgical Movement* [my italics] is in full progress' along with 'much awakening in the East.'[24] Indeed, it was entirely natural that one who had taken such an active role in the Malines Conversations from 1921 to 1927 should be aware of continental developments in liturgical thought.[25] Both Frere's historical methodology and his conclusions closely resemble those of the principal writers of the Liturgical Movement, notably the following generation who had direct influence on the reform of the Roman Liturgy in the 1960s, particularly Josef Jungmann, the author of the authoritative thousand-page study, *The Mass of the Roman Rite: Its Origins and Development* (1948), and a principal author both of Vatican II's constitution on the liturgy, *Sacrosanctum Concilium*, and of its official commentary.

Eamon Duffy has argued recently that an 'exercise of the historical imagination', exemplified in Jungmann's work, 'served within twentieth-century Roman Catholicism to reshape the fundamental and constitutive act of the Christian community, the celebration of the liturgy'; an exercise rooted certainly in 'wide and deep historical scholarship' but consequently in 'a *particular* set of historical assumptions':[26] first, that the early liturgy embodied 'kerygmatic purity',[27] corporate public worship with universal lay communion, expressing the Christian dignity of the baptized, and

---

23 Cuming, *Anglican Liturgy*, pp. 193–4.

24 Frere, *Anaphora*, p. v.

25 See W.H. Frere, *Recollections of Malines* (London: Centenary Press, 1935). Liturgical matters are not mentioned directly, but there are hints of a common awareness of an impetus for change, such as Cardinal Mercier's comment (p. 26) on the 'signs in the Roman Catholic Church of a desire for the restoration of Communion in both kinds, which was not treated as impossible in itself'.

26 E. Duffy, 'Worship', in D.F. Ford, B. Quash and J. Soskice (eds), *Fields of Faith: Theology and Religious Studies for the Twenty–First Century* (Cambridge: Cambridge University Press, 2005), pp. 119–20.

27 Duffy, 'Worship', p. 121.

'dominated by the Easter motif',[28] an active participation of the redeemed in the life of the risen Christ; secondly, that this purity was unavoidably distorted by the Church's preoccupation with refuting heresy, the 'Teutonic Arianism' of Jungmann's 1947 seminal article;[29] thirdly, that this led to a clericalization of the liturgy characteristic of the Middle Ages and after, when the laity were silenced and reduced to spectators, lay communion became rare, private masses proliferated, and the devotional focus switched to Christ's suffering and death 'historically bound, essentially commemorative', and the conception of the Church as the Body of Christ disappeared. This was reflected in the development of art and architecture.[30] Duffy has his own anti-Jungmann agenda, the rehabilitation of the medieval liturgy as the possession of the laity,[31] but his summary of Jungmann's arguments is fair. In his *The Early Liturgy*, Jungmann uses an architectural analogy:

> in essentials [the liturgy] is the same building in which Christians were already living ten or 15 or even 18 or more centuries ago. In the course of all these centuries, the structure has become more and more complicated ... and so the plan of the building has been obscured ... Hence we must look up the old building plans, for these will tell us what the architects of old really wanted.[32]

On one level, his aim is simple: to establish as far as possible, given limited evidence, the earliest forms of the liturgy, 'the old building plans', assuming that these were the purest and closest to the intention of the apostles themselves; and assuming also that in any forthcoming reform adapting the liturgy 'to the needs of our own people ... nothing of the precious heritage of the past will be lost';[33] assuming that the tradition in this oldest form is sufficient for the needs of the contemporary church. The end of the exemplary period is set, somewhat arbitrarily, as the

---

28 Duffy, 'Worship', p. 121.

29 Duffy, 'Worship', p. 121.

30 Duffy, 'Worship', pp. 122–3.

31 See E. Duffy, *The Stripping of the Altars* (New Haven and London: Yale University Press, 1992) and especially pp. 91–130.

32 J.A. Jungmann, *The Early Liturgy, to the Time of Gregory the Great* (English edn, London: Darton, Longman and Todd, 1960), p. 2.

33 Jungmann, *Early Liturgy*, p. 2.

papacy of Gregory the Great (c.540–604).[34] He acknowledges the difficulties inherent in this quest, particularly that within the 'living tradition' of these early 'days of fervor [sic] ... practically no written texts were used'.[35] Nevertheless, he stresses how discoveries in the past hundred years have enhanced the available evidence, especially by unearthing more pre-fourth-century texts: notably the *Didache*, from the early second century, and the *Apostolic Tradition* of Hippolytus, dated to around 215.[36]

Comparing this with Frere's writing on the Eucharistic Canon, the preface to *The Anaphora* expresses very similar concerns to those of Jungmann: that in spite of the obvious gaps in knowledge, the 'fresh evidence' of the previous 50 years needs to be 'assimilated' so that 'current popular ideas' on the shape and content of the liturgy, which he evidently considers defective, may be rectified 'in consequence of the new light'.[37] 'Popular ideas', specifically the attachment of a group of Anglicans to the Tridentine form of the Roman Canon, are defective in the light of a set of historical assumptions almost identical with those of Jungmann: their position is '*historically* untenable' [my italics], because it represents a eucharistic theology 'not truly that of SS. Chrysostom, Ambrose, and Austin [sic] but only that of their *decadent* successors';[38] views 'fathered upon them' during the 'Dark Ages',[39] that ill-defined period of ignorance which most scholars, if they have not abandoned the term, would place somewhere after the papacy of Gregory the Great, Jungmann's cut-off point for the period of primitive liturgical purity. For Frere, as for Jungmann, the liturgical standard is set by the 'patristic heyday'.[40]

Frere is convinced of the 'uniformity of the earliest outlines' of the Eucharistic Prayer, illustrating how its structure is informed by the development of Catholic eucharistic theology, in the light of which both

---

34 He describes 'the sixth century Roman Mass' as 'worthy ... still in the fullest sense, a community exercise, a rite in which the whole Christian people had a part. The members of the congregation were still conscious of their role as the *plebs sancta*', Jungmann, *Early Liturgy*, p. 307; presumably the last generation when this was so.

35 Jungmann, *Early Liturgy*, p. 3

36 Jungmann, *Early Liturgy*, p. 6; for a discussion of both Jungmann and Frere's use of this document, see below.

37 Frere, *Anaphora*, p. v.

38 Frere, *Anaphora*, p. vi.

39 Frere, *Anaphora*, p. v.

40 Frere, *Anaphora*, p. v.

the Roman Canon, in its later form, and the 'Consecration Prayer' of the Book of Common Prayer from 1552 onwards are deemed deficient.[41] *The Anaphora* traces the developing theology of the Eucharist in the apostolic and patristic eras, as the Christian 'Sacrifice of Thanksgiving',[42] a participation in the one atoning Sacrifice of Christ superseding the sacrifices of the Old Covenant.[43] In Judaism and to a lesser extent in paganism, sacrifice had embodied three aims: propitiation, self-surrender and, as the outcome, communion between God and man.[44] Thus, in the primitive Eucharistic Prayer the Anamnesis, the most crucial part of the Anaphora, recalls Christ's work of propitiation particularly through the Institution narrative; supported by the Preface with its 'Recital of the accumulated mercies of God'.[45] The Anamnesis, the act of sacrifice, must be followed by the Oblation, the prayer for its acceptance and of self-surrender. The act of Communion completes the sacrifice by 'seal[ing] the union of the worshipper with God'.[46] Moreover, tradition illustrated that these three elements must be set within a Trinitarian framework: the sacrifice offered to the Father, through the merits of the Son, and sanctified by the Spirit. Frere asserts that 'There is a continuous tradition of triple form in the building up of Christian worship, whether for prayer, praise, or confession of faith',[47] and traces the development of this triple form in baptismal rites, liturgical greetings, doxologies, and in the texts of the *Gloria*, the *Te Deum* and the Apostles' and Nicene Creeds. The development of Trinitarian forms was a natural outcome of the increasing definition in Trinitarian theology, as Frere makes particularly evident in his consideration of Irenaeus.[48] This 'threefold scheme', originally 'universal' in the eucharistic canon as elsewhere,[49] can be maintained only with 'the commemoration of the Holy Spirit in some form' in its proper

---

41 The peculiar problems of the Anglican 'Consecration Prayer' are discussed below.

42 The Eucharist, or 'Sacrifice of Thanksgiving' was a 'continuance of [its antecedent] the old Jewish plan of offering a sacrifice in thankful remembrance of any great event or mercy'; Frere, *Anaphora*, p. 9.

43 He cites Justin Martyr, in his Dialogue with Trypho, and Tertullian in support of this view of the finality of the Eucharist; Frere, *Anaphora*, pp. 33 and 37.

44 Frere, *Anaphora*, p. 2.

45 Frere, *Anaphora*, pp. 24–5.

46 Frere, *Anaphora*, p. 25.

47 Frere, *Anaphora*, p. 19.

48 Frere, *Anaphora*, p. 36.

49 Frere, *Anaphora*, p. 22.

place, that is, after the act of sacrifice, the Anamnesis.[50] Yet, he perceives this 'acquired unity' of doctrine to have been subsequently 'broken up through disruptive forces in some areas',[51] particularly through the unique development of Latin theology which, even as it emerges distinct from the Greek in the third century, notably in the nuances of its Latin terminology and emphasis on the transformative function of the Dominical Words above all else, Frere perceives as already 'getting out of centre',[52] ultimately producing the Roman Canon in its medieval form, without an epiclesis or overall Trinitarian structure.

Jungmann and Frere then, have different concerns about the 'decadence' of eucharistic theology, liturgically expressed, in the post-patristic era. Jungmann is concerned with 'clericalization', Frere with a distortion of Catholic sacrificial theology, yet their concerns overlap. Jungmann's clericalization thesis hangs on the premise that 'it is well known how little the thought of the Church as the Body of Christ flourished in the Middle Ages';[53] that as the devotional focus shifted from the risen to the crucified Lord, so the social reality of the Eucharist became obscured by a subjective and passive devotional focus on the miraculous transformation of the elements and on the eucharistic presence of Christ.[54] Frere expresses similar concerns at a perceived distortion of sacrificial eucharistic theology. He notes that an exclusive emphasis on the Passion is a peculiarly Western, Latin development from the third century onwards, particularly in the writings of Cyprian'.[55] He explores the relationship of 'consecration' to the central act of sacrifice, pointing out that, whilst in Catholic doctrine bread and wine are indeed hallowed to be the body and blood of Christ, transformation 'is no

---

50 Frere, *Anaphora*, p. 25; he is more explicit in a later note, pp. 27–8, that a Catholic understanding of eucharistic sacrifice and particularly of the transformation of the elements, 'should be especially associated in the Anaphora with the work of the Holy Spirit': the Eucharistic Prayer thus necessarily involves an epiclesis, an invocation of the Holy Spirit upon the gifts and upon the people.

51 Frere, *Anaphora*, p. 22.

52 Frere, *Anaphora*, p. 40.

53 J.A. Jungmann, 'The Defeat of Teutonic Arianism and the Revolution in Religious Culture in the Early Middle Ages', in Jungmann, *Pastoral Liturgy* (London: Challoner Publications, 1962), cited in Duffy, *Worship*, p. 127.

54 See Aquinas' hymn, *Adoro te devote*.

55 Frere, *Anaphora*, p. 39.

essential part of consecration in general':[56] the sacrificial act of propitiation, oblation and communion must always be prior in any orthodox eucharistic theology. Hence, he traces an apparent corruption of Western terminology:[57] whereas 'Anaphora', derived from the Greek verb commonly used in the Septuagint for the offering of sacrifice, refers properly to the *whole* sacrifice, including the Offertory and Communion as well as the Anaphora so-called (the Eucharistic Prayer), the equivalent term of Latin origin, 'Canon', he attaches to the 'alternative view' that the 'consummation of the sacrifice ... depended on the recitation of certain Dominical Words', in contrast with the earlier Latin 'prex' which, like 'Anaphora' referred to the prayer as a whole. Interestingly, he locates the earliest use of 'Canon' in Pope Gregory's letter (598), defending 'innovations'.[58] Gregory's papacy, for both Frere and Jungmann, is the turning point, conveniently situated where the collapse of the Roman Empire is traditionally seen to have initiated the Dark Ages.

For both Frere and Jungmann, the most important proof text for the form and content of the early liturgy is the Anaphora found in the *Apostolic Tradition* attributed to Hippolytus of Rome; the earliest extant complete text of a Eucharistic Prayer, which Jungmann, stressing the interchange between the Christian communities of Rome and Alexandria, considers 'a picture of the Church's liturgical life as it existed in the centers [*sic*] of Christendom in the third century'.[59] He stresses the text's sacrificial character, concisely expressed, illustrating that 'from the very beginning, the mass has been understood as a sacrifice which we offer to God';[60] he outlines what he sees as a clearer perception of the Paschal mystery, 'characteristic of Christian Antiquity'[61] as a 'war of liberation ending with the splendid victory of the Resurrection' rather than 'stop[ping] short at a sympathetic meditation' on the Passion 'as the later Middle Ages were wont to do';[62] he highlights the use of an epiclesis, echoing Frere's concern for Trinitarian form; and gives several instances where he considers the Latin text of the Hippolytan prayer superior to the Roman Canon in its

---

56 Frere, *Anaphora*, p. 28.
57 Frere, *Anaphora*, p. 28.
58 Frere, *Anaphora*, p. 28.
59 Jungmann, *Early Liturgy*, p. 57.
60 Frere, *Anaphora*, p. 69.
61 Frere, *Anaphora*, p. 72.
62 Frere, *Anaphora*, p. 72.

theological precision.[63] As early as 1922, Frere had brought the Hippolytan prayer to the Alcuin Club's attention in a lecture,[64] emphasizing the theological neatness of its structure: three main verbs, 'We thank Thee', 'We offer unto Thee', 'We ask Thee to send Thy Holy Spirit', representing the prayer's 'three great motives',[65] and corresponding to the three elements of the sacrifice identified later in *The Anaphora*; and with the 'recital of the Institution which has come in the West to be regarded as the operative part' merely a 'portion of narrative' grammatically and theologically subordinate to the first of these main verbs.[66] Later he asserted that the rediscovered Hippolytan prayer 'caused something of a revolution among many cherished and Western notions and assumptions about the course of liturgical tradition';[67] a revolution whose full effects were only to be seen 30 years afterwards. The Hippolytan prayer forms the basis of the Second Eucharistic Prayer in the 1970 Roman Missal.[68]

Ecclesiastical statesman, scholar and man of God

There are clear parallels in the methodology employed and the conclusions reached by Jungmann and Frere, demonstrating how Frere's place within the development of European liturgical scholarship has been neglected. Both wrote within an historical framework, viewing the eucharistic forms and practices of the patristic era as a lost ideal, but reawakened by recently rediscovered liturgical texts, knowledge of which necessarily challenged the Church's understanding of its own traditions. Both believed that the tradition, in its oldest, 'purest' form, contained

---

63 Frere, *Anaphora*, p. 70.

64 Published as W.H. Frere, *The Primitive Consecration Prayer* (Alcuin Club Prayer Book Revision Pamphlets VIII, London: Mowbray, 1922). Like Jungmann, he depends on the fourth-century Latin text, as the most complete, rather than the fragmentary Greek original. Frere here uses the text first published by Hauler in 1900, but Jungmann uses that of Dix, 1937.

65 Frere, *Primitive Consecration Prayer*, p. 12; on p. 14 he goes on to highlight how the last of these represents the widespread primitive form of the epiclesis.

66 Frere, *Primitive Consecration Prayer*, p. 13.

67 Frere, *Anaphora*, p. 47.

68 See article on the Apostolic Tradition in F.L. Cross and E.A. Livingstone (eds), *The Oxford Dictionary of the Christian Church*, (3rd edn, revised, Oxford: Oxford University Press, 2005), p. 92.

sufficient riches to meet the liturgical and didactic purposes of the twentieth-century church. An influential link between the two is Gregory Dix, who, as Cuming points out, is the more obvious bridge figure between the liturgical scholarship of England and Europe and whose works were certainly well known to European scholars. Jungmann uses Dix's 1937 edition of the Latin text of the *Apostolic Tradition* and makes wide reference to his work, adopting wholesale Dix's account of how the seven different actions of the Last Supper became compressed at an early date into the fourfold action of Eucharist.[69] Duffy suggests that Jungmann's historical account was widely shared by other liturgists such as Ildefons Herwegen, and by Dix in his *The Shape of the Liturgy*;[70] and even a cursory reading of Dix's 752 pages seems to support this. To him the medieval development of the Western liturgy consisted in 'the isolation of the priesthood of the priest from the corporate offering, the false theory of a separate value of the sacrifice of the mass from the sacrifice of Calvary', the elimination of the laity's role, and consequently 'the placing of the whole devotional emphasis ... on the consecration and conversion of the elements',[71] all of which reflect the concerns of both Frere and Jungmann. As for the relationship of Dix to Frere, Dix's memoir demonstrates a great filial affection, recalling how on hearing of Frere's death he 'felt as [he] had not felt since the death of [his] own father';[72] and reverence for his reputation as a scholar, vindicated by the Europe-wide acclamation of his *Studies in Early Roman Liturgy* 'setting the seal upon his whole life's labour of learning in a way which no publication of purely Anglican interest could have done'.[73]

Possibly this Anglican context explains why Frere's impact has been limited. Dix asserts that 'There were in him three men, the ecclesiastical statesman, the scholar, and the man of God.'[74] Perhaps at times the churchman and the scholar co-existed uneasily. Certainly, the extent of his historical knowledge, and his grasp of the latest European developments,

---

69 G. Dix, *The Shape of the Liturgy* (London: A. and C. Black, 1945), cited in Jungmann, *Early Liturgy*, p. 33.
70 Duffy, *Worship*, pp. 123–4.
71 Dix, *The Shape of the Liturgy*, p. 598.
72 Dix, 'The Liturgist', in Phillips, *Frere*, p. 143
73 Dix, 'The Liturgist', p. 144.
74 Dix, 'The Liturgist', p. 144.

combined with his perception of the Church's current needs, made him a brilliant Anglican polemicist. In *Some Principles of Liturgical Reform*, effectively his manifesto for all the debates of the following 20 years, he asserted with regard to the post-1552 Prayer of Consecration: 'the present state of our liturgy at this point is gravely at variance both with the oldest and most universal liturgical tradition, and also with the practical needs of the Church of today.'[75]

No church that claimed a truly Catholic understanding of the Eucharist, as he was to argue consistently until his death,[76] could continue to use a Eucharistic Prayer without a complete Anamnesis[77] and lacking some form of epiclesis, especially given Anglican precedents otherwise in the 1549 Book, and in the Scottish and American liturgies. This stricture included, by implication, the Roman Catholic Church, whose Canon represented 'an ancient but rather clumsy and inconsequent blending of the various elements.'[78] His tone is almost iconoclastic, and yet he goes on to prove himself sufficiently the 'statesman' to anticipate and counter his (especially Evangelical) opponents' arguments: reform need only proceed at first by rearranging the existing material following precedents such as that advocated by Bishop Overall in 1603;[79] a restored Canon would discourage Anglo-Catholics from interpolating sections of the Roman rite,[80] and that the Consecration as it stood was 'more Roman than Rome by [tying] the act of consecration more narrowly to the words of the original administration than any other Christian liturgy',[81] a particularly brilliant sideswipe at Protestant attachment to the rite of 1662. This is coupled with a pastoral and didactic concern, shown throughout the *Principles*, for the way in which the Church's liturgy might relate to the ordinary and occasional churchgoer, even if expressed in terms some would find distasteful today: here he pleads for 'simple people' who

---

75 Frere, *Principles*, p. 186.

76 The last chapter of *Anaphora*, maintains a very similar argument on the Canon from 1552 onwards, see pp. 199 ff.

77 The 1662 Canon commemorated only the 'full perfect and sufficient sacrifice, oblation and satisfaction' of Christ's death, ignoring the Resurrection and Ascension.

78 Frere, *Principles*, p. 186.

79 Frere, *Principles*, p. 194.

80 Frere, *Principles*, p. 194.

81 Frere, *Principles*, p. 190.

should be able to follow the 'dramatic action' of the Eucharistic Prayer, without 'dislocation'.[82]

Yet if both the 'statesman' and the pastor in him were nurtured by the scholar, perhaps the scholar was sometimes compromised by his default position as an Anglican apologist. Dix sees Frere's interpretation of church history and of doctrine as determined exclusively by an Anglican Catholicism 'which was not only justified but rather strictly limited by the historic Anglican formularies', lending an element of 'advocacy' to his work which had been 'much criticized'.[83] Nevertheless, Frere's vision of Anglicanism was unique. In his lecture on the Hippolytan prayer, he sees the Church as 'happy in having recovered in this Canon an earlier and more indefinite invocation of the Holy Spirit upon the elements';[84] 'happy' because here was a concrete example of eucharistic practice prior to the division between East and West over how consecration was effected. If the Church of England and her daughter Churches[85] could recover this form of prayer, in which both the Institution narrative and an epiclesis were included, then Anglicanism could 'stand as a mediator between the East and Rome, comprehending the parts of truth for which each is contending'.[86]

His is a self-confident vision of Anglicanism's place within Christendom; with its own integrity in liturgical practice[87] but also providing an example of comprehensiveness to both Rome and Constantinople by espousing the theological and liturgical positions of the undivided Catholic Church of the Fathers, even if he sometimes reveals himself as

---

82 Frere, *Principles*, p. 192.

83 Dix, 'The Liturgist', pp. 129–130.

84 Frere, *Primitive Consecration Prayer*, p. 17.

85 In the *Church Quarterly Review*, July 1920, he praised the new South African rite for adopting the Gallican form of the epiclesis: an early Western form, and less explicit as to the effect than later Greek forms, allowing a variety of interpretations in the context of the 'great controversies' on the subject. Reprinted in J. Arnold and E.G.P. Wyatt (eds), *Walter Howard Frere: A Collection of his Papers on Liturgical and Historical Subjects* (London: Oxford University Press, 1940), p. 126.

86 Frere, *Principles*, p. 190.

87 The chapter on the 'Kalendar' in *Principles* illustrates this: the Church of England should be free to choose its own commemorations, with reference to historic calendars, local custom and didactic value, and to freely adapt Roman practice to its own use. See especially pp. 43–8. One reviewer saw this as the Church of England potentially overthrowing its Reformation principles (*CQR*, No. CXLIV, July 1911, p. 459).

more Eastern in sympathy.[88] To regard Anglicanism as the rightful inheritor of a 'pure' patristic tradition is hardly new, being inherent in the Tractarian writings of the 1830s.[89] To see Anglicanism, however, as the active agent of reconciliation rather than as an island or a branch of truth was rather more novel: at times comically naive[90] yet founded on the deeply irenic spirit that characterized all his work towards liturgical reform. It is this spirit which is most striking in Frere's work, along with a freshness, an undogmatic enthusiasm for the 'beauty of holiness' wherever it manifested itself in the church's history. A musical Troper was for Dix, and no doubt for Jungmann, symptomatic of 'medieval decadence of liturgical principles', in subordinating the structure of the text to the needs of the chant,[91] but to Frere it was worthy of minute scholarly fascination; an attitude which perhaps has saved the Church of England from the dogmatism and iconoclasm in liturgical reform suffered by the Roman Catholic Church, even if it perhaps cost Frere a reputation as a consistent scholar; a natural outlook from one who lived for worship above all else, and who in monastic obedience subjected every other aspect of his life to this supreme vocation.[92]

---

88 Notably in dialogue with 'Romanisers': see his lecture on the Eastern Orthodox Church to the 1920 Anglo-Catholic Congress, an exhortation 'to look eastward "to the rock whence we were hewn"'. D. Stone (ed.), *Report of the First Anglo-Catholic Congress* (London: SPCK, 1920), p. 97.

89 'I fancied that there could be no rashness in giving to the world in the fullest measure the teachings and writings of the Fathers. I thought that the Church of England was substantially founded upon them.' Newman on the Tractarian proposal to produce a 'Library of the Fathers', in W. Oddie (ed.), *Apologia Pro Vita Sua* [1864] (London: Dent, 1993), p. 128.

90 See his proposal for negotiations between the churches concerning fixing the date of Easter; Frere, *Principles*, p. 19.

91 See Dix, 'The Liturgist', p. 127.

92 See Bernard Horner's recollection of Frere's last days at Mirfield, cited in A. Dawtry, 'Walter Frere', in C. Irvine (ed.), *They Shaped Our Worship: Essays on Anglican Liturgists* (London: SPCK, 1998), p. 49.

9

'Like an elephant waltzing'

PETER ALLAN CR

Walter Frere is, as others have noted, something of an enigma. His interest in church music and particularly the work he did on the medieval English chant manuscripts deepens rather than resolves the mystery. A keen amateur musician, he nonetheless showed himself well equipped for the painstaking, detailed work of analysis when he turned his energies to the Sarum manuscripts; a liturgist, whose enthusiasm seemingly knew no bounds and who was forever dashing off in pursuit of some new lead; a priest, a bishop, a brother of the Community of the Resurrection with a passion for the life of the Church: but, in such a complex and gifted character, does his liturgical musicology provide evidence of increasing integration of these disparate strands? The evidence rather firmly suggests not, though it could be argued that there were particular mitigating factors. Before turning to what might be missing, let us give attention to the source of Frere's enduring reputation in the field of Western chant studies, confident at least of his wholehearted commitment to the project. An obituary article in *The Sign* for January 1940 says of him:

> He would run an obscure antiphon to earth even if it meant a search through the glory-holes of half the churches of France. 'Why do you do it' someone would say, and he would reply, 'Why not? Other people collect stamps.'

This chapter seeks to do no more than sketch a context for understanding Frere's work in the field of Western chant and, out of the considerable corpus of completed and published work, takes notice of only a handful of publications: the two major Sarum facsimiles, Frere's contributions to *The Elements of Plainsong*, first published by the Plainsong and Mediaeval

Music Society in 1895, and his collaboration with H.B. Briggs, *A Manual of Plainsong*, often affectionately referred to simply as 'Briggs & Frere'. Of these the *Elements of Plainsong* is particularly important for it gives a clear summary of the extent to which interest in the chant amongst Frere and his contemporaries was keeping abreast of the unfolding story on the continent, that story that is so intimately bound up with the restoration of Benedictine life at the Abbey of Solesmes.

Some 116 years after the publication of Frere's facsimile edition of the Sarum *Graduale* (1894) and some 86 years after the completed publication of the *Antiphonale* (1901–24), both editions remain authoritative landmarks known and respected far and wide by chant scholars and liturgists. Their significance is manifold. There is the sheer technical achievement, represented by the high quality photographic plates; there is the pioneering element, for recognition of the importance of making historic manuscripts available for scrutiny and analysis was still in its infancy; and there is Frere's own immensely detailed examination reflected most especially in his introduction to the *Antiphonale*. Yet immediately the element of mystery strikes us. Was Frere a liturgist with an enthusiasm for music that, by sheer hard work, he turned to musicological skill? Or should he be regarded equally as a musicologist and a liturgist? There is, certainly, a marked difference between the two introductory essays: that to the *Graduale* is very much the work of the liturgist, but the introduction to the *Antiphonale* contains painstaking analyses of antiphon formulae and a minute examination of the invitatories that remain models of their kind and exemplars of work that has still to be carried out for parts of the chant corpus.

By the time Frere began work on the *Graduale*, renewed interest in the Sarum rite was already high. Wiseman, in 1842, had celebrated Easter using the Sarum rite, 'aware of its appeal to Young England and the Oxford men'[1] (something that had delighted the architect Pugin, who happened to be there). In Anglican circles, the Sarum rite represented access to the pre-Reformation tradition in a way that allowed both connection with, and separation from, Rome and thus had special appeal for those who were realizing the consequences of the Oxford Movement.

---

1 R. Hill, *God's Architect: Pugin and the Building of Romantic England* (London: Allen Lane, 2007), p. 264.

Almost without exception, the Anglican religious communities supplemented the official prayer of the Church of England with material from the Sarum office books. As a liturgist Frere thus had much reason to begin the facsimile project.

Shortly after publication of the *Graduale*, an anonymous review appeared in the *Church Times*.[2] The article is remarkable in its own right. It contains only one, somewhat laconic, reference to Frere, 'the book is admirably edited by the Rev. W.H. Frere', and the opening sentence (rightly) makes much of the extraordinary technological and artistic advances represented by the photographic plates:

> It has been an incalculable advantage that concurrently with the revived interest in ecclesiastical antiquities and the spread of the Catholic movement there should be such rapid progress in art, and especially that of photography. In antique documents, such as this under consideration, accuracy is of the very highest importance, and the reproduction by such processes of these treasures, clearly conduces to that end in a very high degree.

The article then continues with a detailed description of the pre-Reformation Mass. Clearly driven by a sense of widespread ignorance, the author makes no attempt to describe the variety of the music or even the character of the various scribes' hands that created the MSS. The two, brief references to music are themselves worth quoting for the extent to which they reveal the general level of understanding of the chant tradition:

> The book is fully supplied with music in the square note, and usually on a stave of four lines; but occasionally a stave of five lines is used, and we cannot refrain from saying here that we think if it had been generally, many inconveniences would have been avoided, such as changing the position of the clef, in consequence of the notes going off the stave if it were retained in its original place. It may be mentioned that there is in St John's College Cambridge, a fine Antiphonarium in which the stave is of five lines throughout, with scarcely an exception;

---

2 *Church Times*, 21 and 28 June, 1895.

and in these days of much musical knowledge, we believe the advocates of Plain-song handicap themselves unnecessarily by the retention of the four-line stave.

The second reference is still more amusing:

But the music of the 'Verses' of the Gradual, which correspond to the preceding [i.e., the Psalms of the Office], is of a much more elaborate type; being apparently a Psalm Tone with insertion and embellishment producing a result differing little, if at all, from an Antiphon. This treatment necessarily produced the assignment of many notes to one syllable of text, a practice which doubtless was considered a just exploit of art, and therefore became fashionable, until by unreasonable excess, it created a revulsion of feeling. We cannot avoid sympathising with Archbishop Cranmer in directing that the adaptation of Plainsong to the English Prayer Book should be 'syllable for note' as nearly as possible; although we do think that in some cases this rule has been too rigidly adopted.

In devoting the bulk of the article to liturgical form the reviewer is, to some extent, following a lead given by Frere himself. He makes it plain that a primary purpose is to arouse the interest of liturgists in what might seem at first sight something for musicians only.[3] Indeed, the whole of his introductory essay treats of the liturgical evolution of the eucharistic rite. There is no analysis of the music, no reference to significant differences in the musical text in other traditions. We note that the Preface was written at Radley in 1895, in other words, in the very early years of Frere's life in the Community of the Resurrection. He writes with the passion and enthusiasm of the young liturgist, but gives no hint of any appreciation of the spiritual or affective significance of the chant in question and shows no apparent interest in the evolution of musical form represented in the manuscripts. His focus is rather on encouraging the view (now significantly less favoured) that Sarum (like other regional

---

3 Preface: 'it is hoped that at least the index, and perhaps the dissertation too, may in some degree facilitate the work, and be serviceable to liturgical scholars, who have no special interest in the music as such, and have on that account been slow to grapple with books which primarily are musical'.

rites) is primarily to be understood as the transmission of the Roman wellspring, the fundamental liturgical source, than a creation in its own right.

The enduring value of the published facsimile lies then not so much in the way in which it made available and encouraged familiarization with the melodies of the Sarum rite, but above all in the detailed indexing of the available MSS. As the palaeographical workshop at Solesmes was now well established, this facsimile (together with the careful references to the other available sources) was a significant addition. The technical demands involved in making such a volume had only recently been resolved, yet Frere's two volumes are of a very high standard and the photographic plates are, almost without exception, extraordinarily good.

Yet for all the obvious focus on the liturgical questions, the facsimile *Graduale Sarisburiense* is not entirely bereft of insights into the musical text. Characteristically, the gems are mostly to be found in the notes to the index of MSS. Thus we read on p xxxvi:

A careful comparison with Sol.[4] would shew [*sic*] many little ways in which the English Tradition differed uniformly from the foreign, *e.g.* (i) in the avoidance of the quilisma and the various alternatives adopted in its place; (ii) regular variant interpretations of the same pneum, *e.g.,* a pes sub-bipunctis resupinus beginning a.c.b.a in England returns to c but in Sol and most French books to b. (*see* P.M.[5] ii., facsimiles of 'Justus ut palma', where both customs are represented). But in the following notes no attempt has been made at this minute criticism, but only at indicating the major points in which our MS. differs from some other Graduals.[6]

Much is conveyed in this short note.

Frere acknowledges the pre-eminence of the new Solesmes editions: the 1883 *Gradual* marks another important step along the way to recovering reliable texts for performance. He also hints at his own preference for the retention of differing strands of the tradition in suggesting that the differences are not major, but proper for a national

---

4 *Liber Gradualis in Usum Congregationis Benedictinae Galliarum* (Tournai, 1883).

5 *Paléographie Musicale*, Solesmes, 1889– .

6 *Graduale Sarisburiense*, 1894, p. xxxvi.

development; and he demonstrates his technical fluency in citing one of the more complex neums as an example of such difference (not many of his contemporaries would have been able to recognize a pes sub-bipunctis resupinus if they saw one). This much we acknowledge, but it is the result of Frere's painstaking attention to detail and his careful observation of what lay before him. At another level there is a lack of curiosity that is, we may suppose, the result of a combination of factors: the immense scale of his general work and interest, allowing only comparatively little time for this musicological research; and the limited extent and availability of other useful research. This was, in so many ways, still unexplored territory. Nonetheless we may be forgiven for wishing that he had chosen to make a detailed comparison of the Sarum MSS with the English Benedictine and Cistercian MSS. Arguably, this would have provided clearer evidence of what was indeed 'English', but might also have suggested that the importance of the Cistercians in England had led to some characteristics of the Cistercian chant tradition finding their way into the Sarum MSS.

The facsimile edition of the Sarum Antiphonal is an altogether more monumental undertaking. The 1925 introduction concentrates on the music and provides a model of close analysis of the responds (responsories), the invitatories and the antiphons, concluding with a marvellously detailed consideration of the available manuscripts. Frere chooses to treat of the responds first because of their roots in recitation, which he rightly regards as a primitive strand, despite the fact that the responds he examines are all of the later, developed kind. Here a real desire to help the reader appreciate the intricacy of the compositional method is evident, emerging from Frere's own deep familiarity with the material. The modern reader is struck immediately by the depth of observation and yet, at the same time, by its limited usefulness since it is (inevitably, given the historical moment) based solely on the post-Guidonian manuscripts (see further below). There is also no weight given to the way in which the very structure of the language of the text might have influenced the subtle adjustments of the melodic formulae. The section on the Invitatories, though brief, is a model of clarity and makes the form so attractive that it is all the more to be regretted that it is now almost impossible to hear Psalm 95 sung with its proper Invitatory antiphons anywhere. The last part is Frere at his most fluent. He knows the antiphon corpus intimately and all is handled with deftness and efficiency. In the bound volume in the Community library a sheet of manuscript paper (ruled in four line staves) sets out some of the models (actually referring to some of the responds, but placed in the midst of the antiphon section) in his own minute hand with a note for the printer, hoping that it can be set just so, with lines to indicate the points of correspondence. When it comes to antiphons of the *tetrardus* and he is discussing the eighth mode, he says of one of the very simple, early forms, 'This is a neat little theme that comes a good many times in the Psalter'[7] and how right he is. However, while noting one or two eighth mode patterns that are particularly associated with Easter he makes no further attempt to suggest reasons for such a connection. On the fourth mode, he unsurprisingly makes much of the series of antiphons found particularly in Advent, but occurring very generally throughout the Antiphonal. Here the modern reader is struck by the comparison with Cardine's discussion of the same set of antiphons in his *Sémiologie Grégorienne*[8] and it is immediately apparent that Frere is viewing the variants simply as musical adaptations. At one level, this makes Frere's work all the more remarkable, but we cannot help notice his apparent blindness to the unique relationship between word and text that finally makes it impossible to speak of the chant simply as music. Rather, we are reminded of Godehard Joppich's description of the chant as 'articulated text'.

One of the strengths of Katherine Bergeron's[9] study of the Solesmes' revival of the chant lies in her characterization of the different phases of the restoration. It is clear that Frere found himself well equipped to contribute to the second, 'scientific' phase. His exceptional capacity for tenacious precision (albeit developed as a counter to his swift mind's 'weakness for the quick theory' as Dix recalled[10]) was exactly the kind of forensic study that would open up the treasury of English medieval chant for wider study and appreciation. Indeed, there is more than a hint that Frere believed there were technical arguments that, if correctly applied, led to the elucidation of an accurate musical text. His own liturgical sensibilities would, however, have limited such accuracy to a particular

---

7 *Antiphonale Sarisburiense, 1901–24*, Introduction, p. 75.

8 E. Cardine, *Sémiologie Grégorienne* (Solesmes, 1970).

9 K. Bergeron, *Decadent Enchantments: The Revival of Gregorian Chant at Solesmes* (Berkeley: University of California Press, 1998).

10 G. Dix, 'The Liturgist', in C.S. Phillips (ed.), *Walter Howard Frere, Bishop of Truro* (London: Faber & Faber, 1947), p. 121.

location, for he saw each, Roman, Gallican, Sarum, etc., as having their own proper characteristics even though he understood all to derive from the Roman wellspring.

Yet there remain at least two major puzzles. Nowhere does Frere suggest even an awareness of the lived experience of the chant, the effect of being washed in its ebb and flow for a lifetime in one of the monastic houses of Europe; no sense of the consequences of being caught up in the spiritual world it evoked; and, similarly, there is no sense of the manner in which that way of life nurtured the development of the chant and partnered it in a symbiotic relationship of quite extraordinary fruitfulness: the way in which the tradition of Benedictine monasticism shaped the emerging European culture through its theology and spirituality and for both of which the chant proved such a powerful vehicle.

To some extent this is unsurprising. Benedictine monasticism was itself only just emerging from the shadows of Napoleonic suppression on the continent. In England, despite the return of monks from Douai to England in 1795, it was not until the passing of the Catholic Relief Act of 1829 that a securely grounded restoration could begin to become effective. Even then, for all the proud, unbroken witness of the English Benedictine Congregation, it was not until the twentieth century and Abbess Laurentia McLachlan's reign at Stanbrook that something of the dynamism of a Benedictine community shaped by the mysterious language of the chant was once again made visible, or, more appropriately, audible.

Without intending any irony, it was into such a monastic wilderness that the Anglican communities of the nineteenth century emerged. Romantic enthusiasm for the medieval and the powerful Gothick Revival ensured an assiduous search for the appropriate forms and patterns of life. It was from just such enthusiasm that the project of making the chant of the Sarum rite available in English adaptations was undertaken: this was a proper tool for a religious congregation. (The fact that the Use of Salisbury was a secular rite appears never to have been a significant consideration.) Such a labour did indeed produce good fruit, but the foundations of the exercise were always shaky. There was a technical conviction: this is what should be done; but it was unsupported by any appreciation of the theological and spiritual significance. As the task developed, more and more complex pieces of chant were set to English texts, sometimes with disastrous results. As recently as 20 years ago,

Anglican sisters could be heard singing a melisma of some 27 notes to the little word 'of', without the slightest awareness that the Latin original set the same melisma to the second syllable of the word *amor* (love).

Yet Frere's own community had a growing experience of singing the chant, albeit in English, and Frere contributed significantly to that. He championed the use of Palmer's *Sarum Psalter*[11] and relied on it heavily in producing the more modest *Manual of Plainsong* (1902) with H.B. Briggs that stood in direct succession to Helmore's *The Psalter Noted* of 1849.[12] Given Frere's passion for antiphons it is curious that he was willing to put his name to a psalter that is entirely without antiphons, and musically ungrammatical as a result. There is no satisfactory explanation for this: Frere himself, ever the pragmatist, implies that it is a matter of beginning with the most basic elements and gradually expanding. Thus, in the 1902 Introduction he writes, 'When the chanting of a simple Tone has been perfected, it will be easy to apply the principles to the more elaborate Tones and Endings.'[13] But the absence of the antiphons is only underlined by his early remark in the Introduction

> It is the Antiphons, indeed, which, strictly speaking, should determine which Tone is to be sung, and complete the Tone (which of itself more often than not is incomplete), and should thus serve as a melodic cadence in the Mode, or what in modern music would be called a *Coda*.[14]

He was clearly persuaded by the theoretical approach Palmer had evolved for adapting the chant to the English text and there is, indeed, no reason why it cannot be sung with a fair degree of musicality. However, this is to set aside what is surely the most fundamental achievement of the Latin psalm tones: the creation of a melodic and rhythmic frame that succeeds

---

11 G.H. Palmer, *The Introduction and Tone-Table to the Sarum Psalter* (2nd edn, London: George Bell & Sons, 1898).

12 Thomas Helmore, *Accompanying Harmonies to the Psalter Noted* (London: Novello, 1849). The modern reader is inclined to forget just how many worked at producing adaptations of the psalm tones for English texts. Palmer lists Dyce, Oakley, Heathcote, Helmore, Shaw, Sargent, Ravenscroft and Monk in his essay on Psalmody in H.B. Briggs (ed.), *The Elements of Plainsong* (London: Plainsong and Mediaeval Music Society, 1895).

13 H.B. Briggs and W.H. Frere, *A Manual of Plainsong* (London: Novello, 1902).

14 Briggs and Frere, *Manual of Plainsong*.

in holding the attention of the singers and grounding them simultaneously in the deep meaning of the text (a meaning beneath the surface
sense of the words) and in the divine reality out of which they come. It is
certainly not that the singers are transported to the heavenly kingdom,
but the stability of the underlying rhythm opens up a space-time
dimension beyond the present reality. Palmer, in the *Sarum Psalter*, had
lost this at a stroke: he treats each tone differently for each text and the
strong and weak syllables of each psalm are differently handled in the
different tones. There is a strong argument for suggesting that the irregu-
larities of the English language demand such a treatment, but any serious
immersion in the Latin tradition demonstrates the much richer and more
complex way in which a deep, underlying stability of rhythm is given a
priority that actually serves attention to the text. A classic illustration is
the device employed by Palmer, and also by Briggs and Frere, of the so-
called abrupt mediation. In psalm tones 2, 5 and 8 the mediation simply
rises a tone and falls back to the reciting note. Faced with the many
mediations in the English text that ended with a single strong syllable
(Lord, soul, Son, seen) the adaptors chose to omit the final note and leave
the melody hanging. This clearly makes sense in relation to the actual
words, but it undermines that still more important underlying, tidal
rhythm. In practice, it proved a reasonably successful solution when the
chant was accompanied, but it provides yet another illustration of the
way in which a theoretical approach dictated Frere's teaching of the chant
rather than a deeply lived experience of singing it.

Certainly missing from the story of the use of the chant in England (in
either Latin or English) was any sustained reflection on some of the more
remarkable elements of the history. We must allow for the extent to which
the history of both the chant and the evolution of St Benedict's Rule is
understood so differently in the light of increased knowledge, but the
absence of any serious attention to the spiritual qualities of the chant is
astonishing. If Gore's Community of the Resurrection is in any way typical of the late nineteenth century then it can perhaps shed light. When, in
the 1980s, the Community gave serious attention to its founding documents for the first time in the Community's history, we were surprised by
the underlying positivism. That this was characteristic of the late nineteenth century is not in doubt, but it is more surprising that it should have
such a presence here. The confidence, if not arrogance, that prefaced the
Rule of the Community thus, 'The Community of the Resurrection shall

consist of celibate priests who combine together at the call of God to reproduce the life of the first Christians' is just one of the more dramatic evidences. Yet perhaps this too gave rise to Charles Gore's oft-quoted anxiety lest 'appearance outstrip reality'. Insofar as both influenced Frere, this may give some indication of the reason for his refusing to stray beyond observation and analysis in all his work on the chant. In the Introduction to the Sarum Antiphonal (p. 62) Frere notes that the Hereford Tonal[15]explains that the Eighth Mode is the only one without an invitatory tone and 'ventures on a mystical reason for the fact'. His obvious dissatisfaction with the explanation is more broadly puzzling. He clearly knew of the earlier medieval facility for mystical and allegorical exegesis of both Scripture and liturgy, but is seemingly determined that contemporary chant scholarship shall be free of such limitation. He certainly pursues such a course without any apparent anxiety as to what might be lost.

This prompts mention of the extraordinary relationship between Scripture and the chant. It is little exaggeration to say that the worship of the Western church in the first millennium was totally dominated by the chant and Scripture. Even those texts that were not themselves Scripture, in almost every case, remain verbally closer to Scripture than, say, even the most inspired of Charles Wesley's hymns. This fundamental dialogue is itself deeply bound up with the very business of doing theology. How is it that we come to speak of monastic theology as a distinct model of theological discourse? Primarily, it is because the experience of being immersed in the texts of Scripture through the medium of the chant in the seemingly timeless ebb and flow of the monody facilitated a kind of attentive listening, both conscious and subconscious that remains unrivalled.

This quality of attention is fundamental: we marvel at the oral transmission of the chant repertoire. It is not the discrepancies between the manuscripts that is astonishing but the convergence. The care taken to ensure that melodies were faithfully remembered and passed on from community to community and from country to country is a fruit of a kind of serious listening that is itself theologically grounded. The pregnant word 'Listen' with which St Benedict begins the Prologue of his Rule for monks proves an inexhaustible source of reflection. For Benedict

---

15 Hereford Breviary, III. liii.

the whole life of the community was an attentive listening to the voice of Christ, an expectant openness to encounter with Christ present in that carefully presented series of sacramental encounters: in the Word of Scripture, in the Eucharist, in the Abbot, in the guests, in the brothers, in prayer, study and work. In communities thus expecting daily encounter with the Risen Christ the chant emerged as a uniquely supple vehicle that could both carry the texts that communicated such presence and, increasingly, become a bearer of that presence in its own right. The evidence of such development in the Western chant also reveals moments of delight and humour. The Magnificat antiphon for the feast of the Apostle Andrew is the text from Matthew's Gospel telling of the call of the first apostles and speaking of Simon and Andrew leaving their boat to follow Jesus. In the manuscript the Latin of the Vulgate has the word *navis* and the neum for the first syllable is a porrectus. Even a quick glance at the Barnwell manuscript in Frere's facsimile suggests that the scribe was caught by the connection between the image of the boat in the text and the way the shape of the porrectus hinted at a sketch of a boat with a sail.[16] Or, in an altogether different register, the Introit for Corpus Christi sets the text from Psalm 81 'Cibavit eos' and includes reference to the honey from the rock. Here the Latin for honey 'melle' (in the ablative) is precisely notated with a liquescent to ensure the pronunciation of the first 'l'.[17] The effect is much greater and, once again, the scribe must have delighted in such a graphic representation of the stickiness of honey. These are but two of the countless examples of the fruits of the kind of listening nurtured simultaneously by obedience to the Rule of St Benedict and painstaking attention to the faithful transmission of the chant, first orally and subsequently in the manuscripts.

The collection of lectures edited by Briggs and published by the Plainsong and Mediaeval Music Society in 1895 under the title *The Elements of Plainsong* does much, however, to restore our appreciation of the extraordinary work achieved by Frere and his colleagues in advancing an understanding of Western chant in England. Henry Briggs himself contributed three lectures to the printed text, but Frere writes on tonality, hymnody, the music of the Holy Eucharist and accompaniment, with Abdy Williams and Palmer contributing just one lecture each. Briggs's

---

16 *Antiphonale Sarisburiense*, vol. III, p. 345.
17 *Graduale Triplex* (Solesmes, 1979), p. 377.

fine essay on notation includes a serious engagement with the pre-Guidonian notation that serves to underline just how many layers of interpretation need to be uncovered before certain conclusions become possible. Thus, the raw materials with which Cardine and others laboured in the mid-twentieth century are here laid bare, but the gulf between Briggs and Cardine is great. Tucked into the back of the Community's copy is correspondence between Frere and Percy Sankey, of the Plainsong and Mediaeval Music Society, concerning a reprint of *Elements*. After Briggs's death in 1901 Frere was the major figure. He writes to Sankey in July 1908 with his suggestions:

> In the first place I think that practically the whole of it ought to be reprinted except Abdy Williams' chapter on Rhythm which can be wholly omitted I think and Briggs' general outline, of which only a part need be kept.

He gives no detailed explanation for leaving out Abdy Williams on Rhythm, but it is a very significant omission. Williams's piece is dependent on the general approach to the performance of the chant that derived from Dom Pothier's labours and his experience as choir master at Solesmes. But Pothier had been succeeded in 1889 by Dom Mocquereau and the *méthode bénédictine* (as the Solesmes approach had become generally known since 1901) was undergoing a serious revision. Like Frere, Mocquereau was not content with an interpretation based on feeling: he looked for the scientific evidence. A century later we recognize the shrewd judgement that led Frere to recommend the omission of an essay on rhythm that was on the cusp of becoming anachronistic, even as we are better able to distinguish between the shortcomings and the pioneering insights of Dom Mocquereau's work.

Lest the tone become too serious, it is Frere's own essay on accompaniment that provides the title for this piece. He carefully puts the case for and against accompanying the chant, beginning with the assertion that 'the extreme purist is theoretically unassailable. When plainsong was at its zenith, it was always sung unaccompanied.'[18] The case against begins:

---

18 Briggs, *Elements of Plainsong*, p. 86.

The extreme vandal on the other hand has nothing to back him. If he wishes to use in Church-worship all the resources of modern harmony, by all means let him do so; there is plenty of good music written for the purpose: but let him keep clear of plainsong.[19]

In the end, his concern is for the 'safeguarding of the old tonality in its purity'[20] and this suggests a minimalist approach. After all, he notes, 'we have most of us heard plainsong so sung that it sounded like an elephant waltzing: this is generally the fault of the accompaniment'.[21] In considering a reprint he clearly felt these observations still worth making.

Painstakingly precise observation, moments of dazzling acuity and insight: there is no shortage of evidence of Frere's astonishing capacity. Yet there is cause for regret. For, as we have seen, historical accident, the particular character of the Community of the Resurrection (that so largely bears the mark of Frere's influence) and the absence of significant experience of living the chant (apart from the monastery of Solesmes) leaves the Frere legacy distinctly lop-sided. It is useless to speculate on what might have been, but we cannot help but wonder how differently Walter Frere's spiritual and affective life might have developed had he been able to discover the resources that later generations are now rediscovering. There was clearly a deep hunger in him for a living liturgy. As early as 1893 he had written:

We go to Church with a hymn book (an unauthorized supplement to our Prayer Book) in hand prepared to sing at any service any hymn that may be given out when the time comes: & in fact hymns have come to be looked upon so much as part of the services that they tend to obscure other & more important parts: eg at many services we are content lazily to read our psalms canticles Creed Sanctus Gloria &c instead of singing them & think we have done all that should be if we sing a hymn somewhere 'to brighten up the service'.[22]

This is an astonishing plea from the young liturgist and it does

---

19 Briggs, *Elements of Plainsong*, p. 87.
20 Briggs, *Elements of Plainsong*, p. 90.
21 Briggs, *Elements of Plainsong*, p. 90.
22 *Plainsong Hymnody*, 21 June 1893.

significantly anticipate the guidance issued from Rome some 70 years later on the implementation of the liturgical reforms of Vatican II.[23] Perhaps the ineffectiveness of the modern document in reforming practice suggests that a theoretical appreciation of what *should be* is still not sufficient to encourage change unless it results in a renewal of the encounter with the risen Christ, without which liturgy is an empty shell.

---

23 *Musicam Sacram*, 5 March 1967 AAS 60 (1967) 300–320; Not 3 (1967) 87–105; Vatican Polyglot Press (§ 27–36) in *Documents on the Liturgy*, 1963–1979.

10

Life in Community

GEORGE GUIVER CR

At first he wanted to be a friar. While a curate in Stepney he thought of forming a parish-based community, and took an interest in a local attempt to start a group of friars. He paid a visit to the Society of St John the Evangelist at Cowley. He got to know Charles Gore, and he joined the Society of the Resurrection while thinking something more demanding was needed. Then, in February 1892, Walter Frere left Stepney and joined the small group at Pusey House, Oxford, who were to form the first nucleus of CR. He would be the key figure in shaping the new Community once Gore had departed from the scene.

His character

Frere is intriguing. Piecing together what we know about him, it is difficult to conjure up in our minds a coherent picture from the ingredients. Behind a serenely delightful exterior was a firmly reined-in impatience that began to make itself evident only in his last years. We might expect that behind such a controlled exterior lay a deeply affectionate person, and people's accounts of working with him, and his own easy way with children, suggest this. His vision of the Community as a family that must avoid becoming too male in its habits comes out in genuine signs of love for the brethren. His letter to the Community on becoming Bishop of Truro starts: 'Brethren greatly beloved and never more dearly than now'. In his *Commentary* he writes on the Community's relation to each brother that 'It is responsible for having originally elected him, and it continues responsible for retaining him, for influencing him and for loving him.'

Charming, attractive, a pleasure to be with, his ability to entertain audiences, sometimes hilariously with singing, dancing and imitations, was because of the unstuffy 'toff' that he was. It went, too, with a lack of any common touch at all in his preaching in parishes, while for people of his own cultural background his sermons are lucid, human and enlivened with down-to-earth illustrations. He could never be called superficial, for, as we shall see, his view of the religious life was serious and demanding, and his scholarly work showed a daunting level of application; and yet it is difficult to find in his writings any sustained questing or probing. His immense work on medieval chant manuscripts was never brought together in any synthesis. Gregory Dix, in sorting through his liturgical papers after his death, found masses of material that was unusable because only Frere had the key, and masses more falls out of books on the Community's shelves today. He was a scholarly squirrel, delighting in collecting, cataloguing and storing all over the place vast piles of nuts that might never again see the light of day, with no apparent thought for any who might come after to benefit from this labour and build upon it. He had toyed with being a composer, yet 'Most of [his songs] ... have a good melodic line ... But there is little in the way of thematic development and too often the good start seems to "peter out".'[1] One can feel the same about his *Commentary on the Rule* (on which, more below): a good start, but his Community was left with no follow-up or deeper reflection. An extraordinary fact is that he showed little interest in studying the religious life as such. His tidy view of the Church of England as the Catholic Church in this land on a par with Rome on the continent and Orthodoxy in the East seemed to be troubled by no spirit of exploration, no anguished questioning of this watertight vision. If Keble Talbot, when newly arrived at Mirfield, described Frere as 'much the biggest man here',[2] that is an indication of his spiritual stature, intelligence, integrity and clear strength of character, but not necessarily of ability to husband his gifts and many talents into creations of lasting and penetrating worth – except, we would have to say, in his nursling, the Community of the Resurrection. In that at least we see signs of greatness, as well as other enduring traces of his curious character. Without Walter, there can be no

---

1 C.S. Phillips et al., *Walter Howard Frere, Bishop of Truro* (London: Faber & Faber, 1947), p. 160.

2 Quoted in A. Wilkinson, *The Community of the Resurrection: A Centenary History* (London: SCM Press, 1992), p. 124.

doubt that the Community would have had far less about it. We read that after a discussion on celibacy in 1896 'it was felt on the whole that the discussion rather suffered from the absence of Walter'.[3]

He had a deep resistance to making his inner life and feelings accessible to others. Supremely self-contained, he harboured, probably without being fully aware of it, an aversion to being set in a frame, portrayed or pigeonholed; we cannot help but see here one of those deep 'tapes' set running in childhood, ever to condition thereafter a person's actions and responses until their last breath. He was difficult to pin down, serpentine, even, it has to be said, devious when the occasion required. In the wider world of church politics he could come over as mercurial, shifting his position and engagement in a discussion, leaving people unsure what to expect. He cannot have been fully aware of the degree to which this deep drive made him come over as undependable or maverick in the public sphere. People who hoped to profit from his contribution could find themselves reduced to a puzzled silence. One wonders how this played out in Frere as Superior; according to Wilkinson:

> He appeared to govern CR with a light hand, but his clear mind was always two moves ahead and he often advanced obliquely, like a knight in chess evading capture by partisans (as Talbot put it in Phillips' biography of Frere), a 'strange mixture of saintliness and foxiness'.[4]

Whatever else comes across from accounts of him or from reading his writings, it is clear he was a born leader.

Frere and Community

Walter Frere was so closely bound up with the genesis of CR that this account will be as much concerned with the Community as with him. It is difficult to see how far the CR vision emerged from a ferment of thinking in the Community, and how far from him. He certainly espoused and promoted it with conviction. Not only did his vision of a form of priestly community life predate the Community, but so did the core of the

---

3 *Chronicle of the Community of the Resurrection* (Mirfield: CR), I.99.
4 Wilkinson, *Centenary History*, p. 80.

CR Rule, which had started off as a devotional rule for clergy in the parish. This is a key to understanding both Walter and CR: a gradual transition from parish ministry to that of a religious community, rather than a complete break in order to embark on a new way of life. This origin in the parish lay behind the Community's vivacity and social engagement, but also led to weaknesses and shadows.

If we want to know what Walter Frere was like as a member of the Community, there is very little to go on; and if we want to learn of his understanding of the Community's way of life, neither is that a straight-forward matter. The fullest source for exploring Frere's relation to community life is his *Commentary on the Rule*, completed in 1907 when CR was 15 years old. It was formally approved by Chapter after vetting by a committee of which Frere was not a member, and privately printed for internal use without being published. It remained a living document for CR. Occasionally, as when a novitiate was first created in 1919, the Community adapted its wording; it had sufficient standing to be regarded as a document to be studied alongside the Rule. A slim volume, only 55 pages in small pocket format, its style is slightly academic, sometimes inspiring, even stirring, sometimes prosaic bordering on the prim. It opens by attempting to show what makes the religious life distinctive:

> The Religious Life in its essence is one; but it presents itself in many different forms. It is a life which aims at union with God in Christ by means of certain bonds and detachments, which are not those of ordinary Christian life; they are not indeed different from them in kind, for everywhere and in all circumstances the love of God and man is one, detachment from the world is one, hostility to evil is one; but in the Religious Life such bonds and detachments appear to such a degree in an emphasized form that they must be more rightly regarded as special than as general.[5]

This raises the question of where CR finds itself among the 'many different forms'. It is often said in CR that Walter consolidated the monastic aspects of our life, and in this way was complementary to Gore, but the matter is not so simple as that. Walter had a strong sense of what

---

5 W. Frere, *A Commentary on the Rule* (unpublished, 1907), p. 175.

was needed to sustain community, trying for instance to dissuade Gore from taking up the post at Westminster Abbey. His high notion of community is essentially monastic, but we need some clarification here on the misleading ways in which the word 'monastic' is often used.

Monastic?

CR brothers do not habitually refer to themselves as monks, and from the beginning have often wanted to make a distinction between their own life and that of monasteries. It has not been properly recognized, however, that the monasticism from which they sought to distance themselves was that of the nineteenth century. They shunned its terminology and outward trappings, and yet at the same time developed a liturgy more monastic than that of most monastic communities today. The discipline and structures, too, that evolved in the Community were more monastic than those of some Benedictine communities today. In trying to understand this dichotomy we need to realize that the difference between the CR founders and nineteenth-century monasticism turns on CR's anthropology, that is, their understanding of what it was to be a human being in modern times. The monasticism of the nineteenth century seemed to ignore that anthropology. CR's founders envisaged something new: a community of mature, educated adults, with a life based on certain standards of liberty, its decision-making as far as possible based on discussion among equals. They sought to replace child – parent relationships with adult – adult relating. This was new for its time, while today it has become general almost everywhere in religious communities. CR was ahead of its time, and because of that differed radically from the monasticism it was familiar with. That monasticism from which the founding brothers wished to distance themselves has disappeared – nowadays the careful balance evolved in CR between monastic life and modern expectations about human maturity and liberty is the common task of all healthy religious communities.

This sets the scene for building a picture of Walter Frere in relation to community: he firmly believed in an anthropology ahead of its time in the church at large. CR was a very Victorian – Edwardian foundation, born in times of confidence, optimism and energy, embarking on an audacious range of undertakings while still small in numbers (spurred on by Walter's daring and vision): the College, the South African Mission, the building of an enormous church (the present one is perhaps two-thirds of the size intended), the founding of the Hostel in Leeds. It was an era of confidence in democracy and gradually extending suffrage; of original and bold re-imagining of traditional structures. Children of their age, the founders eschewed the documents of the monastic tradition, except as important points of reference among many others: they sought a new creation that would bypass monastic history to draw inspiration directly from the picture of the primitive church portrayed in Acts 2 and 4, producing an equivalent to that early fervent life with modern means. In his *Commentary* Walter writes:

> It is not at all surprising to note that [monastic systems of government] have been profoundly influenced by the general theories of government prevailing at the time. A modern community such as ours very naturally has much that is democratic in its system of government.[6]

CR took many practices and conventions from inherited monastic tradition, but Frere adds that 'We have adopted also other features which are characteristic of family life as we know it now in our own English homes, such as the use of the simple Christian name, the habit of conversation at meals, and so forth.'[7] A notion that recurs in the early decades is that of family, and Walter himself repeatedly takes it as one of the touchstones of the Community's life. In this context there is an emphatic treasuring of the individual. Walter has this to say about individual self-expression in the public arena: 'The Community ... will do all it can to secure for each of its brethren as large an area of liberty for self-expression as is possible.'[8] This self-expression within and outside the Community related to the world of ideas – it was not expected to include public talk about the life of the Community itself, where the reticence appropriate to any human family was expected. With that proviso, the Community was unusual in encouraging freedom of expression on the questions of the day.

In these and other ways CR aimed to create *de novo*, drawing on what it was to be a human being in the contemporary world. This would lead

---

6 Frere, *Commentary*, p. 216.
7 Frere, *Commentary*, p. 210.
8 Frere, *Commentary*, p. 225.

to something distinctive, with a freshness and life that opened up new possibilities in the long story of Christian community life. We can see with hindsight, however, that while the early brethren thought they were creating something new, they were in fact ahead of their time, initiating a renewal of something old: in a nineteenth century not fully ready for it, they were doing a Vatican II on an ancient tradition. We should not be surprised to discover, however, that they did not get it quite right. Walter and his brothers failed to realize the degree to which liberty of this kind needs a well-founded maturity of vision if it is not to invade and weaken the living of the life itself. We only realize too late perhaps the need for careful monitoring and touches to the tiller in matters of this kind.

Leadership

Another element in this new start was a rejection of abbatial government: here again the Community was ahead of its time, evolving a subtle combination of individual leadership with exhaustive consultation and an assumption of equality. The usual approach to a Benedictine abbot's role today is much closer to what has always prevailed in CR. We may ask, however, whether the change in the Roman Catholic Church has yet gone far enough – abbots and mothers superior often have major difficulties in readjusting to life as ordinary members of community on retiring from office. This may in part be due to the continuing survival of 'monarchical' elements in their role, where the person is still too much of a persona, with a status, trappings and approaches to decision-making not yet fully attuned to a modern anthropology. Walter and the early brethren were clear that something new was needed. The matter was not straight-forward, however: a community's leader needs to be a spiritual father or mother, and responsible for taking certain kinds of decision; a difficult discernment is needed if that is to be held together in right balance with joint decision-making, proper accountability and a need for constant consultation. Walter was far from indecisive as a superior: he could be peremptory when occasion required it. In 1910 for instance he announced that he would require each brother to have a definite scheme of theo-logical study, and he would also visit rooms to inspect. In his *Commentary* he writes:

In respect of work to be undertaken by the brethren, the responsibility rests not with the Chapter but with the Superior or his representative. In this then, and in some other respects, there is personal government even in a system generally democratic; for matters that are personal to a brother, and only more remotely concern the Community as a whole, are best settled personally.[9]

It has never been easy in CR to find a balance of proper spiritual leadership with adult-to-adult relating, and that has led to travails and even real suffering. In common with many communities today, the quest goes on in what is new territory for everyone. The founders knew that what they saw in nineteenth-century abbots was not for them, but there is at least one very good reason why it has been extraordinarily difficult for CR to find a path it could tread securely. That reason will shortly become apparent.

The nature of a Rule

If we now turn to CR's Rule we immediately meet some of the limitations inherent in the whole approach. One of the prime functions of rule is to be a deposit of the wisdom of the tradition as it has accumulated over the centuries. Its role is inspirational before it is legislative. 'Constitutions' are then needed to provide an up-to-date legal framework (the word is plural, each chapter or unit being a 'constitution'– not therefore to be confused with the secular notion of 'a constitution'). A third document, a 'Customary', provides for lesser areas of the life, such as the timetable, that might change fairly frequently. CR used to have two documents: the Rule and 'The Constitution' (betraying here the secular presuppositions at work), both of them to be abandoned in the final years of the twentieth century. Frere will have had a large part in the framing of both documents, and often in them we hear his characteristic style. He speaks of the Rule as follows:

A Religious Rule comprises both the statement of an ideal and the enactment of a specific code of regulations. These two are related to one another like soul and body, the one being the inner reality and the

---

9 Frere, *Commentary*, p. 217.

other being the outward embodiment of it. There must be a necessary harmony between the two, but the ideal must always transcend the code. A brother is bound by loyalty to the first and by obedience to the second; but loyalty is greater than obedience. He lives therefore under a threefold obligation: – of obedience to his community's regulations, of loyalty to its ideal (both of these being defined by its rule), and further of personal fidelity to Christ.

The ideal, like all ideals, cannot adequately be expressed in words. But apart from the actual phrases of the rule it is expressed also in the life and tradition of the Community. These two forms of expression therefore are complementary, just as the written revelation and the living tradition are complementary to one another in the Church.

Every brother therefore has his share in the upholding of the ideal of the Community and in the handing on of its tradition. This is a sacred task; and let each one often reflect upon his own performance of it, with a great sense of shortcoming but a lively hope of amendment.[10]

This passage is interesting: he recognizes two aspects of the Rule, ideal and code. There is an abstract 'ideal', set out in the Rule but also to be found currently in the Community's life and its oral tradition (we shall return to this shortly). On the 'ideal', Walter is specific: 'The chief ideal of the Community is a renewal of the first fervour of the apostolic church in the primitive era.'[11] In the early decades of CR this picture portrayed in Acts was the controlling vision above all others, rather than monastic tradition.

Frere had come to the Community convinced that life vows were necessary, but soon changed his mind:

I feel my views about our rule much modified. I came here with strong feeling in favour of vows: discouraged by what seemed to me too medieval at Cowley [the Society of St John the Evangelist, or 'Cowley Fathers'] I hoped for something as binding but less monkish: more in

10 Frere, *Commentary*, pp. 176 f.
11 Frere, *Commentary*, p. 183.

the world, frankly and openly, but as tightly bound. But as we have
discussed, other views have become more strict and mine less in favour
of final bonds, so that we can meet heartily in our rule which demands
the idea of permanence in its obligation (I insisted on this) but will
not enforce it at the last resort ... We thus throw St Benet [Benedict] to
the winds and return to Apostolic freedom and community ideals
which I am more and more convinced is right, especially in view of the
hazy views among us as to what dispensing power there is and in view
of the troubles Cowley has experienced.[12]

Here we can see that he understood 'monkish' life as not being much 'in
the world frankly and openly'. With such thoughts in its mind the
Community specifically turned away from intervening monastic history:

It differs alike from communities which have sought their ideals in the
examples of religious life in subsequent eras,–as S. Benet founded his
rule upon the teaching of his predecessors and left it as an example to
his successors,–and also from those which have taken as their model
the three evangelical counsels.[13]

It was an audacious project, to bypass everything in order to rely solely on
the New Testament. All the time, however, so much of the monastic
tradition is there in the background. On Gore's proposed move to a
canonry in Westminster, Frere writes:

Poverty and obscurity are what we want ... Both Radley and
Westminster are too respectable to attract the sort of person we want
... If we do not take care we shall become a little body of middle-aged
Clergymen of unimpeachable respectability ... but no community –
much: no poverty – much: no obedience – much ... retrograde for us
who desire the development of a stricter and poorer house than Radley
and an opening for real parish work among the poor.[14]

---

12 Martin Jarrett-Kerr, 'A Lost Journal of +Walter Frere CR', *CR Quarterly* No. 325, St
John Baptist 1984, pp. 12–19 at p. 14.
13 Frere, *Commentary*, p. 183.
14 Quoted in Wilkinson, *Centenary History*, p. 57.

Walter's vision of what the Community should be was an open one, and we can see in the early years how his thinking changed this way and that. Before he had come to Pusey House he revealed a basic urge in a letter to Gore in 1891, writing of Cowley:

> I think I saw enough to shew that their ideal and the one I humbly pursue are very different: they seem to be so much monks and even monks of the Carthusian type, hermits; while the idea before me is rather that of friars – men detached by Vows from three at least of the bonds of the world but living in the world and actively ministering to its masses of untouched men and women.[15]

That was to remain the basis of what he sought. Predominant is a vision of a group of priests sharing a demanding and disciplined life of real community while very active in the service of the church in pastoral, missionary and teaching work. He took a lot of convincing on whether to admit lay brethren: he thought the real test was whether they were able to take a proper part in Chapter; in a second discussion shortly afterwards he added more: the test should be their capacity for priesthood.[16]

Obedience

There are attempts at community life today that aim first to write a rule and then to live by it, but the advice given by more experienced hands is to live the life first in order to gain the ability to write a rule. Classically a monastic rule is a distillation of a life already lived: an egg laid after the journey is under way, not a basis from which to start. For Frere this question takes a particularly stark form, for it is to the Rule that obedience is due: 'Obedience is the very essence of our profession; and the particular form of it that we profess is obedience to Rule.'[17] The classic understanding of obedience is a mutual listening between two parties. It is a way of relating, not only to those in leadership but also horizontally to one another. Obedience as mutual listening is a form of love – love of the other, of God and of the life. Obedience to Rule alone cannot but be

---

15 Wilkinson, *Centenary History*, p. 33.
16 *Chronicle* III, 26 and 28.
17 *Commentary*, p. 214.

individualistic and impersonal, and cannot be a living process in the classic sense – it is static and limited to prescribed formulas. It presents the vision, not of two people facing each other and listening (obedience) but of solitary individuals each following a text with a magnifying glass (compliance).

Walter now shows a surprisingly poor knowledge of monastic history: 'Herein we adhere to the old monastic tradition, before feudalism introduced into the system a more personal form of obedience, which was further developed by the Friars and pressed to its extreme by the Jesuit Order.'[18] His knowledge on this could not have been more inaccurate. Obedience is personal from the earliest beginnings of monasticism, from the Abba of the desert who was supposed to give the disciple a word, to Benedict and beyond, while the picture of the Jesuits given here is simply caricature. It was indeed St Benedict who first introduced the notion of obedience to Rule as a check to abuse of authority by abbots – his is a new notion of obedience to abbot and Rule rather than abbot alone. The Rule for Benedict, however, is an objective standard for Abbot and brothers, not something to which one makes profession, as was the case in CR.

What Frere does take from Benedict is the notion of minimum rather than maximum prescription: the Rule is to set a minimum beyond which the Community should seek to aspire, rather than stringent maximum demands for all to comply with. It is at this level that Benedict recognizes each person's individuality: the life has to be flexible enough to be workable with a wide variety of people, 'that the strong may have something to strive after while the weak are not discouraged'.[19] Rules on their own cannot achieve that, a point Frere shared with Gore, who hated rules and prescription.

All a bit contradictory, and there is some evidence that Walter was not fully comfortable with the Community's decision in favour of obedience to the Rule – he urges brothers to go beyond the thing they have vowed obedience to:

Let us provoke one another to good works in spiritual rivalry; and

---

18 *Commentary*, p. 214.
19 *Rule of St Benedict*, 64.19.

count that those things which are required of us are the least that we can do, or rather that they are to be the starting-point from which we are to aspire and ascend to better things. So by the inspiration of the Holy Spirit there may be among us a spiritual enthusiasm for progress; and even the best that God has taught us in the past, and that which we have learnt so slowly and so painfully, we shall soon leave behind us, as we reach forth to the things that are before and press on untiringly towards the prize of our high calling in Christ Jesus.[20]

On more than one point we feel Walter cannot be pinned down. He was passionate about engaging in demanding and almost nose-to-tail pastoral, missionary and other work, and yet asserts that work to be secondary. At one point in the Commentary he seems to equate the life with monastic life: outside work is a secondary element to that, vital to those for whom it is vital:

There has come into the religious life a secondary ideal and a secondary vocation, connected not with life as a whole, but with that special part of life which we call work. A community has its special work or works, which it seeks to carry out on the general basis of the religious life; and similarly there is to be taken into account in the case of the individual, not merely his call to the life in general, but the particular calling or occupation to which he can best devote himself, with that life as his basis and support. The work that our Community sets before itself is, in the main, priestly work and other activities ancillary to that work.[21]

Ideal versus concrete Grace

There are other strange contradictions. Postulating an abstract 'ideal' is characteristic of the Renaissance and Enlightenment, revealing a shadow side to CR's anthropology. The old CR Rule presumes first and foremost the mature individual adult – excellent so far. But a telltale phrase constantly recurs: 'each brother'. There is a danger here of a collective of clergymen individually just trying to be good in a humanly planned

20 *Commentary*, p. 178.
21 *Commentary*, p. 185.

cooperation. To this extent the founding of CR was an Enlightenment project, showing undue confidence in the human capacity to arrange things, to devise 'ideals', and privileging the rational over the incarnational. It is as if the Community were a machine that could simply be evolved by human experimentation. Gore had even said to James Nash in 1889 on the projected Community that 'friendship with a few wise rules well kept, makes the machine function'.[22] A German author once coined the term 'concrete Grace' to indicate that divine grace, rather than being just an abstract influence, comes in concrete forms and practices within the genetic transmission of tradition.[23] CR knows well what concrete Grace is, and has often got its hands dirty in the living of it (pastoral work, schools, colleges, the struggle against apartheid), but for a long time it did not think this applied to itself and the life it led. Having invented the life, it could not easily see that such a life in reality takes its birth from elsewhere, and is, as the Orthodox put it, a 'Mystery': it is sacramental, not just a human arrangement.

A curious fact about much of CR's early approach is in surprising contrast with Catholic religion: an intention to bypass all intervening history to get back to a New Testament ideal is characteristic of Protestantism. Frere would have fiercely resisted this principle in liturgy, doctrine or church order. The Community were trying to write out of their life the genetic code of the Church. From an admittedly privileged position, we can be struck by the lack of joined-up thinking at many levels, and an inability to pull together the whole at the foundations. It was not thought through, and these things are not capable of access or ordering by thinking alone.

Charism and ethos

By 1984 the Community's Chapter had decided the Rule and Constitution were no longer usable. A committee was set up that was to spend 17 years working towards replacing them. In the course of its work, the 'Rule and Constitution Revision Committee' came to recognize a distinction between what it called charism and ethos: charism was the essential

22 Wilkinson, *Centenary History*, p. 31
23 Arno Schilson, *Theologie als Sakramententheologie* (Mainz: Matthias-Grünewald, 1982), p. 141.

calling of the Community, the gift given it by God, while ethos represents those elements in its life that merely reflect practices and presuppositions of a particular age, inevitably subject to change. This notion of ethos helps us in sifting out what is enduring in the Community's early vision. For instance, a team of young boys in the early years did much of the manual work. At a certain moment we read in the Chapter minutes: 'Sanction was given to brethren blacking their own boots if they desired to do so.'[24] The 'ethos' was evolving.

The early members of CR came from one side of the great social divide that marked British society until recent times. They were middle to upper class and had already received a double formation: first in public school, with all the presuppositions it instilled in them about life together, and then in the pathways of the Church by which they were prepared for ordination, consolidated thereafter in some years of parish ministry. They knew who they were. In coming together, they wanted to put all of that to best use; that was fine, but miles away from a life whose history spoke of leaving everything and being radically re-made. That never quite happened in the early CR, for the marks of public school remained vigorous, and the priestly culture men brought with them approximated in so many ways to monastic life that they could easily believe it to be sufficient. The Church of England was, after all, littered with monastic debris: a living tradition of daily office in choir, choir stalls themselves, the sedate liturgical praxis of cathedrals and college chapels, the learned retirement of cathedral closes, the devout spiritual life of clergy produced by the Oxford Movement, and behind all that the tough askesis, discipline and esprit de corps of life in a public school. These elements could easily be brought together, and in CR some of the terminology from these worlds passed over too, such as the cathedral term of 'residence' for a team serving its stint of responsibility for certain duties. Ronald Knox was to write: 'When you were with the Cowley Fathers or the Community of the Resurrection at Mirfield, a sort of common-room atmosphere prevailed; you had the same background of College traditions, College loyalties, anecdotes about the dons.'[25]

Any individual first coming to the Community would find no

---

24 *Chronicle* I, 171.

25 Quoted in P.F. Anson, *The Call of the Cloister* (rev. edn, London: SPCK, 1955), p. 124.

corporately held apprehension of a wisdom and praxis to do with total conversion, a leaving behind of all that has been in order to start again from square one in apprenticeship to a great and ancient tradition. Rather did you come already formed in one thing and now had it 'topped up'. Walter even says as much: 'Our priestly vocation had already brought us some way along that road and laid upon us corresponding requirements in the way of devotion; this additional call carries us yet further in the same direction.'[26]

There was at least one moment when the brothers made a qualitative leap, apparently just as the project for a community was taking shape. It is recounted in a paper presented by Cyril Bickersteth at the Community's 'Quiet Time' in 1905, 'A Retrospect', in which he looked back over the 13 years since the Community was founded, making fascinating observations, and among them this:

> Perhaps the decisive moment came when we resolved to adopt the principle of a common purse and surrender all claim to the private use of our annual income. To this we were led not only by a will to make real the vow of poverty but by the strong leaven of Christian Socialism which made us long to reproduce the life of the early Christians described in Acts IV.32.

A life evolved in this heuristic way will necessarily have its contradictions and opposites held in tension. What it needed and did not begin to find until the 1980s was some attempt to draw it all together and discover what would enable it to cohere.

Relationship to the Church

An unnoticed contradiction is found in the key area of ecclesial consciousness. CR as a child of the Oxford Movement took a strong stand on the Catholic tradition, not least on the ordained ministry and sacraments. It was not possible to live the life of the gospel fully unless fully part of the fabric of the Church Catholic, with its threefold order of bishop, priest and deacon. Every Christian by his or her baptism was under authority,

---

26 *Commentary*, p. 197.

under episkopé. It is amazing therefore that for much of its history CR never noticed it was living a life of sovereign independence, subject to no bishop or any equivalent (the Visitor has little authority and the diocesan only a vague say on 'the services of the altar'). It was run by a Chapter, with the Superior as executive officer. In a truly Catholic eucharistic community there is a graced ministry of oversight that is more than practical, more than democratic. In the theology of monastic life in both East and West, each community is a 'little church', replicating the Church in miniature. Except at the level of piety, CR's governance lacked the dimension of grace. The Rule and Constitution Revision Committee came to recognize this; without actually saying so it showed the Community's ecclesiology to have been little other than congregationalist. Amongst much that could be said about the ethos that marked the early years of the Community, we can see again what is in fact an underplaying of grace, both in structures and governance, and in the self-understanding of the individual brethren.

This leads us to add a third element to charism and ethos: vocational context.

Context

Among Frere's papers is a small notebook which throws light on his thinking about religious community life. It contains lectures on monasticism in the form of over 100 pages of notes tabulated in headings and sub-headings, with occasional elucidations and expansions, sifting through the history in minutest detail. From New Testament beginnings, through early ascetics, Antony, and on, it lists every possible monastic figure great and small, from Augustine and Cassian to Paul of Leon or Deiniol, with details of their Rules, their foundations, their lives, right on, through the Reformation, Napoleon, and onwards to modern revivals. On reaching the Middle Ages he begins to revel in primary sources and their details about daily life. Of one unnamed monastery he writes:

Mattins midnight – 3am. Bell rung. Lights lighted. Sleep in dormitory clothed. Rise in nocturnality as custos ... rings small bell. Come to church through dorter down stairs to south transept ... 6.00 sit in cloister and read quietly while boys read aloud and sing.

These lectures show an extraordinarily detailed knowledge of monastic life in all its historical manifestations (mostly in the West). His interest is in names, places, dates, basics. On the 'object and significance' of Benedict's Rule he notes six things: 1. Milder and considerate; 2. Enforces stability; 3. Closer unity; 4. Solitude and silence ('but never alone'); 5. Supremacy of services; 6. Study – a somewhat strange collection. Governance is by Abbot, with 'the advice of all', plus deans, provosts and cellarer. In referring to reforms, there is little reference to the world of thinking behind them. On the Cistercians, Bernard appears as a name, full stop. These lectures were history lectures, not a course on the spiritual life.

The sources referred to imply the notes were written around 1909, and additions imply the lectures were given more than once. It is difficult to know for whom they were intended: they are far too detailed for novice classes, and, even if given at the College, they would surely have sent most students to sleep. They were composed after he had written his *Commentary*, but he never revised the *Commentary* in the light of them. We realize that it was not until this time that Frere gave close, systematic attention to monastic history, although a strong medieval foundation would already have been there through his vast knowledge of monastic music manuscripts. From here on we see a Walter Frere who has great familiarity with the practices of monastic life as passed down by the tradition. This study was done too late to have had an influence on the early formation of CR, but it may lie partly behind the gradual introduction of more 'monastic' practices from 1910 onwards, when he announced he would start inspecting brethren's rooms and so on (see above).

While the material is all purely historical, Frere could not have immersed himself in it without being affected by the spirit behind it. Perhaps this little book marks a moment of revelation for him. There is little evidence that the young Frere had read much amongst the monastic authors, but some to suggest he was not naturally drawn that way. In the first months at Pusey House when there was little happening, he wrote: '[I] find the want of active work very trying: busy deeper and deeper in MSS but only feel more and more useless; little able to learn from retirement or to discipline self.'[27] Here was a young man who did not know how to use his time in a monastic environment, and without much

---

27 Jarrett-Kerr, 'Lost Journal', p. 13.

sense of the electricity to be found in it. By the time of these notes of 1909 he has clearly moved a long way.

In the *Commentary* he gives a brief sketch of monastic history, attempting to show where CR sits within it in relation to work:

> The ideal of primitive monasticism was escape from the world for the salvation of the individual soul; beyond this the monk's occupation was of little importance; 'doing' was entirely subordinate to 'being'. When the monastic spirit was transplanted from the East to the West, it was natural that there should come some change with regard to this. It was an important part of the reform of S. Benet that he exalted work to a place of special honour. The monk was still to live isolated from the world; but he was to be occupied with two great tasks: first and foremost came the opus Dei – the joyous task of worshipping God – and with it was linked the opus manuum – the manual labour, – which thus began to assume a fresh dignity in the midst of a world which had accustomed itself to leave hard work to slaves ... The monk was a solitary person, who knew no work beyond his monastery, nor any task but the all-absorbing task of worship, relieved by intervals of homely industries and toils.
>
> With the rise of Friars in the thirteenth century there came a new conception of work into the ideals of religious life. The friars were not to forsake the world in order to sing and toil in solitary places for their own souls', or for the world's, salvation; they were to venture deeply into it in order to leaven it, and they were to labour in it in order to re-deem it. This new conception of work rapidly took various forms, as the Franciscans cultivated simplicity and the Dominicans learning ... Then side by side with the old contemplative orders, new ones ranged themselves, which were missionary, evangelistic and, above all things, active.[28]

There are problems with this: in the *Sayings of the Desert Fathers*, duty to brothers and sisters rings from every page, and the monk's pilgrimage cannot be seen as an individual one – and it is frequently said that the

---

28 *Commentary*, p. 184.

disciple's salvation is to be found in his or her relation with their neighbour, which requires constant work. While Benedict does not draw such direct attention to community as we would expect, his rule turns its attention repeatedly to dynamics within the community in which it was not enough for the monk to be a 'solitary person'; there is no such clear distinction for St Francis between 'work' in the world's hurly-burly and the life out of which such work flows – he set up hermitages intending that brothers should spend regular periods in such solitary places.

In this historical passage Frere was struggling to explain the really interesting combination in CR of pastoral and social zeal with a commitment to demanding religious community. Walter presents the rationale for the Community's idea of making a new start in this way:

> Our Community has from the first desired to learn from all good precedents in the religious life, but not to be bound to any particular form of them. Convinced of its divine call, it has also been convinced that the call of the living God is new and fresh to each succeeding age, and that therefore its own rule and life will be conditioned by the circumstances of the time.[29]

The first brethren had studied the most important of the ancient rules and opted to compose something different. There is a danger that in shopping amongst deep traditions the choosers, deep in none of them, will not be equipped to discern, and so it seems to have been. In his *Commentary* the technical term 'stability' for instance becomes 'steadfastness', paring away most of its layers of signification. This is nowhere in the same league as the treatment of the term 12 years later by Cuthbert Butler.[30] When he wrote the *Commentary*, Frere was still 'young' in the life, within a community itself just as young. The early years of the Community as described in its *Chronicle* were delightfully casual. Brethren were always going off elsewhere, gathering only at specific times. There were holidays in Italy, Norway, the United States. The Community was shocked and depressed at a string of brethren who left to get married. One boarded an ocean liner a religious, fell in love and disembarked in

---

29 *Commentary*, p. 176
30 C. Butler, *Benedictine Monachism* (London: Longmans, 1919), pp. 126 ff.

New York a married man. It came to be recognized that a community living after this fashion could not last long, and gradually, piece by piece, elements of a traditional religious community were put into place: specific training for probationers (1904), no reading of newspapers at breakfast, and cassocks to be worn unless undesirable, suggestion of wearing scapulars (1910), Aspirancy (1911), the office of Prior (1916), the term 'novice' (1919), life intention at profession (1922), scapulars (1927).

Not much was done however on the context that was needed, the soil out of which these things could fully live: Hubert Northcott's *Commentary on the Rule* of 1955 is often said to be more monastic than Frere's, but there is nothing specifically monastic in it. It lays weight on the disciplines of the life as instituted by CR, drawing on many popular sources in the general Western spiritual tradition. The great monastic texts might never have existed, were it not for rare allusions.

CR's secular spiritual tradition

Walter's scholarly energies were devoted to liturgy and church history. When he wrote or spoke on spiritual matters for internal consumption, he drew on the spiritual tradition that might be taught to any candidates for priesthood. In essence Walter's spiritual foundation, and the well at which he and the Community drank, was that of the good parish priest – the secular spiritual tradition, not the monastic. In its Chapter meetings CR from the beginning devoted a great deal of its time to presentations and discussions on the issues of the day, contemporary theology, social questions, biblical study, all listed in the Community's *Chronicle*, but rarely was the religious life discussed. From its foundation up to the time of Walter's death 46 years later, there is reference to only five occasions when attention was given to the life itself: in 1897 Walter spoke one evening about communities and 'the need for non-parochial clergy';[31] in 1901 he led a discussion on 'the Religious Life – what is it?'[32] and the brethren asked for it to be published (was this the germ of his *Commentary?*); in 1903 Charles Fitzgerald and George Longridge spoke on Aquinas' defence of his order, and on congregations of the seventeenth

---

31 *Chronicle* I, 145.
32 *Chronicle* I, 239.

and nineteenth centuries;[33] in 1909 Aelred Carlyle gave retreat addresses on the religious life ('This interested the brethren so much that an evening was given to a discussion of the subject, each brother giving his impression of the abbot's addresses');[34] in 1926 Gore gave retreat addresses on the teaching of Cassian on the religious life ('which were most helpful').[35] That appears to be the entire record of the Community's discussion of the religious life in those 46 years. In 1916 Walter led the Community retreat on the theme 'War and Peace'. The addresses contain no allusions to the religious life, though they do manage to bring in one of his favourite themes: ornaments and ceremonies.

The Community library is helpful here. Books on monastic tradition in its first two decades are few and basic. It did take the *Revue Bénédictine* from 1895 to 1946 but this was of interest to Walter for its articles on liturgy, the chant and monastic manuscripts. With the set is a single volume for 1890 which he must have possessed as a curate. It was one of the early volumes that did not have an index, and on the fly-leaf Walter supplied a list of selected articles. They are all liturgical, except for one that gives an overview of monastic history prior to Benedict, and a two-page hagiography on Eusebius of Vercelli, a strange one to single out were it not for that fact that Eusebius, unusual for his time, founded a monastery of diocesan clergy with pastoral responsibilities – almost a fourth-century CR.

All of this suggests four key elements in Frere's approach to CR's vocation: (1) Pastoral zeal and engagement for and with the Church; (2) a powerful commitment to community as closely bound family; (3) the spirituality of a good parish priest; (4) an abiding delight in researching and listing the details of medieval manuscripts. The last influenced greatly the evolution of the Community's liturgy and its disciplines, but it was chiefly the externals of monastic life that were drawn on, while the spirituality remained that of the parish.

Two wings

There have always been two currents in CR: those who felt an apostolic, pastoral vocation, and others, sometimes in the past called the 'spiritual

---

33 *Chronicle* I, 283.
34 *Chronicle* I, 421.
35 *Chronicle* III, 36.

wing', who saw the life to be more monastic. Cyril Bickersteth, in his 'Retrospect' of 1905, said that from the early days

> some of us were inclined to lay stress on the Religious life as a vocation independent of any particular external activity, while others frankly acknowledged that they were drawn to the life because they felt it was the ideal background which would enable them to do special work to which they were called in happiness and safety. [However], in the early days we did little or nothing to encourage the adhesion of brethren whose strength lay chiefly in pastoral or parochial work ... [and only more lately has it been] possible to include every variety of ministerial capacity.

The two 'wings' in the Community have for long lived in (mostly good-humoured) friction with one another. What prevented them from working in more fruitful harmony was the fact that neither of them fully grasped what was required: an attention to the life itself within its specific 'context', worldwide and through time.

Monastic theology

We can come closer to this notion of context by looking at what has been called 'monastic theology', much discussed in recent years, and well outlined in Jean Leclercq's *The Love of Learning and the Desire for God*.[36] It rests on a distinction between academic theology done in universities (for instance) and theology as lived in the monastic world. The one treats theology as a human science, the other as a more all-encompassing approach to knowledge of God. The scholastic theology of the later Middle Ages – the ancestor of what today we could call academic theology – 'seeks in secular learning and philosophy', according to Leclercq, 'for analogies capable of expressing religious realities. Its purpose is to organize Christian erudition by means of removing any subjective material so as to make it purely scientific.' The term monastic theology, on the other hand, while used in a variety of ways, really refers to the whole way of life of religious communities.

---

36 J. Leclercq, *The Love of Learning and the Desire for God* (New York: Fordham, 1974).

According to Evagrius, 'the theologian is one who prays in truth'. For him, theology cannot be done in separation from prayer; indeed in a sense it is prayer. This theology furthermore is a way of life – it prospers as a person's life becomes more and more a life that is prayer, a life inhabited by God. It encompasses everything: the common table, the daily chores, the silence, the liturgy, study, lectio, contemplation, obedience, simplicity, the vows and their consequences, manual labour and so on. Out of this comes a picture of God and the things of God; out of it comes a frame of mind. This is difficult to describe. In it there is a basic simplicity, and a shunning of power, constantly close to the breaking out of humour, partly related to a permanent awareness of sin. Many modern monastic writings (such as those of Michael Casey) bubble with a strange humour about the difficulties of living with our frequently irritating and difficult brothers and sisters. It is a life not quick to take tasks by the scruff of the neck, but rather to watch and to pray, knowing that there is more than the organizing intellect can take account of; and even where things go wrong, that itself is grist to God's mill of the conversion of souls and communities. The foundation out of which this 'theology' springs is faith, the experienced journey of faith into God, with and in God. Monastic theology is sapiential before it is intellectual – it is a wisdom before it is ratiocination.

The two theologies are complementary and need each other. Academic theology left to itself would lose sight of the divine Person who cannot be accessed by reason alone. Monastic theology left to itself would go off in fanciful flights leaving reason (and common nous) too far behind. Leclercq falls into this trap in setting monastic theology higher, 'the contemplative's love, possessing greater penetration, makes him a bold, avant-garde scout';[37] the examples he gives show just how unreliable this is.

The College of the Resurrection at Mirfield has shown all along a better balance: commitment to the academic theology of the University, held in tandem with theological study in a 'monastic' setting of liturgy, prayer and the common life, something it clearly owes to the Community's founders, and not least to Walter Frere. Walter was aware of the problem – he recognized two dangerous tendencies in Western Chris-

---

37 Leclercq, *Love of Learning*, p. 134.

tianity: over-reliance on Aristotle in theology, and a legalism in dogmatic thought and ecclesiastical organization. There was an 'exaggerated self-confidence of the man of the West in his own intellectual ability and power',[38] criticisms as true of the church in the twenty-first century as they were then. Frere knew by instinct what monastic theology was, but in the Community's life it was never taken to its necessary conclusion, something that could only have been done had CR had the right equipment, which was to be found in the venerable (Catholic) tradition of the religious life

Drinking from the well

We are at this point compelled to ask what attention to the monastic tradition might involve in practical terms. If one sets aside for a moment the vast corpus of literature produced by monastic communities, the basic 'context' can be seen to consist of two things: (1) awareness of being set within a great tradition, imbibing much of its wisdom through spoken word and praxis, and (2) being bound to a specific document or documents. Benedictines have Benedict's Rule, Franciscans a wealth of tradition and literature on Francis, Jesuits the writings of Ignatius, Augustinians have Augustine's Rule and all his other writings. CR has had nothing of the kind and has turned to nothing. This is to a considerable extent true of much Anglican religious life: while it has had its scholars and wise men and women, it has produced almost no respected authorities on the life itself. The approach was overwhelmingly practical.

CR has never had a theology of its own life – it has simply got on and done it, all of this leading to a lack of powerful perception of being an element in something much bigger. True, it has always been aware that other communities existed, but it has never had a very strong sense of being one manifestation of a much bigger, overarching reality in whose light it would be judged, and to which it must attend. Thereupon would follow a need for reflection on key terminology, attention to the thinking current in the wider world of similar communities, and regular study of the life as such, individually and corporately.

It might be objected that there are any number of Roman Catholic

---

38 Phillips, *Frere*, p. 189.

communities with much the same history, and who pay little attention to all this historical stuff. They are not, however, communities living a close life with strong stability of place, a demanding liturgical round and a basically coenobitic understanding of obedience, manifesting into the bargain all those monastic externals with which Walter was fascinated. The more the life is centred on these people in this place, the more the individual and the group need to be fed by attention directed to that life. Without that they can simply feel a lack of sufficient meaning in it, and end by leaving. An alternative is to turn to inappropriate sources of satisfaction and fulfilment that can manifest themselves in a variety of ways. People can be hurt as a result of such lack of focus, and can fail to have their gifts properly developed (lack of attention to the life as such leads easily to insufficient attention to the individual). For much of CR's history, Walter's notion of 'family' turned out not to be enough. As the Community became bigger, not all of its aspects were sustainable. There were never the mechanisms for sustained mutual engagement. The Rule Revision Committee thought that some of the many brothers who left did so through loneliness. While exalting the model of the family, Frere, very secure in himself, underestimated what was needed to sustain it for lesser mortals. Keble Talbot commented that, 'It seemed sometimes that he underrated the need that others less detached and free have of external bonds to preserve their stability.'[39] It had to wait for the Community to shrink to a couple of dozen in recent times: then many defective habits of relating became too apparent, and CR began to make use of professional facilitators, which at the present time it continues to do to its great benefit. The modern age expects high standards of interpersonal relating, and, if young people are to join, they will rightly expect a coherent integrity right through the life which also faces directly all its flaws. It is a way of life that needs to be backed up by sustained reflection on it, and a strong sense of orientation within its greater context.

All that we have uncovered now shows why the role of Superior has so often worked out unsatisfactorily in CR: insufficient understanding of it as a graced role, enabling the Community to be a truly Catholic eucharistic community, a role that cannot be conceived through human planning and construction, in place of being received from the Catholic

---

39 Phillips, *Frere*, p. 48.

tradition. The positive side was that the early brethren were on the right track in rejecting abbacy as known in the nineteenth century. The more difficult task was to evolve structures that did not throw out the reality of grace, and concrete (historical) grace at that.

The fruits of drawbacks

The imbalance in self-understanding would mean a tendency for CR to contain rich individual characters and a lively tension between individual sparkle and that mutual submission necessary for life together, things that have stayed with CR throughout its subsequent history. It would also mean a lively and somewhat unstable ride, in a framework less firm than normal. This came into its own in South Africa, where a particularly swashbuckling spirit flourished in the cowboy environment of Johannesburg and the Rand to great and lasting effect – literally contributing to transformation of the world, in the huge contribution made to creating the new South Africa. Lives of great simplicity and self-denial were led, and there built up a fund of wisdom and insight derived more from lived experience than a deliberate project. The rest was carried along by tremendous energy and enthusiasm. The Community was like a self-taught person, patchily equipped but not without appropriate nous, and inspired in some of its innovations.

In its early decades CR had much of the liveliness of youth. Brethren seemed to be away very regularly, and it is not always clear what they could be doing. Around 1914 Charles Gore, who was Visitor for a time as Bishop of Birmingham, chastised them for too much levity in conversation, and in 1923 the Visitor (the Bishop of Lichfield) drew the Community's attention to: 1. A tendency to levity in the general life; 2. Difficulties of living together perhaps not fully faced; and 3. The need of preserving carefully a right measure of time spent at home.[40]

It seems that Walter in his later years was not happy with the way some things were going in the Community, including the private masses, the increasing association with 'advanced' Anglo-Catholicism by at least some of the brethren, and the use for the Eucharist of the 'Interim Rite', which he called 'deplorable'. In 1935 the chronicler reports the setting up of a

---

40 *Chronicle* III, 30.

special dining room for elderly brothers (five at the time, including Walter), with its own cooking equipment and a special boy to look after it. Was it to give them time to eat without feeling rushed? How would Walter have lived with this apparent contradiction of community? Would he have felt relief at escaping increasingly churchy Anglo-Catholic talk? We have to hope he was not disappointed by where the Community had arrived by the 1930s.

Walter's legacy

The reader may feel by the end of this chapter that Walter Frere has taken a dent. His stature, however, can take it. We have perforce said little about the life that animated him, and the way it pervaded the Community through the way he lived the life. We have not touched on many intangibles. In Gore and Frere, in true monastic fashion, we have real bits of dented concrete Grace. This is what God sent, and he did amazing things with it. Between them these two incarnate CR's charism more than any documents. Through some divine deftness beyond our ken, God brought CR into our own time with a unique if flawed gift.

When in 1967 a deputation of Benedictines from the venerable St Matthias' Abbey in Trier, Germany, came looking for an Anglican community to twin with, they visited various Benedictine communities but found they had most in common with CR, and the close relationship that resulted still flourishes warmly today. Over the years we have shared many things and supported each other through difficulties and challenges. CR is not Benedictine, and, despite the self-realization that has come about as a result of intense study over the last 20 years or more of the questions that I have raised, some key distinctive elements of its charism go back to the call that Walter and the early brethren sensed to create something new that took account of the new world born of the Enlightenment, the Industrial Revolution and the growth of democracy. But in some key respects they discovered St Benedict by the back door without realizing it.

As I sit in choir in what is probably Walter's church, I wonder how the sense of sitting under things greater than us, and of having great things expected of us, would have survived had we been worshipping somewhere manageable and normal; and as we sing the plainchant day by day I wonder where we might have been without this testing lifeline to the tradition; and as I reflect on the close similarity not only of practice but of spirit that we share with our brothers in Trier I cannot help but agree with those in the Community who see Walter as having steered the Community along this road when it might have followed a different course. What he wrote in a small volume early in his time in community has to be held together with the stature of his presence in the Community over almost half a century, as it comes over in the other chapters in this book. When Keble Talbot died in October 1949, the Community's Chronicler wrote:

> In his account of the Community's growth written at the Jubilee in 1942, Keble spoke of the 20 years since the election of Walter Frere to the Episcopate as being a period in which there was no one figure who dominated the Community as the Senior [Gore] and then Walter had done'.[41]

When in 1930 Walter Tapper produced a modified design for the church nave in brick (never to be carried out), Osmund Victor was moved to write that Walter, who was at the time in Truro, 'has gone into these plans carefully and it is everything to know that he approves of them and is prepared to vote for them'.

Shortly after Frere's death, Mervyn Haigh, Bishop of Coventry, wrote a letter painting a picture of him that is impressive, delightful and attractive, showing us a clear-eyed, gifted and immensely likeable saint. He then adds:

> But, but, but, in the main and increasingly towards the end, there was no doubt that he really staggered the Bishops by the increasingly paradoxical and seemingly 'clever', subtle and even insincere kind of way in which he commended his views, not for the reasons that everybody felt must be his reasons, but sometimes for almost diametrically opposed reasons which looked like the reasons that he thought would commend themselves to those out of sympathy with him ... I believe [he] intensely disliked the whole process of having to commend his views to anyone else who did not readily agree with him,

---

41 *Chronicle* IV, no page number.

and developed a kind of nonchalant, 'puckish' method of commending them.[42]

We might see something else here too – a man formed by life in community: first, a long habit as Superior of seeking to give voice to all, and so to build up community, and second, the undeniable fact that religious are left by their life unable to take themselves seriously in the way that is usual in other walks of life. They are too aware of the humorous nature of their predicament. This can be a real problem when seeking to address people who do take themselves more seriously – it can be existentially impossible to change gear. There is not a whiff of these problems in the Community records, but everything to indicate a man who succeeded in building up an effective and fruitful community. Such is the difficulty of holding together all the aspects of this unusual man.

Walter's posterity

And what of the Community today? It has the task of discerning in what it has received from Charles Gore, Walter Frere and the early brothers and their heirs those things that are divine gift (charism), in distinction from those peculiar to those people and that time (ethos), in order to stay faithful to the former while also looking to complete what they did not finish, as we grow in awareness of the tradition (context), or, as CR's new Constitutions put it, we 'take forward that ecumenical vision which unites members of all religious communities, as we find our place in the mainstream tradition of the religious life'. In the modern world the task includes grasping the potential of renewing the church building Walter inspired and the worship offered within it, equally indebted to him, and, as Walter did with such commitment in another time, zestfully throwing ourselves into those new ways of supporting the Church in mission, teaching and pastoral care that the Lord now sets before us.

---

42 Borthwick Institute.

Walter Howard Frere: representative bibliography

BENJAMIN GORDON-TAYLOR

This bibliography is not exhaustive: for a more complete version, see the 'List of Writings' in *Walter Howard Frere, Bishop of Truro* by C.S. Phillips et al. (London: Faber & Faber, 1947), pp. 204–13, although in the course of preparing the present book we have found one or two omissions. Indeed, a complete annotated bibliography of the works of Frere is needed – available space has, unfortunately, precluded this here. Instead we offer a representative list of Frere's principal publications in the hope that those unfamiliar with his work will explore further; readers are also, of course, provided with many references in the chapters of this book. Some titles below have been abbreviated for ease of communication.

Liturgy

1896   *The Wells Office Book: Prime and Hours with Other Services for the Use of Wells Theological College.* London: J. Hodges.

1898–1901   *The Use of Sarum*, ed. W.H.F. 2 vols. Cambridge: Cambridge University Press.

1899   *Exposition de la Messe from La Legende Dorée of Jean de Vignay*, ed. W.H.F. Alcuin Club Collections 2. London: Longmans, Green.

1901   *Pontifical Services Illustrated from Miniatures of the Fifteenth and Sixteenth Centuries*, ed. W.H.F. Alcuin Club Collections 3 and 4. London: Longmans, Green.

1901   *A New History of the Book of Common Prayer ... on the Basis of the Former Work by Francis Procter, M.A.*, revised and rewritten by W.H.F. London: Macmillan.

1903   *The English Liturgy: Being the Office for Holy Communion...with Additional Collects, Epistles, and Gospels for the Lesser Holy-Days and for Special Occasions ...* ed. Percy Dearmer, W.H.F., S.M. Taylor. London: Rivingtons.

1903–4   Daniel Rock, *The Church of Our Fathers*, ed. W.H.F. and W. Hart CR. 4 vols, London: John Hodges.

1904–15   *The Hereford Breviary*, ed. W.H.F. and L.E.G. Brown. 4 vols, London: Henry Bradshaw Society 26, 40, 46.

1906   *The Principles of Religious Ceremonial*. London: Longmans.

1911   *Some Principles of Liturgical Reform: A Contribution Towards the Revision of the Book of Common Prayer*. London: John Murray.

1914   *English Church Ways Described to Russian Friends*. London: John Murray.

1921   *The Leofric Collectar*, vol. 2, ed. and compl. by W.H.F. London: Henry Bradshaw Society 56.

1930   *Studies in Early Roman Liturgy*, vol. 1: *The Kalendar*. Alcuin Club Collections 28. London: Oxford University Press.

1934   *Studies in Early Roman Liturgy*, vol. 2: *The Roman Gospel-Lectionary*. Alcuin Club Collections 30. Oxford: Oxford University Press.

1935   *Studies in Early Roman Liturgy*, vol. 3: *The Roman Gospel-Lectionary* Alcuin Club Collections 32. Oxford: Oxford University Press.

1935   *Collects, Epistles, and Gospels for the Lesser Feasts according to the Calendar Set out in 1928*. London: SPCK.

1938   *Black Letter Saints' Days*. London: SPCK.

1938   *The Anaphora, or Great Eucharistic Prayer: An Eirenical Study in Liturgical History*. London: SPCK.

The following important collections of scholarly papers (excluded above) and correspondence were compiled and published after the death of W.H.F. in 1938. Both are essential to the study of his work:

1940   *Walter Howard Frere: A Collection of his Papers on Liturgical and Historical Subjects*, ed. J.H. Arnold and E.G.P. Wyatt. Alcuin Club Collections 35. London: Oxford University Press.

1954   *Walter Howard Frere: His Correspondence on Liturgical Revision and Construction*, ed. R.C.D. Jasper. Alcuin Club Collections 39. London: SPCK.

2. History

1890   *A Sketch of the Parochial History of Barley, Herts*, ed. A.H. Frere and W.H.F. Stepney Green: G. Reynolds.

1890–91   *Memorials of Stepney Parish*, ed. W.H.F. and G.W. Hill. Guildford: Billing.

1896   *The Marian Reaction in its Relation to the English Clergy: A Study of the Episcopal Registers.* London: SPCK.

1904   *The English Church in the Reigns of Elizabeth and James I*, vol. 5 of *History of the English Church*, ed. W.R.W. Stephens and W. Hunt. London: Macmillan.

1907   *Puritan Manifestoes. A Study of the Origin of the Puritan Revolt*, ed. W.H.F. and C.E. Douglas. London: SPCK.

1910   *Visitation Articles and Injunctions of the Period of the Reformation*, 3 vols, Alcuin Club Collections 14, 15, 16. London: Longmans, Green.

1918   *Some Links in the Chain of Russian Church History*, London: Faith Press.

1928–35   *Registrum Matthei Parker, Diocesis Cantuariensis, AD 1559-75*, ed. W.H.F., 3 vols, Canterbury and York Society 35, 36, 39. Oxford: Oxford University Press.

1935   *Recollections of Malines.* London: Centenary Press.

     Also papers in the posthumous collection ed. Arnold and Wyatt (see above, section 1).

3. Music

1894   *The Winchester Troper from MSS of the Tenth and Eleventh Centuries*, ed. W.H.F. London: Henry Bradshaw Society 8.

1894   *Graduale Sarisburiense: A Facsimile of a MS of the Thirteenth Century*, ed. W.H.F. London: Plainsong and Mediaeval Music Society.

1901–25   *Antiphonale Sarisburiense: A Facsimile of a MS of the Thirteenth Century*, ed. W.H.F., 26 fascicules. London: Plainsong and Mediaeval Music Society.

1901–32   *Bibliotheca Musico-Liturgica: A Descriptive Handlist of the Musical and Latin-liturgical MSS of the Middle Ages in the Libraries of Great Britain and Ireland*, ed. W.H.F. 2 vols, London: Plainsong and Mediaeval Music Society.

1902   *A Manual of Plainsong*, new edn of T. Helmore original, by

H.B. Briggs and W.H.F. under the superintendence of J. Stainer. London: Novello.

1909   *Hymns Ancient and Modern: Historical Edition*, with Notes on the Origin of both Hymns and Tunes and a General Historical Introduction by W.H.F. London: William Clowes and Sons.

4. Devotional

1896   *The Stations of the Passion of Our Lord and Saviour Jesus Christ*. Oxford and London: Mowbray.

1898   *Sursum Corda: A Handbook of Intercession and Thanksgiving*, arranged by W.H.F. and A.L. Illingworth. Oxford: A.R. Mowbray & Co.

1936   *A Devotionarie Book of John Evelyn of Wotton 1620-1706*, with introduction by W.H.F. London: Murray.

5. Theological Education

1910   'The Training and Examination of Candidates for Orders', part III, *Church Quarterly Review* 70, 333–44.

Modern works wholly about or referring in detail to Frere

1947   Phillips, C.S. et al. *Walter Howard Frere, Bishop of Truro: A Memoir*. London: Faber & Faber. [includes Obituary by E.K. Talbot CR which appeared in the *CR Quarterly* after the death of W.H.F.]

1949   Thompson, A.H., 'Walter Howard Frere', in *Dictionary of National Biography 1931–40*. London: Oxford University Press.

1984   Jarrett-Kerr, M., 'A Lost Journal of +Walter Frere CR', *CR Quarterly* No. 325, St John Baptist.

1992   Wilkinson, A., *The Community of the Resurrection: A Centenary History*. London: SCM.

1998   Dawtry, A., 'Walter Frere', in *They Shaped Our Worship*, ed. C. Irvine. Alcuin Club Collections 75. London: SPCK.

2004   Green, H.B. 'Walter Howard Frere', in *Oxford Dictionary of National Biography*. Oxford: Oxford University Press.

General Bibliography

Andrewes, L. *Preces Privatae*, trans. F.E. Brightman (London: Methuen, 1903).

Anson, P.F., *The Call of the Cloister: Religious Communities and Kindred Bodies in the Anglican Communion* (rev. edn, London: SPCK, 1955).

Armstrong, C.J.R., *Evelyn Underhill* (London: Mowbray, 1975).

Arnold, J.H., and E.G.P. Wyatt, (eds), *Walter Howard Frere: A Collection of his Papers on Liturgical and Historical Subjects* (Alcuin Club. London: Oxford University Press, 1940).

Avis, P., *Anglicanism and the Christian Church* (Edinburgh: T&T Clark, 2002).

Ayris, P., 'The Challenge of Interpretation: Using Documents of the Early English Reformation Period', *Reformation & Renaissance Review*, vol. 6.2 (2004).

Baker, W.J., 'Hurrell Froude and the Reformers', *Journal of Ecclesiastical History* 21 (1970).

Barlow, B., *A Brother Knocking at the Door: The Malines Conversations 1921–1925* (Norwich: Canterbury Press, 1996).

Bell, G.K.A., *Randall Davidson, Archbishop of Canterbury* (2 vols, London: Oxford University Press, 1935).

Bergeron, K., *Decadent Enchantments: The Revival of Gregorian Chant at Solesmes* (Berkeley: University of California Press, 1998).

Bowers, R., 'The Chapel Royal, the First Edwardian Prayer Book and the Elizabethan Settlement of Religion 1559', *The Historical Journal* 43.2 (2000).

Burne, R.V.H., *Knutsford: The Story of the Ordination Test School, 1914–40* (London: SPCK, 1960).

Burns, A., *The Diocesan Revival in the Church of England, c.1800–1870* (Oxford: Oxford University Press, 1999).

Butler, C., *Benedictine Monachism* (London: Longmans, 1919).

Cameron, J.M., 'Editor's Introduction', in J.H. Newman, *Essay on the Development of Christian Doctrine* (Harmondsworth: Penguin, 1974).

Cardine, E, *Sémiologie Grégorienne* (Solesmes, 1970).

Carr, E.H., *What Is History?* (Harmondsworth: Penguin, 1964).

Chadwick, O., *The Reformation* (3rd edn, London: Pelican, 1972).

Chandler, A., *A Dream of Order: The Medieval Idea in 19th Century English Literature* (London: Routledge, 1970).

Clark, J.W., *The Observances in Use at the Augustinian Priory of S. Giles and S. Andrew at Barnwell, Cambridgeshire* (Cambridge: Macmillan and Bowes, 1897).

Cobbett, W., *A History of the Protestant Reformation in England and Ireland* (London, 1824–7).

Collinson, P., *The Elizabethan Puritan Movement* (London: Jonathan Cape, 1967).

Crankshaw, D., 'Preparations for the Canterbury Provincial Convocation of 1562–63: A Question of Attribution', in S. Wabuda and C. Litzenberger (eds), *Belief and Practice in Reformation England* (Aldershot: Ashgate, 1998).

Crankshaw, D., and A. Gillespie, 'Matthew Parker (1504–1575)', in *Oxford Dictionary of National Biography* (Oxford: Oxford University Press, 2004).

Cropper, M., *Life of Evelyn Underhill* (London: Longmans, 1958).

Cross, F.L., and E. Livingstone (eds), *The Oxford Dictionary of the Christian Church* (3rd edn, Oxford: Oxford University Press, 2005).

Cuming, G.J., *A History of Anglican Liturgy* (2nd edn, London: Macmillan, 1982).

Dark, S., *Lord Halifax: A Tribute* (Milwaukee: Morehouse, 1934).

Dawtry, A., 'Walter Frere', in C. Irvine (ed.), *They Shaped Our Worship: Essays on Anglican Liturgists* (London: SPCK, 1998).

Dearmer, N., *The Life of Percy Dearmer* (London: Book Club, 1941).

Dickens, A.G., and J.M. Tonkin, *The Reformation in Historical Thought* (Oxford: Basil Blackwell, 1985).

Dix, G., *The Shape of the Liturgy* (London: A. and C. Black, 1945).

Dixon, R.W., *History of the Church of England* (6 vols., London: Routledge, 1878–1902).

Dorran, S., 'Elizabeth I's Religion: The Evidence of Her Letters', *Journal of Ecclesiastical History* 51.4 (2000).

Dowland, D.A., *Nineteenth-Century Anglican Theological Training: The Redbrick Challenge* (Oxford: Oxford University Press, 1997).

Duffy, E., *The Stripping of the Altars* (New Haven and London: Yale University Press, 1992).

——, 'The Shock of Change: Continuity and Discontinuity in the Elizabethan Church of England', in S. Platten (ed.), *Anglicanism and the Western Christian Tradition* (Norwich: Canterbury Press, 2003).

——, 'Worship', in D.F. Ford, B. Quash and J. Soskice (eds), *Fields of Faith: Theology and Religious Studies for the Twenty-First Century* (Cambridge: Cambridge University Press, 2005).

Fedotov, G.P. (ed.), *A Treasury of Russian Spirituality* (New York: Sheed and Ward, 1948).

Fincham, K. (ed.), *Visitation Articles and Injunctions of the Early Stuart Church* (2 vols, Woodbridge: Boydell Press, 1994-8).

Fisher, M., *For the Time Being: A Memoir* (Leominster: Gracewing, 1993).

Fletcher, S., *Maude Royden* (Oxford: Blackwell, 1989).

Freestone, W.H., *The Sacrament Reserved* (Alcuin Club. London: Mowbray, 1917).

Froude, R.H., *The Remains of the Late Reverend Richard Hurrell Froude*, ed. J. Keble and J.H. Newman (4 vols., London and Derby, 1838–9).

Gore, C., *Roman Catholic Claims* (11th edn, London: Longmans, 1920).

Gray, D., *Earth and Altar* (Alcuin Club. Norwich: Canterbury Press, 1986).

——, *The 1927-28 Prayer Book Crisis* (2 vols, Alcuin Club. Norwich: SCM-Canterbury Press, 2005–6).

Green, H.B., 'Walter Howard Frere', *Oxford Dictionary of National Biography* (Oxford: Oxford University Press, 2004).

Haigh, C. (ed.), *The English Reformation Revised* (Cambridge: Cambridge University Press, 1987).

Hall, B., 'The Early Rise and Gradual Decline of Lutheranism in England (1520–1600)', in D. Baker (ed.), *Reform and Reformation: England and the Continent c.1500–1750* (Oxford: Blackwell, 1979).

Haugaard, W.P., *Elizabeth and the English Reformation: The Struggle for a Stable Settlement of Religion* (Cambridge: Cambridge University Press, 1968).

Heal, F., and R. O'Day (eds), *Continuity and Change: Personnel and Administration of the Church in England 1500–1642* (Leicester: Leicester University Press, 1976).

Helmore, T., *Accompanying Harmonies to the Psalter Noted* (London: Novello, 1849).

Henson, H.H., *Retrospect of an Unimportant Life* (3 vols, London: Oxford University Press, 1943).

Herring, G., *What Was the Oxford Movement?* (London: Continuum, 2002).

Hill, R., *God's Architect: Pugin and the Building of Romantic England* (London: Allen Lane, 2007).

Hughes, A., *The Rivers of the Flood: A Personal Account of the Catholic Revival in England in the Twentieth Century* (London: Faith Press, 1961).

Jagger, P., *The Alcuin Club and its Publications 1897–1987* (2nd edn, Norwich: Hymns Ancient and Modern, 1986).

Jarrett-Kerr, M., 'A Lost Journal of +Walter Frere CR', *CR Quarterly* No. 325, St John Baptist, 1984.

Jasper, R.C.D. (ed.), *Walter Howard Frere: His Correspondence on Liturgical Revision and Construction* (Alcuin Club. London: SPCK, 1954).

——, *The Development of the Anglican Liturgy, 1662-1980* (London: SPCK, 1989).

Jeanes, G.P., *Signs of God's Promise: Thomas Cranmer's Sacramental Theology and the Book of Common Prayer* (Edinburgh: Continuum, 2008).

——, 'Early Steps in the English Liturgy: The Witness of the Wanley Part Books', paper delivered to the Society for Reformation Studies Conference at Westminster College, Cambridge, in April 2010 (publication forthcoming).

Jungmann, J.A., *The Early Liturgy, to the Time of Gregory the Great*, trans. F.A. Brunner (London: Darton, Longman and Todd, 1960).

——, 'The Defeat of Teutonic Arianism and the Revolution in Religious Culture in the Early Middle Ages', in Jungmann, *Pastoral Liturgy* (London: Challoner Publications, 1962).

Lake, P., *Moderate Puritans and the Elizabethan Church* (Cambridge: Cambridge University Press, 1982).

——, 'The "Anglican Moment"? Richard Hooker and the Ideological Watershed of the 1590s', in S. Platten (ed.), *Anglicanism and the Western Christian Tradition* (Norwich: Canterbury Press, 2003).

Leclerq, J., *The Love of Learning and the Desire for God* (New York: Fordham, 1974).

Livesley, J., 'John Mason Neale and the Anglo-Catholic Idea of History' (unpublished Oxford History Faculty M.St. thesis, 2003).

Lockhart, J.G., *Charles Lindley, Viscount Halifax* (London: Centenary Press, 1935).

Lowther Clarke, W.K., and C. Harris (eds), *Liturgy and Worship* (London: SPCK, 1932).

MacCulloch, D., 'The Myth of the English Reformation', *The Journal of British Studies*, vol. 30.1 (1991).

——, *Thomas Cranmer: A Life* (New Haven: Yale University Press, 1996).

——, *Tudor Church Militant: Edward VI and the Protestant Reformation* (London: Allen Lane, 2000)

——, *The Later Reformation in England, 1547–1603* (2nd edn, Basingstoke: Palgrave, 2001).

——, 'Can the English Think for Themselves? The Roots of English Protestantism', *Harvard Divinity Bulletin* 30 (Spring, 2001).

——, 'The Church of England 1533–1603', in S. Platten (ed.), *Anglicanism and the Western Christian Tradition* (Norwich: Canterbury Press, 2003).

——, 'Putting the English Reformation on the Map', *Transactions of the Royal Historical Society* 15 (2005).

McGrath, A.E., *Reformation Thought: An Introduction* (3rd edn, Oxford: Blackwell, 1999).

Maltby, J., *Prayer Book and People in Elizabethan and Early Stuart England* (Cambridge: Cambridge University Press, 1998).

Martindale, C.C., *The Life of Monsignor Robert Hugh Benson* (London: Longmans, 1916).

Mason, A., *History of the Society of the Sacred Mission* (Norwich: Canterbury Press, 1993).

Matthews, M., *Both Alike to Thee: The Retrieval of the Mystical Way* (London: SPCK, 2000).

Morris, J.N., 'Newman and Maurice on the Via Media of the Anglican Church: Contrasts and Affinities', *Anglican Theological Review*, vol. 85.4 (2003).

Murray, D.L., *Reservation: Its Purpose and Method*, Alcuin Club Prayer Book Revision Pamphlets (2nd edn., 1953).

Murray, P., *Newman the Oratorian* (Dublin: Gill and Macmillan, 1969).

Newman, J.H., *Apologia Pro Vita Sua*, ed. W. Oddie (London: Dent, 1993 [1864]).

——, *The Via Media of the Anglican Church* (2nd edn, 2 vols, London, 1877).

——, *Tract XC: On Certain Passages in the XXXIX Articles* (London: A.D. Innes and Co., 1893).

Nockles, P., *The Oxford Movement in Context: Anglican High Churchmanship 1760–1857* (Cambridge: Cambridge University Press, 1994).

——, 'A Disputed Legacy: Anglican Historiographies of the Reformation from the Era of the Caroline Divines to that of the Oxford Movement', *Bulletin of the John Rylands University Library of Manchester*, vol. 83.1 (2001).

——, 'Survivals or New Arrivals? The Oxford Movement and the Nineteenth Century Historical Construction of Anglicanism', in S. Platten (ed.), *Anglicanism and the Western Christian Tradition* (Norwich: Canterbury Press, 2003).

O'Day, R., *The Debate on the English Reformation* (London: Methuen, 1986).

Palmer, G.H., 'Psalmody', in H.B. Briggs (ed.), *The Elements of Plainsong* (London: Plainsong and Mediaeval Music Society, 1895).

Palmer, G.H., *The Introduction and Tone-Table to the Sarum Psalter* (2nd edn, London: George Bell & Sons, 1898).

Perriro, J., *'Ethos' and the Oxford Movement: At the Heart of Tractarianism* (Oxford: Oxford University Press, 2008).

Phillips, C.S., et al., *Walter Howard Frere, Bishop of Truro: A Memoir* (London: Faber & Faber, 1947).

Pickering, W.S.F., *Anglo-Catholicism: A Study in Religious Ambiguity* (London: Routledge, 1989).

Prestige, G.L., *The Life of Charles Gore* (London: Heinemann, 1935).

Raikes, E. (ed.), *Agnes Louisa Illingworth: A Brief Memoir* (London: SPCK, 1938).

Read, C., *Bibliography of British History: Tudor Period* (2nd edn, Oxford: Clarendon Press, 1959).

Robinson, H. (ed.), *The Zurich Letters: Second Series* (Cambridge: Cambridge University Press, 1845).

Rowse, A.L., *A Cornish Childhood* (London: J. Cape, 1942; repr. Truro: Truran, 2003).

Schilson, A., *Theologie als Sakramententheologie: Die Mysterientheologie Odo Casels* (Mainz: Matthias-Grünewald, 1982).

Sheils, W.J. (ed.), *The Church and War* (Oxford: Blackwell, 1983).

Smith, H.M., *Frank, Bishop of Zanzibar: Life of Frank Weston* (London: SPCK, 1926).

Smyth, C., *Cyril Foster Garbett* (London: Hodder and Stoughton, 1959).

Spinks, B.D., *Sacraments, Ceremonies and the Stuart Divines* (Aldershot: Ashgate, 2002).

Stephenson, C., *Merrily on High* (London: Darton, Longman and Todd, 1972).

Stevenson, K.W., *Eucharist and Offering* (New York: Pueblo, 1986).

Stone, D., *Report of the First Anglo-Catholic Congress* (London: SPCK, 1920).

Sykes, N., *Old Priest and New Presbyter: Episcopacy and Presbyterianism since the Reformation with Especial Reference to the Churches of England and Scotland* (Cambridge: Cambridge University Press, 1956).

Tyacke, N., 'Rethinking the Reformation', in N. Tyacke (ed.), *England's Long Reformation 1500–1800* (London: Taylor & Francis, 1997).

——, 'Lancelot Andrewes and the Myth of Anglicanism', in P. Lake and M. Questier (eds), *Conformity and Orthodoxy in the English Church c.1560–1660* (Woodbridge: Boydell & Brewer, 2000).

Tyacke, N., and K. Fincham, *Altars Restored: The Changing Face of English Religious Worship 1547–c.1700* (Oxford: Oxford University Press, 2007).

Underhill, E., *Worship* (London: Nisbet, 1936).

——, *Eucharistic Prayers from the Ancient Liturgies* (London: Longmans, 1939).

Wilkinson, A., 'Three Sexual Issues', *Theology*, March 1988.

——, *The Community of the Resurrection: A Centenary History* (London: SCM Press, 1992).

——, *The Church of England and the First World War* (1st edn, London: SPCK 1978, 2nd edn, London: SCM Press, 1996).

——, *Christian Socialism* (London: SCM Press, 1998).

——, 'Charles Gore', in *Oxford Dictionary of National Biography* (Oxford: Oxford University Press, 2004).

——, 'Frere: Ecumenist, Feminist, Socialist', *Church Times*, 28 March 2008.

Williams, C., *The Place of the Lion* (London: Victor Gollancz, 1931).

Wrightson, J., *The 'Wanley' Manuscripts: A Critical Commentary* (New York: Garland, 1989).

Yates, N., *The Oxford Movement and Parish Life: St Saviour's, Leeds, 1839–1929* (York: St. Anthony's Hall Publications, 1975).

Yelton, M., *Anglican Papalism 1900–1960* (Norwich: Canterbury Press, 2005).

Notes on the Contributors

Peter Allan CR studied music at Oxford and theology at Leeds. He is Precentor of the Community of the Resurrection and Principal of the College of the Resurrection, Mirfield, where he teaches moral theology.

Bernard Barlow OSM is a priest of the Servite Order. He taught theology at Ushaw Seminary and has written *A Brother Knocking at the Door: The Malines Conversations 1921–25*. He is at present Chaplain to the Young Christian Workers in London.

Philip Corbett studied theology at the University of St Andrews, Yale University and Keble College, Oxford. He trained for the priesthood at the College of the Resurrection, Mirfield, and is now assistant priest at The Priory of Our Lady and S Cuthbert, Worksop. He is the co-author of the book *Defend and Maintain: A History of the Church Union*, and a priest of the Society of the Holy Cross.

John Davies, after being Succentor at Derby Cathedral and Chaplain at Westcott House, taught theology at Southampton University for 30 years and was Canon Theologian of Winchester. He first encountered Frere via plainsong and proceeded to a lifelong admiration for Frere and all his works.

Alexander Faludy read theology and art history at Cambridge and theology at Oxford, and was trained for the priesthood at the College of the Resurrection, Mirfield. He is now curate at St Paul's, Cullercoats.

Benjamin Gordon-Taylor read history at Durham and theology at Leeds and Mirfield, and returned to Durham to take his doctorate in liturgical studies. He now teaches liturgy at the College of the Resurrection and is Director of the Mirfield Liturgical Institute. He is a Companion of the Community of the Resurrection and a member of the committee of the Alcuin Club, of which Walter Frere was for many years the President.

George Guiver CR is Superior of the Community of the Resurrection. A graduate in music from Durham, he is a noted liturgical scholar with several books to his credit.

John Livesley is Priest in Charge of the parishes of Tudhoe Grange and Cassop cum Quarrinton with Bowburn in the Durham diocese. He studied history at Magdalen College, Oxford, and theology at Leeds University and the College of the Resurrection, Mirfield.

Nicolas Stebbing CR is a priest of the Community of the Resurrection and teaches Greek at the College of the Resurrection. His books include *Bearers of the Spirit: Spiritual Fatherhood in Romanian Orthodoxy.*

Alan Wilkinson was trained at the College of the Resurrection, Mirfield. He was formerly Principal of Chichester Theological College and Ripon Diocesan Director of Lay and Clergy Training. He has taught for the universities of Cambridge, Bristol and Portsmouth and for the Open University. He has written a number of studies of church and society, as well as *The Community of the Resurrection: A Centenary History.* A new edition of his *Dissent or Conform? War, Peace and the English Churches 1900–1945* was published in 2010.

Index